YouTube for Beginners

Navigate, Watch, and Enjoy

Kiet Huynh

Table of Contents

Introduction

1.1 What is YouTube?

YouTube is a video-sharing platform that has transformed the way people consume and share content online. Launched in February 2005, YouTube quickly became one of the most popular websites in the world, attracting millions of users within its first year. Today, it stands as the second-most visited website globally, just behind Google, its parent company. But what exactly is YouTube, and why has it become such an integral part of our digital lives?

A Platform for Sharing and Discovering Videos

At its core, YouTube is a free platform where anyone with an internet connection can upload, share, and watch videos. From educational tutorials to entertainment, music videos to personal vlogs, YouTube hosts an incredible variety of content. Its vast library means that no matter your interest—whether it's cooking, gaming, DIY projects, or fitness—you'll find something that resonates with you.

The History of YouTube

YouTube was founded by three former PayPal employees—Chad Hurley, Steve Chen, and Jawed Karim—who envisioned a platform where people could easily upload and share videos. The first video ever uploaded to YouTube, titled "Me at the Zoo," was posted by Karim and features him standing in front of elephants at the San Diego Zoo. This humble beginning marked the start of a platform that now hosts billions of videos.

In 2006, YouTube was acquired by Google, a move that significantly boosted its growth and integration with other Google services. With the backing of Google's resources and expertise, YouTube expanded its features, improved its algorithms, and introduced monetization opportunities for creators.

YouTube's Mission and Vision

YouTube's mission is simple: "to give everyone a voice and show them the world." This vision highlights its commitment to democratizing access to information and creating a platform where people from all walks of life can share their stories, ideas, and expertise.

YouTube isn't just a video-sharing site; it's a global community. It empowers creators to build careers, educates users through tutorials and lectures, and entertains audiences with a seemingly endless stream of videos.

How YouTube Works

YouTube operates as a digital ecosystem where users can engage with content in multiple ways:

1. **Watching Videos:** This is the primary activity on YouTube. Users can search for specific topics, browse recommended videos, or explore trending content.
2. **Creating and Uploading Content:** YouTube allows anyone to become a creator. Whether you're recording a vlog, teaching a skill, or sharing a hobby, YouTube provides a platform for you to reach a global audience.
3. **Interacting with Content:** Users can like, comment, and share videos, fostering a sense of community. These interactions help content creators understand their audience and improve their videos.
4. **Subscribing to Channels:** Users can subscribe to their favorite creators to stay updated on new uploads. Subscriptions are a key feature that helps viewers personalize their YouTube experience.

Why YouTube Matters in Today's World

YouTube has become more than just a platform for entertainment; it's a tool for education, communication, and even activism. Here are some key reasons why YouTube is significant:

- **Education and Learning:** With countless tutorials, lectures, and how-to videos, YouTube serves as a free educational resource. Whether you're learning a new language, mastering a musical instrument, or studying for exams, YouTube has content tailored to your needs.

- **Entertainment:** From comedy skits and music videos to web series and live streams, YouTube offers endless entertainment options for users of all ages.
- **Career Opportunities:** YouTube has created an entirely new category of careers—content creation. Many individuals earn a living by producing videos on the platform, with some even achieving celebrity status.
- **Community and Connection:** YouTube brings people together. Communities form around specific channels or topics, allowing like-minded individuals to connect and share their passions.
- **Global Reach:** As a platform available in over 100 countries and supporting multiple languages, YouTube bridges cultural and linguistic barriers, making it a truly global community.

YouTube's Key Features

1. **User-Friendly Interface:** YouTube's design makes it easy for anyone to navigate, whether you're a tech-savvy individual or a first-time user.
2. **Search and Recommendations:** The platform uses advanced algorithms to suggest videos based on your interests and viewing history, ensuring a personalized experience.
3. **Channels and Subscriptions:** Creators can organize their content into channels, and viewers can subscribe to their favorites for updates.
4. **Live Streaming:** YouTube supports live broadcasting, allowing creators to engage with their audience in real time.
5. **Monetization Options:** YouTube offers creators the chance to earn revenue through ads, memberships, and merchandise sales.

Who Uses YouTube?

YouTube's user base is incredibly diverse, spanning all ages, professions, and interests. Some of the key user groups include:

- **Casual Viewers:** People who watch videos for entertainment or to pass the time.

- **Learners:** Individuals who use YouTube as a resource for acquiring new skills or knowledge.
- **Creators:** Anyone who uploads videos, from hobbyists to full-time professionals.
- **Businesses:** Companies use YouTube for marketing, brand building, and customer engagement.
- **Educators:** Teachers and institutions use YouTube to distribute educational content.

The Future of YouTube

As technology continues to evolve, so does YouTube. The platform is constantly introducing new features, such as augmented reality (AR) tools, improved analytics for creators, and enhanced accessibility options. With the rise of short-form content and increasing competition from other platforms, YouTube remains innovative to retain its position as a leader in the digital space.

Conclusion

YouTube is much more than a video-sharing website; it's a hub of creativity, learning, and connection. Understanding what YouTube is and how it works is the first step to fully utilizing its potential. Whether you're here to watch, learn, or create, YouTube offers endless opportunities for growth and enjoyment.

1.2 Why Use YouTube?

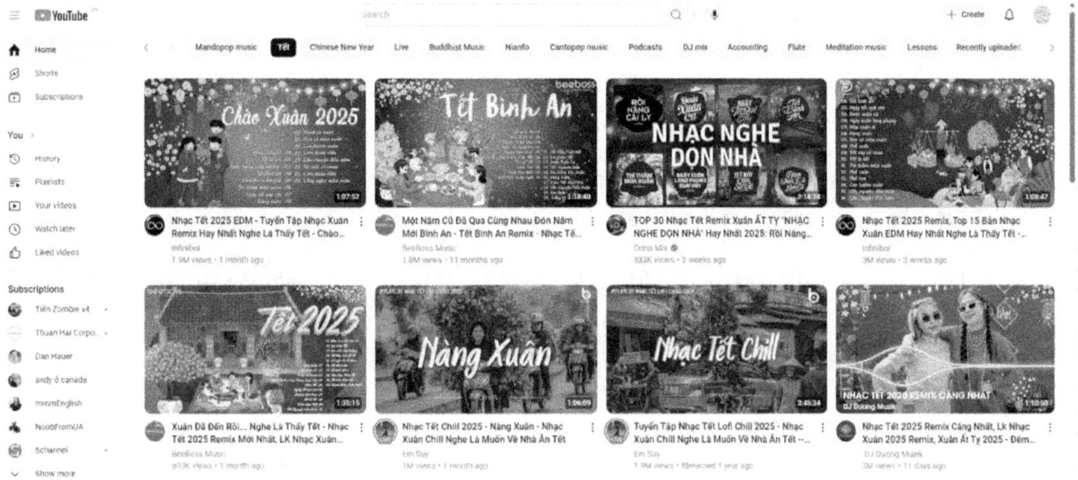

YouTube has become an essential part of our digital lives, serving as a platform for entertainment, education, communication, and even career development. Whether you are looking for inspiration, learning a new skill, or simply enjoying a few minutes of entertainment, YouTube provides unlimited access to content from all over the world. But what makes YouTube such a valuable tool, and why should you use it?

In this section, we will explore the many reasons why YouTube is one of the most popular websites globally and how it can benefit you in different ways.

Access to a Vast Library of Content

One of the biggest reasons to use YouTube is its enormous variety of content. With billions of videos available, you can find almost anything you are looking for. Whether you are interested in technology, cooking, travel, fitness, science, or even niche hobbies, there is always something for you.

Some of the most popular types of content on YouTube include:

- **Educational videos** – Tutorials, lectures, and how-to guides help people learn new skills and expand their knowledge.

- **Entertainment** – Comedy skits, vlogs, movie trailers, and live performances provide endless entertainment options.
- **News and current events** – Stay updated on world events, politics, and technology through reliable news channels.
- **Reviews and recommendations** – Find product reviews, unboxings, and recommendations to help you make informed purchasing decisions.
- **Live streams** – Watch live events, gaming sessions, and Q&A sessions with your favorite creators in real time.

Because YouTube's content is constantly growing, there is always something new to watch and explore.

Free and Easily Accessible

Unlike many streaming services that require a subscription, YouTube is free to use. You can access millions of videos without having to pay anything, making it one of the most accessible platforms on the internet.

Even though YouTube offers a premium subscription (YouTube Premium) for additional features like ad-free viewing and background play, the free version still provides an incredible amount of value. All you need is an internet connection and a device, and you can watch as much content as you like.

Additionally, YouTube is available on multiple devices, including:

- Smartphones and tablets (iOS and Android)
- Desktop computers and laptops
- Smart TVs and streaming devices (such as Roku, Apple TV, and Chromecast)
- Gaming consoles (such as PlayStation and Xbox)

This accessibility makes YouTube a convenient platform that you can use anywhere, anytime.

Learning and Skill Development

YouTube is one of the best free learning resources available today. Whether you want to improve your academic knowledge, develop a new skill, or learn a language, YouTube has thousands of educational channels covering almost every subject.

Examples of Educational Content:

- **Academic subjects:** Math, science, history, literature, and more.
- **DIY projects:** Home improvement, arts and crafts, and building projects.
- **Professional development:** Business skills, coding, marketing, and career advice.
- **Health and fitness:** Workout routines, nutrition tips, and mental health discussions.
- **Languages:** Learn and practice new languages through lessons and real-life conversations.

Some well-known educational channels include:

- **Khan Academy** – Free academic courses on a wide range of subjects.
- **TED-Ed** – Animated lessons on fascinating topics.
- **CrashCourse** – Engaging, fast-paced lessons on history, science, and more.

With YouTube, you can take charge of your own learning and gain valuable knowledge without spending money on expensive courses.

Entertainment and Fun

YouTube is also an amazing source of entertainment. Whether you enjoy watching music videos, stand-up comedy, or gaming content, there is always something to keep you entertained.

Popular entertainment categories on YouTube include:

- **Music videos** – Listen to the latest hits and watch music videos from your favorite artists.
- **Comedy and vlogs** – Enjoy stand-up performances, skits, and personal vlogs from content creators.
- **Gaming** – Watch gameplays, tutorials, and live streams from professional gamers.

- **Movies and trailers** – Discover upcoming movie trailers, short films, and full-length documentaries.

YouTube is not just a passive entertainment platform; it also allows you to engage with content by liking, commenting, and sharing videos with friends.

A Platform for Creators and Businesses

For those who want to share their creativity or promote a business, YouTube provides an excellent platform to reach a global audience.

For Creators

Many people use YouTube to express themselves, showcase their talents, and build a personal brand. Some popular types of content for creators include:

- **Vlogging** – Sharing daily life experiences and personal insights.
- **Tutorials and guides** – Teaching others about various topics.
- **Creative content** – Short films, animations, and storytelling.

Many YouTubers have built successful careers by consistently creating content and gaining subscribers. Some even earn a full-time income through YouTube's monetization features, such as:

- Ad revenue
- Sponsorships and brand deals
- Merchandise sales
- Membership programs

For Businesses

Businesses use YouTube for marketing, customer engagement, and brand awareness. Some ways companies use YouTube include:

- **Product demonstrations and tutorials** – Show how products work.
- **Customer testimonials** – Share positive customer experiences.
- **Behind-the-scenes content** – Give viewers an inside look at the company.

Because YouTube videos can reach millions of viewers worldwide, it is an effective marketing tool for both small businesses and large corporations.

A Global Community

One of the unique aspects of YouTube is its ability to connect people from all over the world. Viewers and creators can interact through comments, live chats, and social media, forming communities based on shared interests.

Some benefits of being part of the YouTube community include:

- **Discovering different cultures** – Watch content from different countries and learn about various traditions.
- **Engaging with others** – Discuss topics with like-minded individuals.
- **Supporting creators** – Help your favorite creators grow by liking, sharing, and subscribing to their channels.

This sense of community makes YouTube more than just a video-sharing platform—it is a place where people can connect and share their passions.

Conclusion

YouTube is more than just a platform for watching videos—it is a tool for learning, entertainment, communication, and business growth. Whether you are a casual viewer, a student, a creator, or a business owner, YouTube offers countless opportunities to engage with content and connect with a global audience.

By understanding the many benefits of YouTube, you can make the most of your experience on the platform and use it to enhance your daily life in meaningful ways.

1.3 How to Use This Book

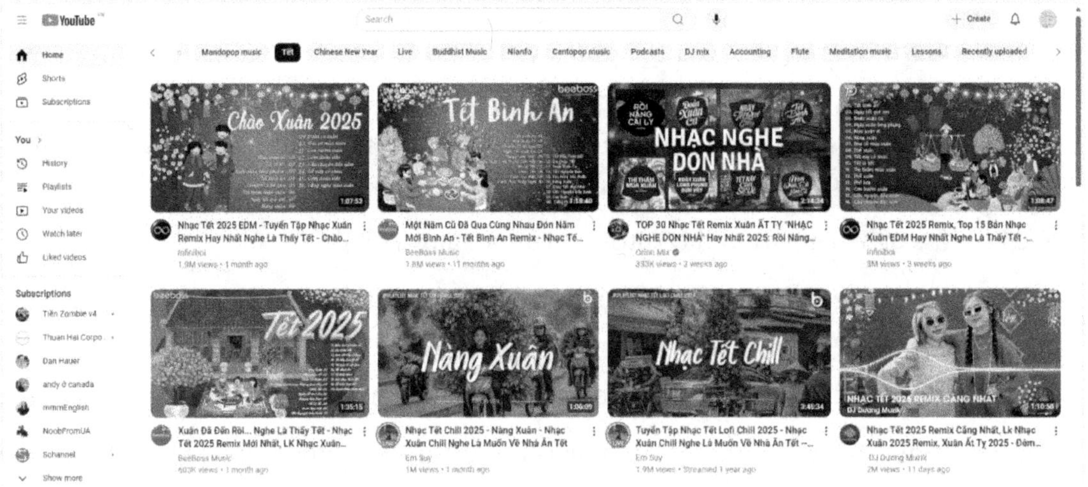

Welcome to *YouTube for Beginners: Navigate, Watch, and Enjoy*! This book is designed to help you understand and make the most of YouTube, whether you are a casual viewer, an aspiring content creator, or someone looking to enhance their knowledge of the platform.

As YouTube continues to grow, so does the variety of features and options available to users. While YouTube's interface is relatively intuitive, many users—especially beginners—find themselves overwhelmed by the sheer number of possibilities. This book aims to break down YouTube into easy-to-understand sections so that you can confidently explore, navigate, and engage with content on the platform.

In this chapter, we will explain how this book is structured and how you can get the most out of it.

Who This Book Is For

Before diving into the details of YouTube, it's important to understand who this book is intended for. Whether you're brand new to YouTube or have been using it for a while but want to deepen your understanding, this book is for you. Below are some of the key types of readers who will benefit from this guide:

- **Absolute Beginners:** If you've never used YouTube before or only watched a few videos, this book will help you start from the basics, such as creating an account, understanding YouTube's interface, and searching for content.
- **Casual Users:** If you already use YouTube to watch videos but want to explore more features—such as subscriptions, playlists, and settings—this book will guide you step by step.
- **Parents and Guardians:** If you want to help your children use YouTube safely, this book will introduce you to parental controls, privacy settings, and YouTube Kids.
- **Aspiring Content Creators:** If you're interested in uploading your own videos but don't know where to start, this book provides foundational knowledge before you move on to content creation and monetization.
- **Seniors and Non-Tech-Savvy Users:** If you're not very familiar with technology but want to enjoy videos online, this book will explain concepts clearly and concisely.

No matter your background, this book will provide you with the tools and confidence to navigate YouTube effectively.

How This Book Is Structured

This book is divided into several chapters, each focusing on a different aspect of YouTube. The chapters are arranged in a logical order, starting from the very basics and gradually moving toward more advanced features.

Here is an overview of what you can expect from each chapter:

1. **Introduction** – This section provides background information on YouTube, why it is useful, and how you can best utilize this book.
2. **Getting Started with YouTube** – Covers account creation, setting up your profile, and understanding the YouTube interface.
3. **Searching and Discovering Content** – Explores how to find videos that interest you, use search filters, and navigate YouTube's recommendation system.
4. **Interacting with YouTube Videos** – Discusses how to like, comment, share, and engage with videos.

5. **Managing Your YouTube Experience** – Guides you through using subscriptions, playlists, history, and watch later lists.
6. **YouTube Settings and Privacy** – Helps you adjust YouTube settings for a personalized and secure experience.
7. **YouTube for Families and Kids** – Explains how parents can set up child-friendly content and use parental controls.
8. **YouTube on Different Devices** – Shows how to use YouTube on smartphones, tablets, smart TVs, and more.
9. **Troubleshooting and Common Issues** – Provides solutions for common problems users may face while using YouTube.

Each chapter contains step-by-step instructions, screenshots, and tips to make learning easy and practical.

How to Use This Book Effectively

This book is designed to be flexible, meaning you can read it from start to finish or jump to specific sections that interest you. Here are a few ways to use this book depending on your needs:

1. Read from Start to Finish

If you are completely new to YouTube, we recommend reading the book sequentially. This will help you build a solid foundation and understand how different features work together.

2. Use It as a Reference Guide

If you already have some experience with YouTube but need help with specific features, feel free to jump to the relevant chapters. Each chapter is structured so that you can understand it without reading the previous sections.

3. Follow Along with a Device

For the best learning experience, keep this book open while using YouTube on a computer, smartphone, or tablet. Try out the features as you read about them.

4. Take Notes and Experiment

Don't be afraid to take notes, highlight key sections, or experiment with different settings on YouTube. The best way to learn is through practice.

Additional Features to Help You Learn

This book includes various elements to enhance your learning experience:

- **Step-by-Step Instructions:** Clear, easy-to-follow instructions to help you complete tasks on YouTube.
- **Screenshots and Visuals:** Images and illustrations to help you understand different YouTube features.
- **Tips and Tricks:** Useful tips to enhance your YouTube experience.
- **Common Issues and Solutions:** Troubleshooting advice for common problems.

By using these features, you will be able to navigate YouTube with ease and confidence.

Common Questions New Users Have

As a beginner, you may have questions about using YouTube. Here are some common concerns that this book will address:

- **Do I need a Google account to watch YouTube?** (Answer: No, but it helps you access more features.)
- **How can I find videos on topics I like?** (Answer: You will learn how to use search tools and recommendations effectively.)
- **Is YouTube safe for kids?** (Answer: We will cover parental controls and YouTube Kids in detail.)
- **Can I watch YouTube without ads?** (Answer: YouTube Premium allows you to watch ad-free content.)
- **How do I save videos to watch later?** (Answer: Playlists and the 'Watch Later' feature help organize videos.)

These are just a few of the many topics covered in this book.

Final Thoughts

YouTube is one of the most powerful and entertaining platforms available today. Whether you want to watch videos, learn new skills, or eventually create content, understanding how YouTube works will improve your experience.

By following the guidance in this book, you will quickly become comfortable navigating YouTube and using its features to your advantage.

Now, let's get started with the first chapter: **Getting Started with YouTube!**

CHAPTER I
Getting Started with YouTube

1.1 Creating a Google Account

1.1.1 Why You Need a Google Account

In order to fully experience everything YouTube has to offer, you need a Google account. While it is possible to browse YouTube and watch videos without signing in, having a Google account unlocks a range of features that enhance your experience. From subscribing to channels and leaving comments to creating and uploading your own videos, a Google account provides access to YouTube's full functionality.

This section will explore the reasons why having a Google account is essential for YouTube users, including the benefits it provides, the features it unlocks, and how it integrates with other Google services.

---

1. The Role of a Google Account in YouTube

A Google account serves as your digital identity across Google's ecosystem, including YouTube. Since Google owns YouTube, your Google account allows you to access and personalize your experience across both platforms seamlessly. Here are some of the main functions that require a Google account on YouTube:

- **Subscribing to Channels** – Stay updated with your favorite creators by subscribing to their channels.
- **Liking and Commenting on Videos** – Engage with content by liking, disliking, and leaving comments on videos.
- **Creating Playlists** – Save videos into organized collections for easy access later.

- **Uploading Videos** – Share your own videos with the world by creating a YouTube channel linked to your Google account.
- **Using YouTube Premium** – If you want to enjoy ad-free videos, background play, and offline downloads, a Google account is required to subscribe to YouTube Premium.
- **Personalized Recommendations** – YouTube's algorithm customizes video recommendations based on your viewing history when you are signed in.
- **Syncing Across Devices** – Your Google account allows you to access your YouTube history, subscriptions, and preferences from any device.

Without a Google account, you can still watch videos, but you will miss out on these valuable features.

---

2. Benefits of Having a Google Account for YouTube

2.1 Personalization and Recommendations

One of the biggest advantages of having a Google account is the personalized experience it offers. YouTube tracks your viewing habits to recommend videos you might enjoy. If you frequently watch tech reviews, for example, your home page will begin to show more related content.

Without an account, you have to manually search for content every time you visit YouTube, and your watch history won't be saved.

2.2 Subscriptions and Notifications

A Google account lets you subscribe to YouTube channels, ensuring that you never miss new content from your favorite creators. Subscriptions allow you to:

- Get notified when new videos are uploaded.
- Easily access content from subscribed channels through the "Subscriptions" tab.
- Support your favorite creators by increasing their subscriber count.

If you don't have a Google account, you would have to remember each channel's name and manually search for new content.

2.3 Engaging with the YouTube Community

YouTube is more than just a video-sharing platform; it's a community. With a Google account, you can:

- **Like videos** to show appreciation and influence video rankings.
- **Comment on videos** to join discussions and interact with creators.
- **Share videos** easily with friends via YouTube's built-in sharing options.

These features help users engage with content and make YouTube a more interactive experience.

2.4 Creating and Uploading Content

For aspiring YouTubers, having a Google account is mandatory. It allows you to:

- Set up your YouTube channel.
- Upload videos.
- Monetize content through ads and memberships.
- Track performance through YouTube Studio analytics.

Without a Google account, you can't post videos or engage with an audience.

2.5 Access to YouTube Premium and Additional Features

If you want an ad-free experience, background play, or offline downloads, a Google account is necessary to subscribe to **YouTube Premium**. Other features, such as **YouTube Music** and **YouTube TV**, also require a Google account.

---

3. How a Google Account Integrates with Other Google Services

Since YouTube is part of Google, a single Google account gives you access to many interconnected services:

- **Google Drive** – Store videos and backups.
- **Gmail** – Receive YouTube notifications and channel updates.
- **Google Photos** – Upload and edit videos directly from your photo storage.
- **Google Search** – See YouTube video results in Google searches.

- **Google Assistant** – Use voice commands to play YouTube videos.

This integration makes managing your digital life easier and more seamless.

---

4. Common Misconceptions About Google Accounts on YouTube

"I Can Watch YouTube Without a Google Account, So Why Create One?"

While this is true, you miss out on all the personalized features, such as watch history, subscriptions, and recommendations.

"I Don't Want My Personal Email Linked to YouTube"

If you prefer to keep YouTube separate from your personal email, you can create a new Google account specifically for YouTube.

"Creating an Account is Complicated"

Setting up a Google account is quick and simple. The process takes only a few minutes, and we will cover the step-by-step guide in the next section (**1.1.2 Step-by-Step Guide to Creating an Account**).

---

5. Conclusion

Having a Google account is essential for unlocking the full potential of YouTube. It allows you to personalize your experience, engage with content, subscribe to channels, and even create and upload your own videos.

In the next section, we will go through a **step-by-step guide** to creating a Google account, ensuring that you can start enjoying all of YouTube's features right away.

1.1.2 Step-by-Step Guide to Creating an Account

Creating a Google account is the first step to accessing YouTube's full range of features, including subscribing to channels, liking videos, creating playlists, and even uploading your own content. Since YouTube is a Google-owned platform, a Google account serves as your login credential for YouTube and many other Google services like Gmail, Google Drive, and Google Photos.

This guide will walk you through the process of setting up a Google account, whether you are using a desktop computer, a smartphone, or a tablet. By the end of this section, you will have a fully functional Google account that allows you to explore and engage with YouTube.

---

1. Understanding Google Accounts and Their Benefits

Before diving into the steps, let's take a moment to understand why a Google account is necessary and how it enhances your YouTube experience:

Why You Need a Google Account for YouTube

- **Personalized Experience:** A Google account enables YouTube to recommend videos based on your watch history and interests.
- **Subscription to Channels:** You can subscribe to your favorite creators and receive notifications when they upload new videos.
- **Playlists and Watch History:** Your account allows you to create playlists and keep track of videos you have watched.
- **Engagement Features:** With a Google account, you can like, comment, and share videos.
- **Uploading Content:** If you want to become a YouTube creator, a Google account is required to upload and manage videos.

---

2. How to Create a Google Account

The process of creating a Google account is straightforward. Follow these step-by-step instructions based on your device type.

Creating a Google Account on a Desktop or Laptop

Step 1: Visit the Google Account Sign-Up Page

1. Open a web browser (Chrome, Firefox, Safari, or Edge).
2. Type **accounts.google.com/signup** in the address bar and press **Enter**.

3. You will see the Google sign-up page with a form to create a new account.

Step 2: Enter Your Personal Information

1. In the first two text boxes, enter your **First Name** and **Last Name**.
2. Choose a **Username** (this will be your Gmail address). If your desired username is taken, try adding numbers or other variations.
3. Create a **Strong Password** that is at least 8 characters long and includes a mix of letters, numbers, and symbols.
4. Confirm your password by typing it again in the second password field.

Step 3: Verify Your Identity

1. Click **Next** to continue.
2. Google will ask for your **Phone Number** to verify your identity. Enter your mobile number and click **Next**.
3. You will receive a **6-digit verification code** via SMS. Enter this code and click **Verify**.

Step 4: Provide Additional Information

1. Enter a **Recovery Email Address** (optional but recommended). This helps you recover your account if you forget your password.
2. Select your **Date of Birth** and **Gender** from the dropdown menus.

Step 5: Agree to Google's Terms and Privacy Policy

1. Read Google's **Terms of Service** and **Privacy Policy**.
2. Scroll down and click **I Agree** to proceed.

Step 6: Account Setup Completion

1. You will now be directed to the Google Account dashboard.
2. Your new Google account is now ready to use for YouTube and other Google services!

Creating a Google Account on a Mobile Device (Android or iPhone)

If you are using a smartphone or tablet, follow these steps to create a Google account through the **YouTube app** or your **device's settings**.

Method 1: Through the YouTube App

1. Open the **YouTube app** on your device.
2. Tap the **Profile Icon** in the top-right corner.
3. Select **Sign in** > **Create account**.
4. Follow the same steps as described in the desktop guide (entering your name, choosing a username, creating a password, verifying your phone number, and agreeing to terms).

Method 2: Through the Device's Settings (Android)

1. Open the **Settings** app on your Android device.
2. Scroll down and select **Google** > **Add account** > **Google**.
3. Tap **Create account**, then enter your name, date of birth, gender, and other required details.
4. Follow the instructions to set up your username, password, and phone number verification.
5. Once completed, your Google account is linked to your device and ready for YouTube.

Method 3: Through the Gmail App (iPhone & Android)

1. Open the **Gmail app** on your phone.
2. Tap your **Profile Picture** (top-right) and select **Add another account**.
3. Tap **Google** > **Create account**.
4. Enter your details and follow the on-screen instructions to complete the setup.

---

3. Setting Up Your Google Account for YouTube

Now that you have successfully created a Google account, there are a few additional steps to optimize it for YouTube.

3.1 Adjusting Privacy and Security Settings

1. Go to **myaccount.google.com** and log in.

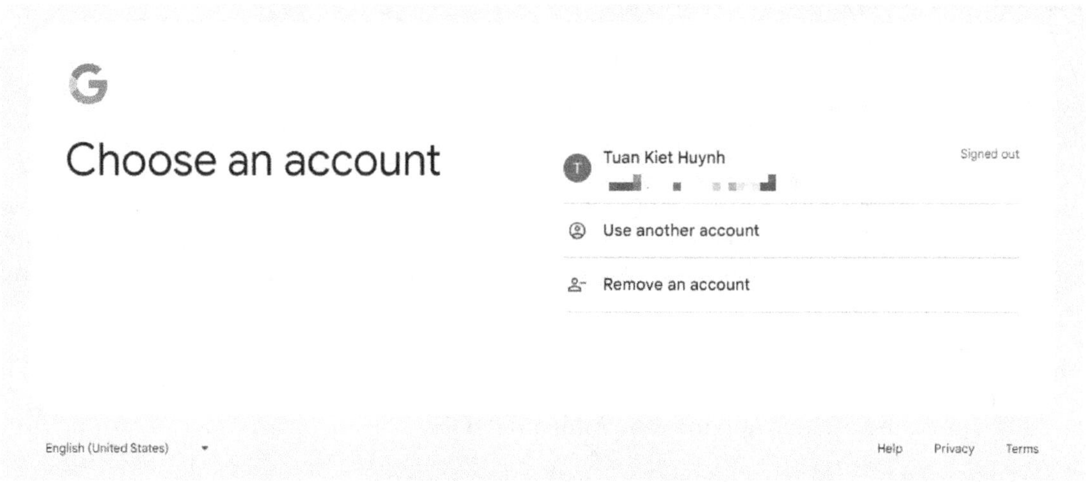

2. Click on **Security** to set up **2-Step Verification** for added protection.

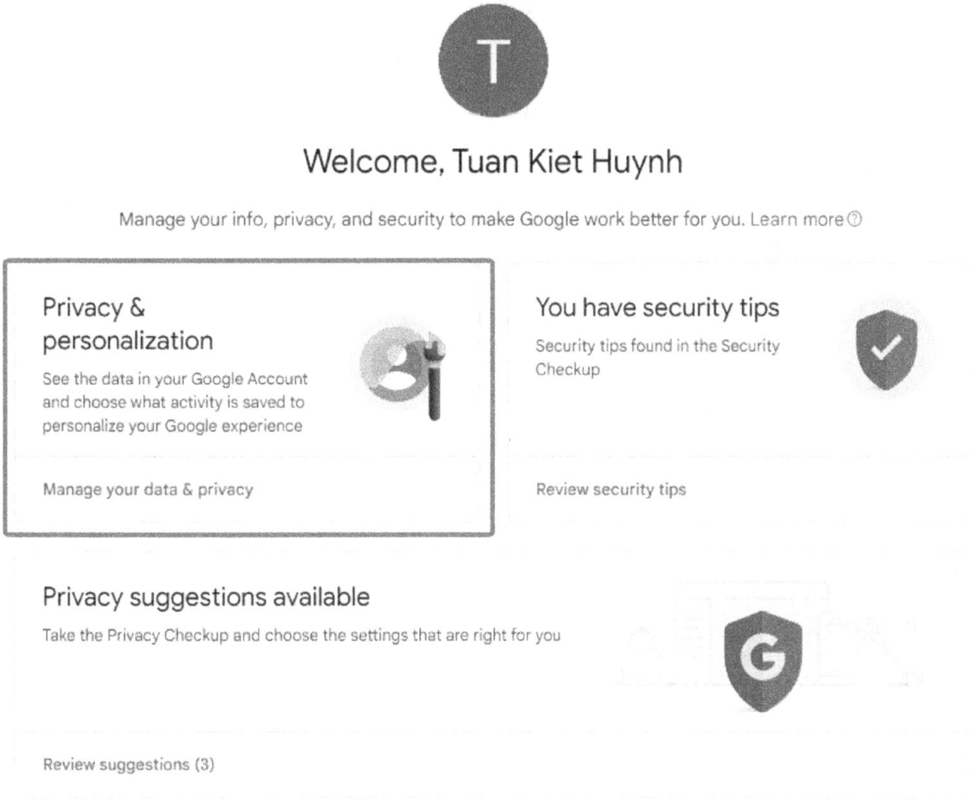
T
Welcome, Tuan Kiet Huynh
Manage your info, privacy, and security to make Google work better for you. Learn more
Privacy & personalization
See the data in your Google Account and choose what activity is saved to personalize your Google experience
Manage your data & privacy
You have security tips
Security tips found in the Security Checkup
Review security tips
Privacy suggestions available
Take the Privacy Checkup and choose the settings that are right for you
Review suggestions (3)

3. In the **Privacy & Personalization** section, review the data Google collects and manage your ad preferences.

3.2 Customizing Your Profile

1. Click on your **Profile Icon** in the top-right corner of any Google service.
2. Select **Manage your Google Account > Personal Info**.
3. Add a **profile picture**, update your **name**, and personalize your **public information**.

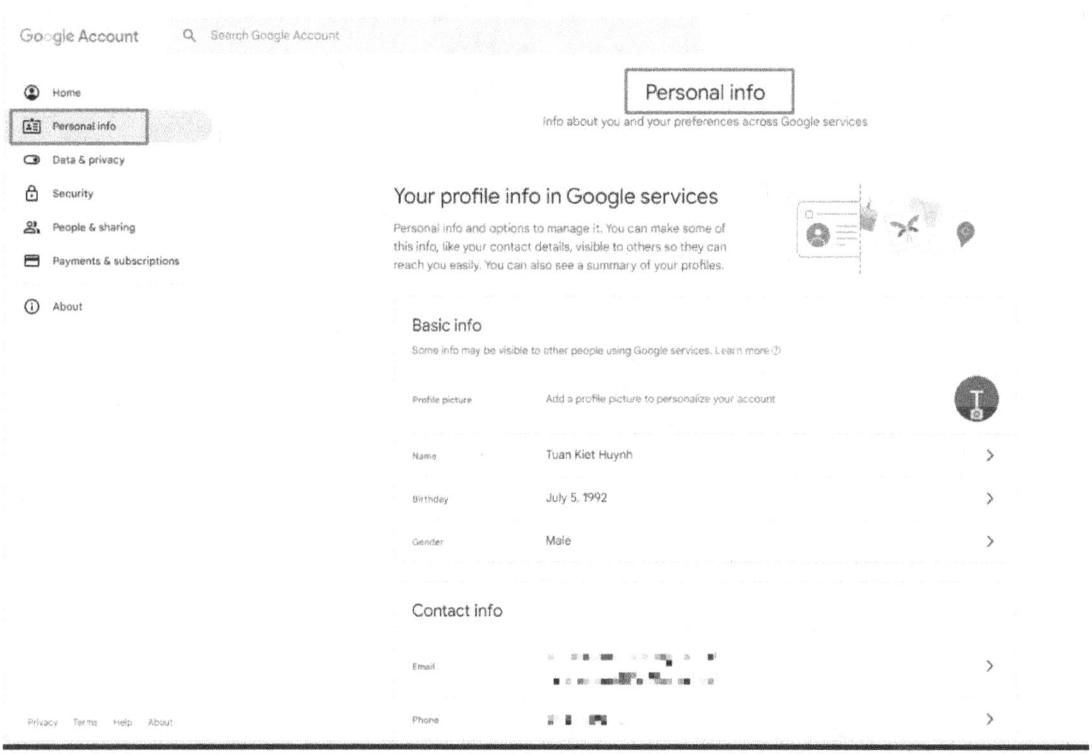

3.3 Syncing Your Account Across Devices

1. If you use multiple devices, sign in with your Google account on each one.
2. Open the **YouTube app**, tap the **Profile Icon**, and ensure you are logged in.
3. Your watch history, subscriptions, and preferences will now sync across all devices.

---

4. Troubleshooting Common Issues

If you encounter issues while creating your Google account, here are some troubleshooting tips:

Issue 1: Username Already Taken

- Try adding numbers or symbols to create a unique username.
- Use a variation of your name (e.g., JohnDoe123 instead of JohnDoe).

Issue 2: Verification Code Not Received

- Ensure your phone number is entered correctly.
- Check for network issues or delays in SMS delivery.
- Request a new verification code after a few minutes.

Issue 3: Forgotten Password After Account Creation

- Visit **accounts.google.com/signin/recovery**.
- Enter your recovery email or phone number to reset your password.

---

5. Conclusion

Creating a Google account is the first step in fully experiencing what YouTube has to offer. By following this step-by-step guide, you now have a working Google account that allows you to explore YouTube, subscribe to channels, and engage with videos. In the next section, we'll cover how to **set up and customize your YouTube profile** to make the most of your YouTube experience.

1.1.3 Managing Your Google Account

A Google account is the key to accessing YouTube and many other Google services, such as Gmail, Google Drive, and Google Photos. Once you have created an account, managing it effectively ensures a seamless experience across all Google platforms. This section will guide you through the essential aspects of managing your Google account, including updating personal information, adjusting security settings, managing privacy preferences, and troubleshooting common issues.

---

1. Understanding Your Google Account Dashboard

After creating a Google account, you can access and manage it through the **Google Account Dashboard** at myaccount.google.com. This dashboard provides a central hub for managing your personal details, privacy settings, and security features.

When you log into your Google account, you will find several sections, including:

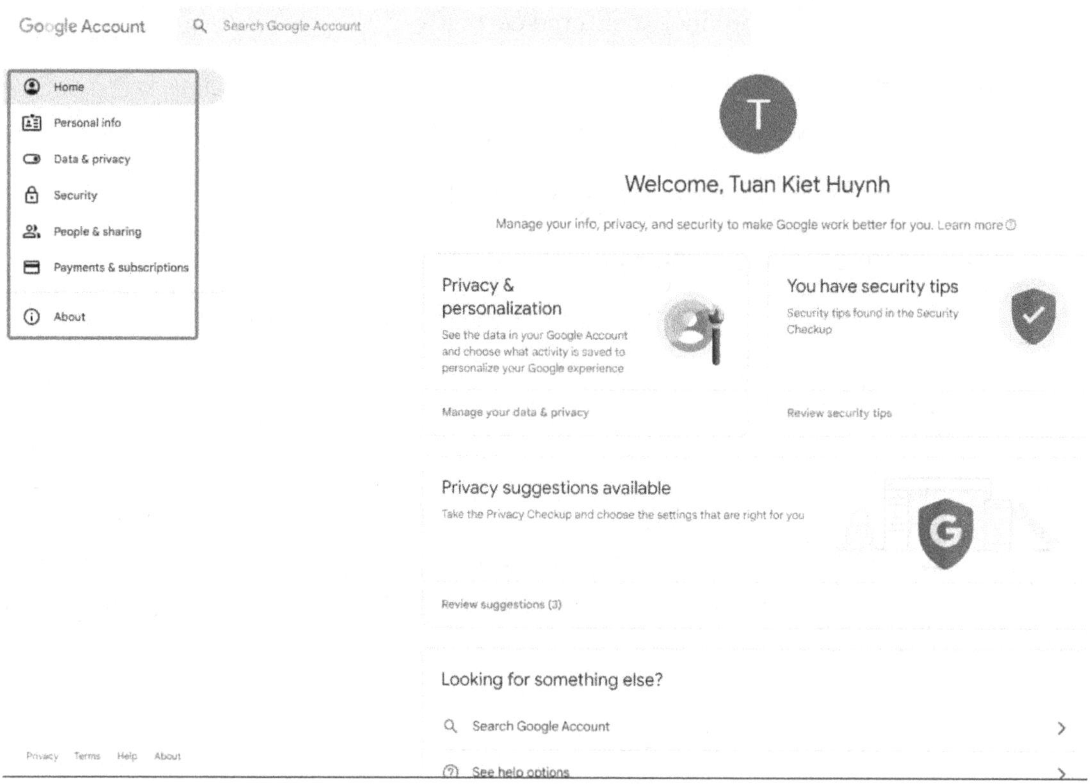
Google Account
Search Google Account
Home
Personal info
Data & privacy
Security
People & sharing
Payments & subscriptions
About
Welcome, Tuan Kiet Huynh
Manage your info, privacy, and security to make Google work better for you. Learn more
Privacy & personalization
See the data in your Google Account and choose what activity is saved to personalize your Google experience
Manage your data & privacy
You have security tips
Security tips found in the Security Checkup
Review security tips
Privacy suggestions available
Take the Privacy Checkup and choose the settings that are right for you
Review suggestions (3)
Looking for something else?
Search Google Account
See help options
Privacy Terms Help About

- **Home:** A summary of your account status, security suggestions, and privacy recommendations.
- **Personal Info:** Where you can update your name, email, phone number, and profile picture.
- **Data & Privacy:** Manage what data Google collects and how it is used.
- **Security:** Control password settings, two-factor authentication, and recovery options.
- **People & Sharing:** Adjust settings related to contacts and sharing preferences.
- **Payments & Subscriptions:** View your purchases, payment methods, and active subscriptions.

2. Updating Your Personal Information

Keeping your personal information up to date is important for account security and recovery. Here's how to update your details:

2.1 Changing Your Name and Profile Picture

1. Go to myaccount.google.com.
2. Click on **Personal Info** in the left menu.
3. Select your **Name** or **Profile Picture** and update them as needed.

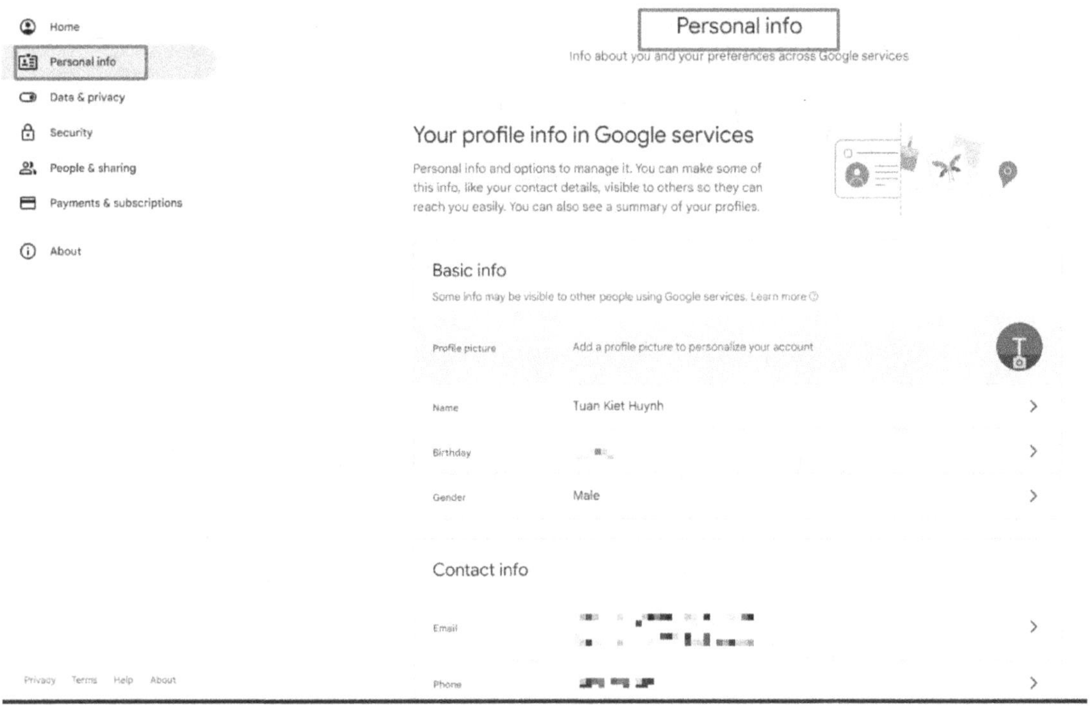

4. Click **Save** to apply changes.

Tip: Your profile picture will appear on YouTube, Gmail, and other Google services, so choose an appropriate image.

2.2 Updating Your Phone Number and Email Address

1. Navigate to **Personal Info** in your Google Account.
2. Under **Contact Info**, select your **Phone Number** or **Email** to edit.
3. Enter the new information and verify it if required.

4. Click **Save** to confirm.

Having a verified phone number and email helps with account recovery in case you forget your password.

---

3. Managing Security Settings

Security is a top priority when managing your Google account. Google provides several options to protect your data and prevent unauthorized access.

3.1 Changing Your Password

It is recommended to change your Google password periodically for better security.

1. Go to **myaccount.google.com/security**.
2. Under **Signing in to Google**, select **Password**.

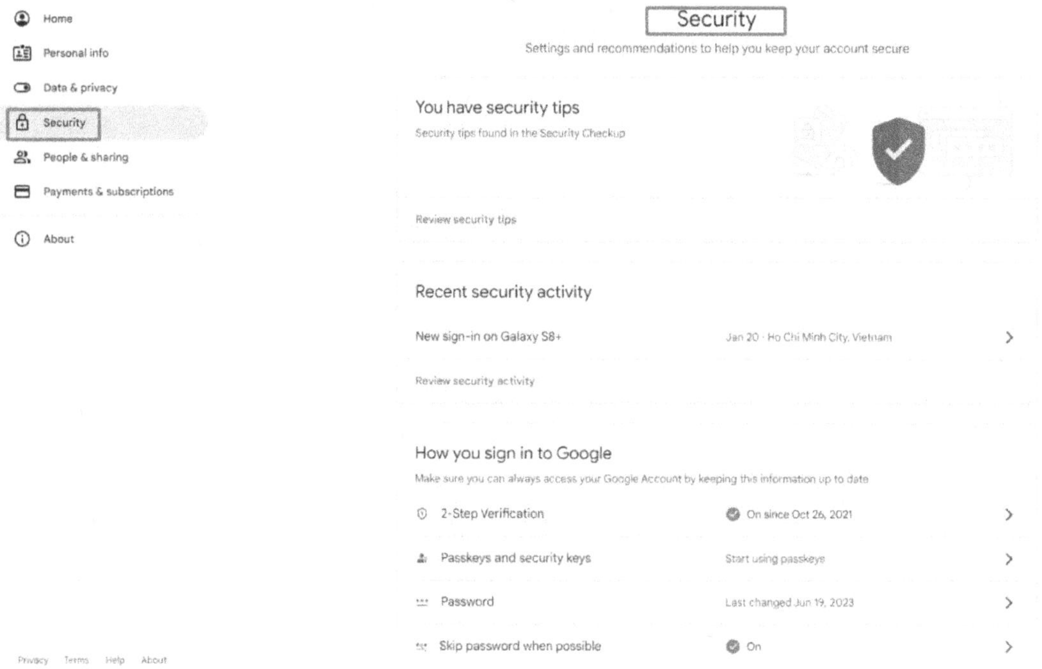

3. Enter your current password, then choose a new strong password.
4. Click **Save**.

A strong password should:

- Be at least 12 characters long.
- Include a mix of uppercase and lowercase letters, numbers, and symbols.
- Avoid common words and personal information.

3.2 Enabling Two-Step Verification (2FA)

Two-Step Verification adds an extra layer of security to your Google account by requiring a second form of authentication (such as a phone code) in addition to your password.

1. Go to **myaccount.google.com/security**.
2. Click **2-Step Verification** and select **Get Started**.
3. Choose a verification method (SMS, authentication app, or security key).
4. Follow the on-screen instructions to complete the setup.

Tip: Using an authentication app (like Google Authenticator) is more secure than SMS-based verification.

3.3 Setting Up Account Recovery Options

Recovery options help you regain access to your account if you forget your password or lose access.

1. In the **Security** section, find **Ways we can verify it's you**.
2. Click **Recovery Phone** or **Recovery Email**.

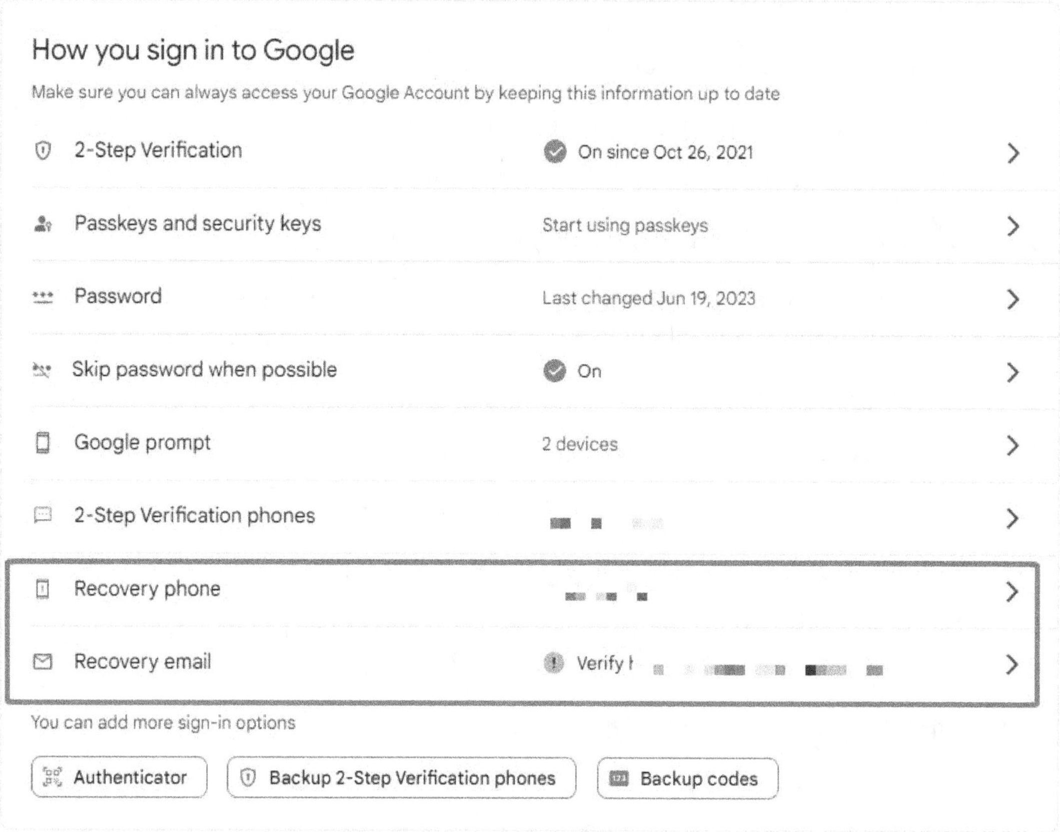

3. Enter a valid phone number or email and verify it.

---

4. Managing Privacy and Data Preferences

Google collects data to personalize your experience, but you can control what information is stored.

4.1 Adjusting Ad Personalization

Google customizes ads based on your activity. You can manage ad settings to control what types of ads you see.

1. Go to **myaccount.google.com/data-and-privacy**.

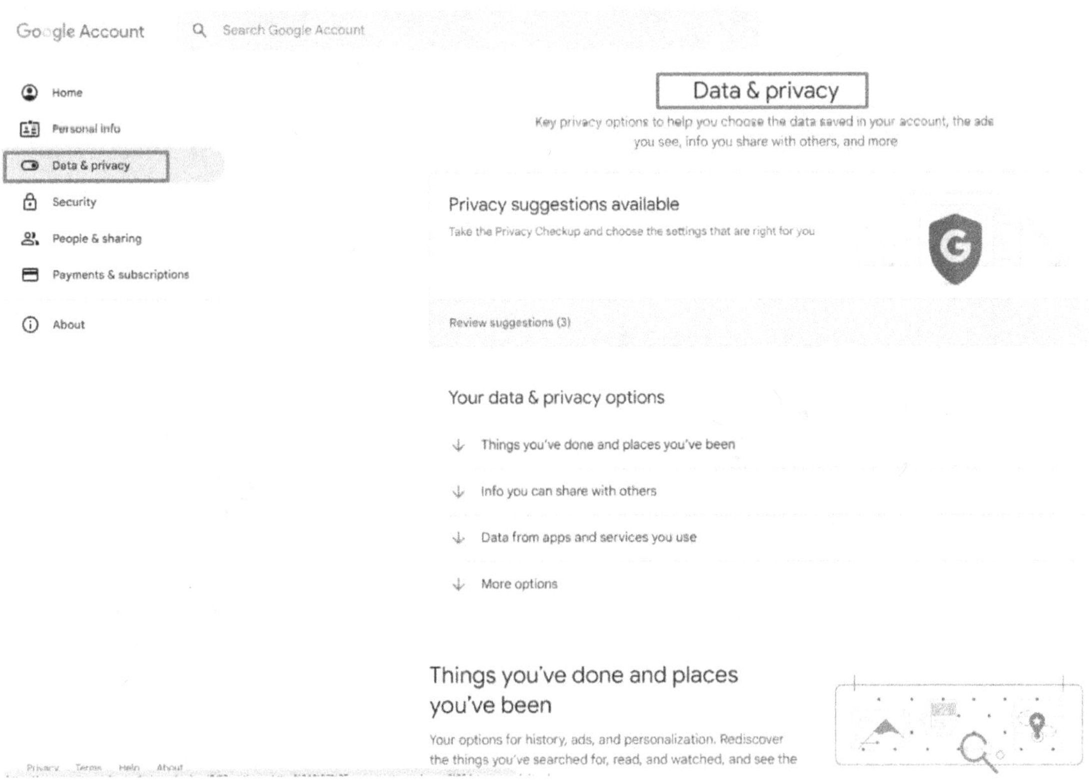

2. Scroll to **Ad Settings** and click **Ad Personalization**.

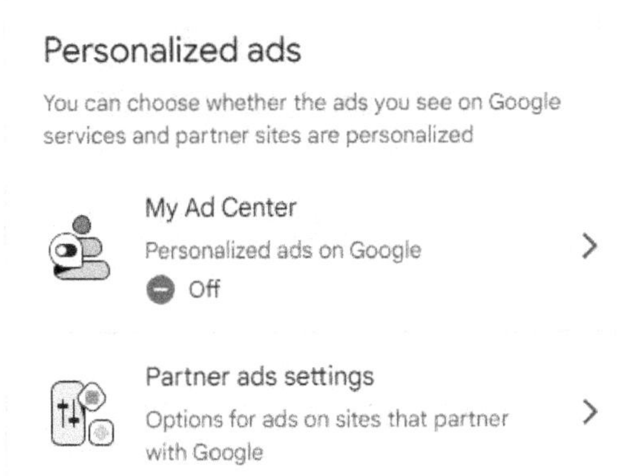

3. Toggle the switch **On** or **Off** depending on your preference.
4. You can also choose what types of ads Google can show you.

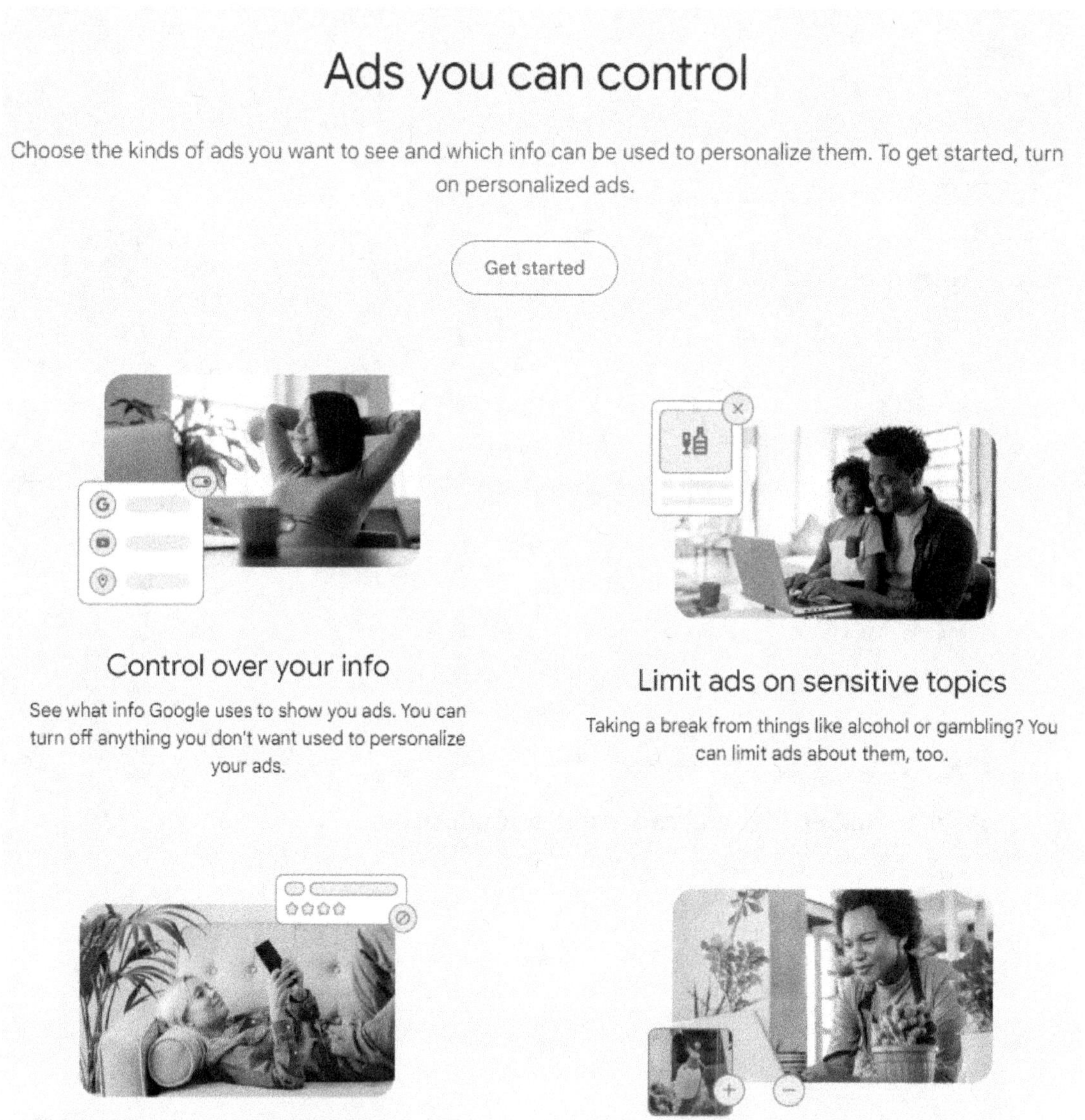
Ads you can control
Choose the kinds of ads you want to see and which info can be used to personalize them. To get started, turn on personalized ads.
Get started
Control over your info
See what info Google uses to show you ads. You can turn off anything you don't want used to personalize your ads.
Limit ads on sensitive topics
Taking a break from things like alcohol or gambling? You can limit ads about them, too.

4.2 Managing YouTube History

Your YouTube history influences video recommendations. You can clear or pause your history as needed.

1. Go to **YouTube History** in your Google Account.

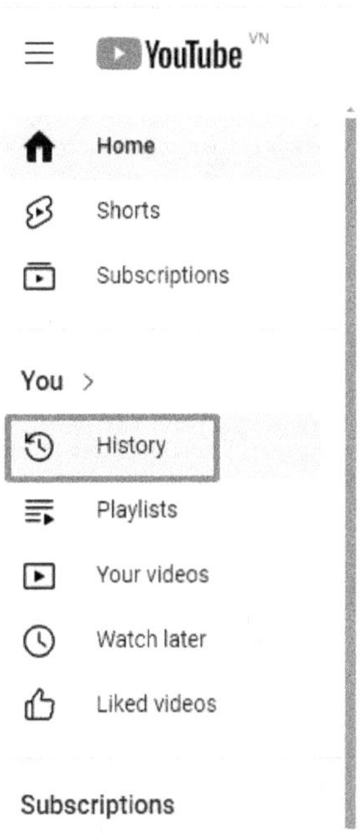

2. Click **Manage history** to delete specific videos or clear all history.

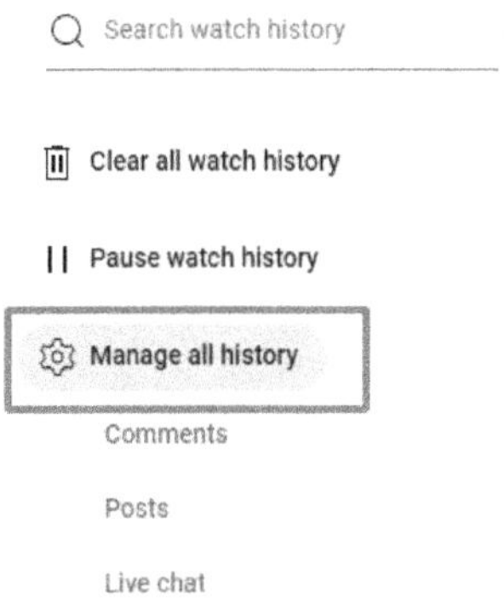

3. Click **Auto-delete** to set automatic history deletion.

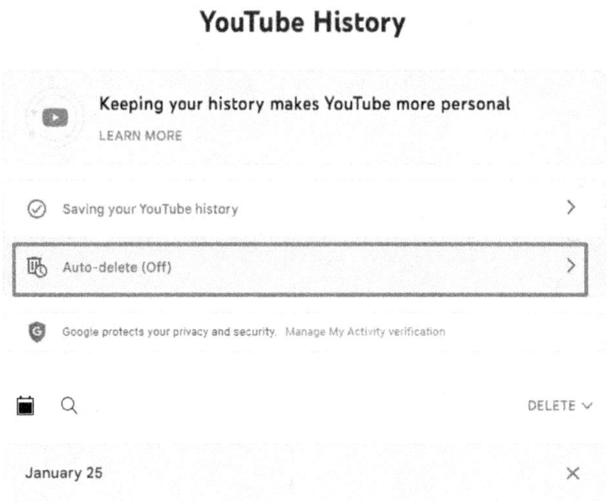

4. Toggle **Pause history** to stop YouTube from saving your watch history.

Tip: Pausing your history may affect YouTube recommendations.

4.3 Controlling Location History

Google tracks location data if enabled. You can turn it off or delete past data.

1. Open **myaccount.google.com/data-and-privacy**.
2. Scroll to **Location History** and click **Manage history**.
3. Toggle location tracking **On** or **Off**.
4. Click **Auto-delete** to remove older location data.

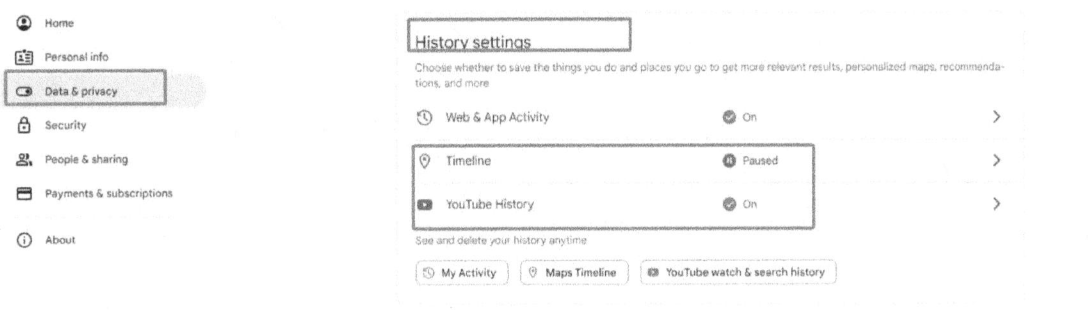

---

5. Managing Account Activity and Subscriptions

5.1 Viewing and Downloading Your Data

Google provides a tool to download your personal data, including YouTube history.

1. Go to Google Takeout. https://takeout.google.com/

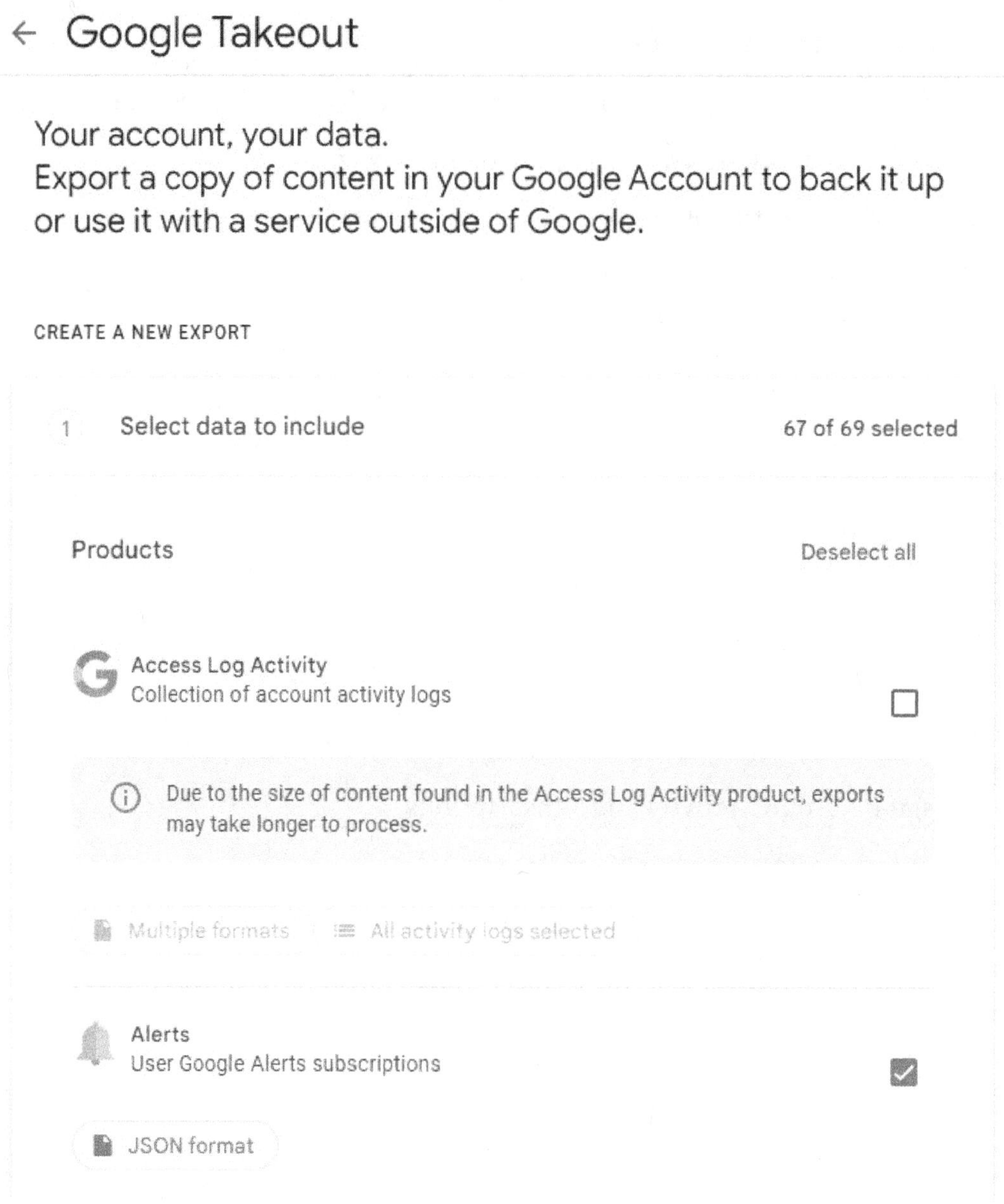
Google Takeout
Your account, your data.
Export a copy of content in your Google Account to back it up or use it with a service outside of Google.
CREATE A NEW EXPORT
1 Select data to include
67 of 69 selected
Products
Deselect all
Access Log Activity
Collection of account activity logs
Due to the size of content found in the Access Log Activity product, exports may take longer to process.
Multiple formats
All activity logs selected
Alerts
User Google Alerts subscriptions
JSON format

2. Select the services you want to download data from.
3. Choose the file format and delivery method.
4. Click **Create Export**.

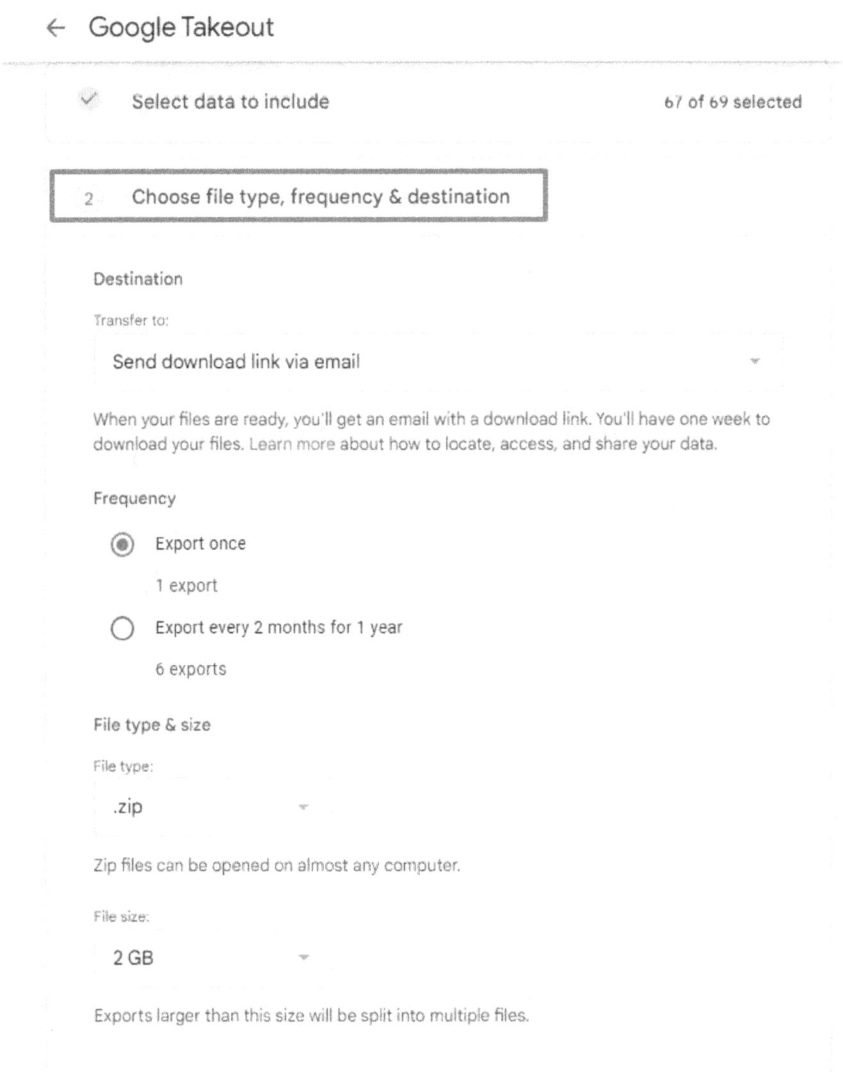

5.2 Managing Google Subscriptions

If you have YouTube Premium or other Google subscriptions, you can manage them in your account.

1. Open **myaccount.google.com/payments-and-subscriptions**.
2. Click **Manage Subscriptions**.

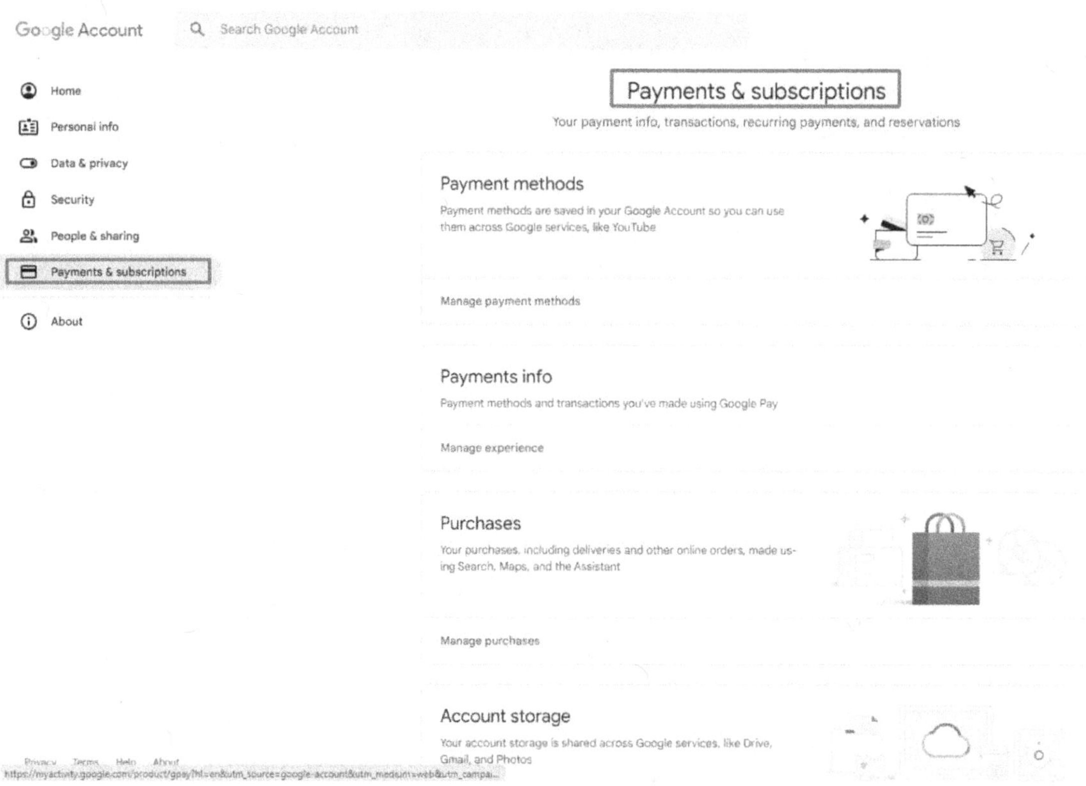

3. View, modify, or cancel any active subscriptions.

---

6. Troubleshooting Common Google Account Issues

6.1 Recovering a Lost Password

If you forget your password, you can reset it using your recovery options.

1. Go to Google's Account Recovery Page.
2. Enter your email and follow the on-screen instructions.
3. Use your recovery email or phone number to reset your password.

6.2 Dealing with Suspicious Activity

If you receive a security alert about suspicious activity:

1. Visit **myaccount.google.com/security-checkup** to review security settings.
2. Check the **Recent Security Events** section for unusual sign-ins.
3. Change your password if necessary.
4. Enable two-step verification for extra security.

6.3 Deleting Your Google Account

If you decide to stop using Google services, you can delete your account permanently.

1. Go to **myaccount.google.com/delete-services-or-account**.
2. Click **Delete your Google Account** and follow the instructions.
3. Confirm your decision by entering your password.

Warning: Deleting your account will remove all your data, including emails, YouTube history, and saved files.

Conclusion

Managing your Google account effectively is crucial for security, privacy, and a smooth user experience across YouTube and other Google services. By keeping your personal details updated, securing your account, and managing privacy settings, you can ensure a safer and more personalized experience. Whether you're a casual viewer or an active creator, taking control of your Google account settings will help you make the most of YouTube and beyond.

1.2 Setting Up Your YouTube Profile

Before you start watching and interacting with videos on YouTube, it's essential to set up your profile. Your YouTube profile represents your identity on the platform, allowing you to engage with content, subscribe to channels, and even upload your own videos in the future. In this section, we'll cover how to customize your profile picture and name, ensuring that your YouTube presence reflects your personality or brand.

1.2.1 Customizing Your Profile Picture and Name

Your YouTube profile picture and name are two key elements that define your presence on the platform. Whether you're using YouTube for personal entertainment, learning, or building a brand, having a well-crafted profile helps enhance your experience and makes your interactions more meaningful.

Why Customize Your Profile?

While YouTube automatically assigns a default profile picture (usually a simple colored letter icon) and your Google Account name when you sign up, personalizing these elements has several benefits:

- **Recognition:** A unique profile picture and name make it easier for others to recognize you.
- **Professionalism:** If you plan to create content or engage frequently, a well-designed profile gives a professional touch.
- **Branding:** For those using YouTube as a platform for business, a customized name and profile picture help in brand identity.
- **Personal Touch:** Adding your own image or a custom name makes your YouTube experience feel more personal and engaging.

How to Change Your Profile Picture on YouTube

Your YouTube profile picture is linked to your Google Account, which means changing it on YouTube will also update it across other Google services like Gmail and Google Drive. Here's a step-by-step guide:

Step 1: Sign in to YouTube

1. Open your web browser and go to YouTube. https://www.youtube.com/
2. Click the **Sign In** button in the upper-right corner.

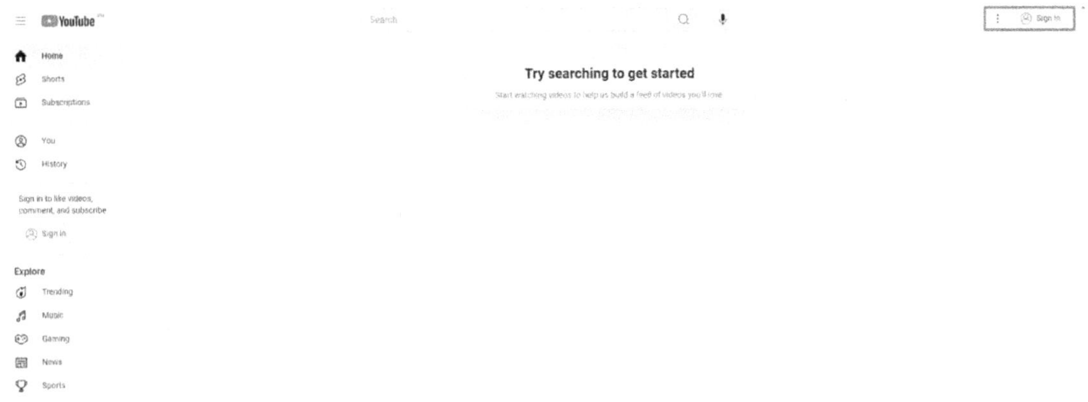

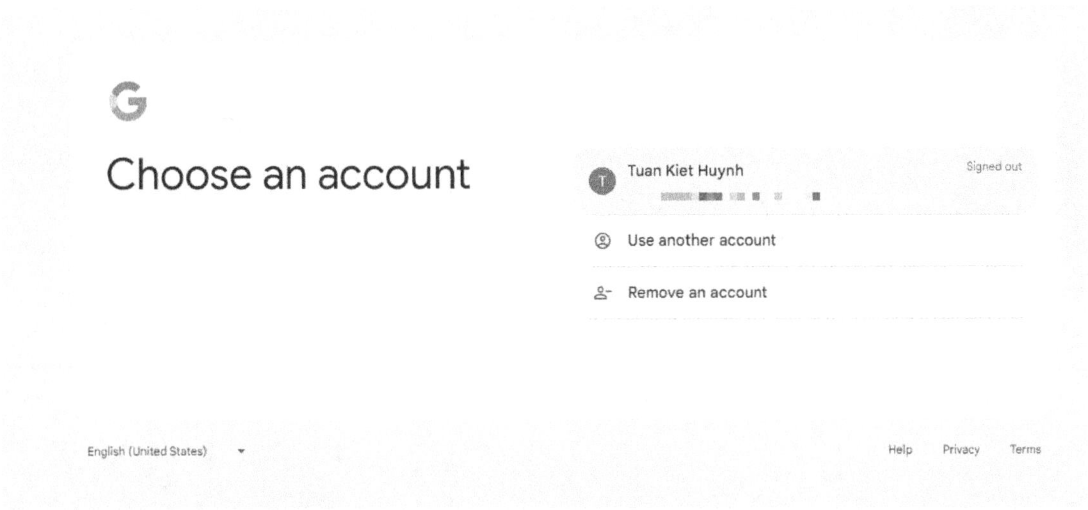

3. Enter your Google Account credentials to log in.

Step 2: Access Your Profile Settings

1. Click on your profile picture (or the default Google Account icon) in the top-right corner.
2. Select **Manage Your Google Account** from the dropdown menu.

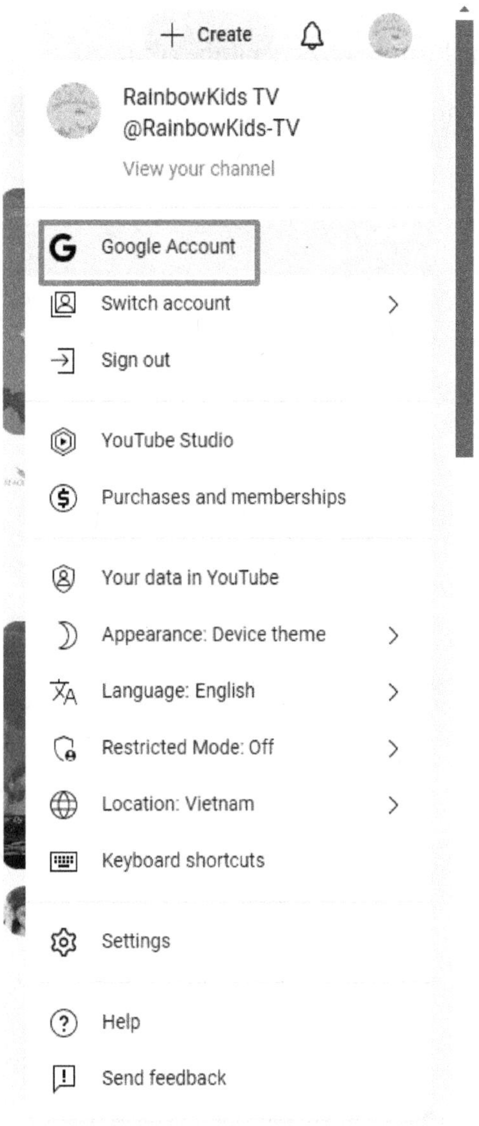

3. You'll be redirected to your Google Account settings.

Step 3: Change Your Profile Picture

1. In your Google Account settings, go to the **Personal Info** tab.
2. Under the **Basic Info** section, click on your current profile picture.
3. Select **Change** or **Upload a New Picture**.
4. Choose an image from your device and adjust it as needed.
5. Click **Set as Profile Photo** to save the changes.

Your new profile picture may take a few minutes to update across YouTube and other Google services.

Best Practices for Choosing a Profile Picture

When selecting a profile picture, keep these tips in mind:
✅ **Use a Clear Image** – A high-resolution picture ensures your profile looks professional and recognizable.
✅ **Keep It Simple** – Avoid overly complex images that may not be visible in smaller sizes.
✅ **Brand Consistency** – If you're a business or content creator, use a logo or an image that represents your brand.
✅ **Face Visibility** – If you're using YouTube for personal engagement, a headshot or a clear image of yourself works best.
✅ **Avoid Offensive or Copyrighted Content** – Make sure your image follows YouTube's community guidelines.

How to Change Your YouTube Name

Your YouTube name is also tied to your Google Account, but YouTube allows you to customize how your name appears on the platform without affecting other Google services. Here's how you can update it:

Step 1: Open YouTube Studio

1. Go to YouTube Studio. https://studio.youtube.com/
2. Click on **Customization** in the left-hand menu.
3. Select the **Basic Info** tab.

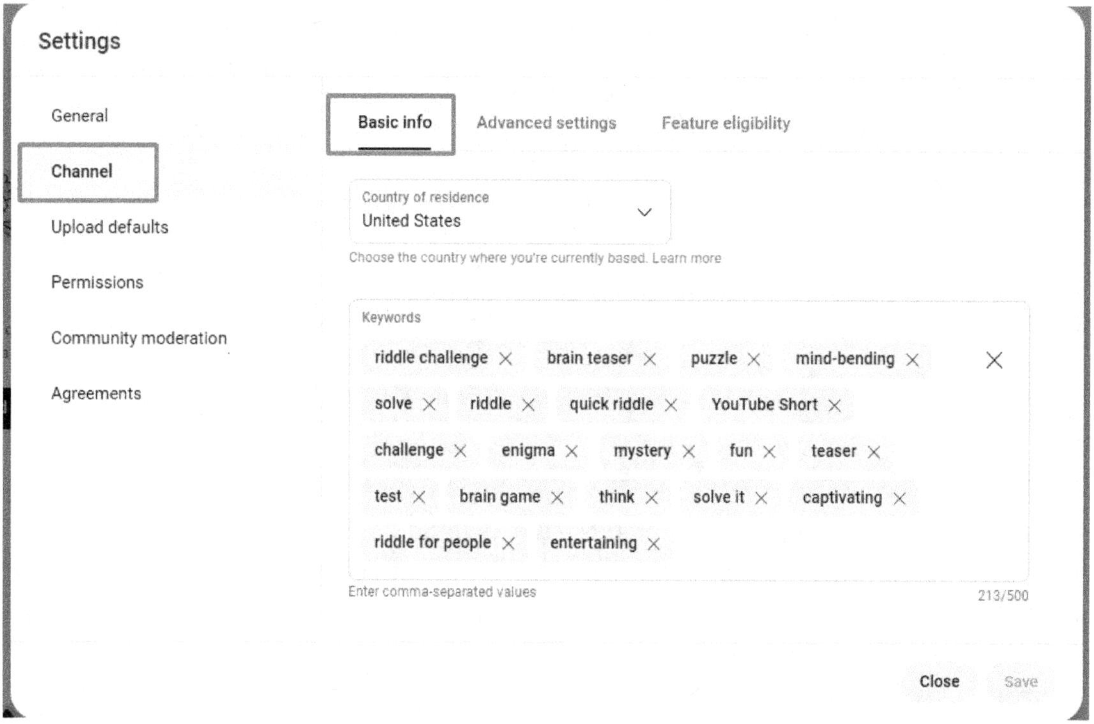

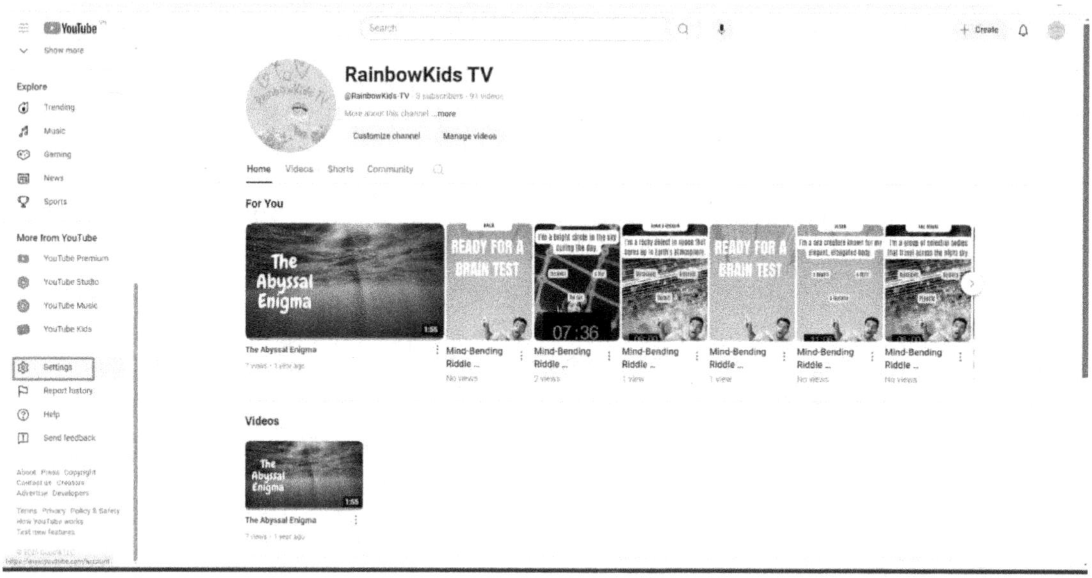

Step 2: Edit Your Channel Name

1. Click the **Edit Icon** next to your channel name.

2. Enter your new name.

3. Click **Save** to apply the changes.

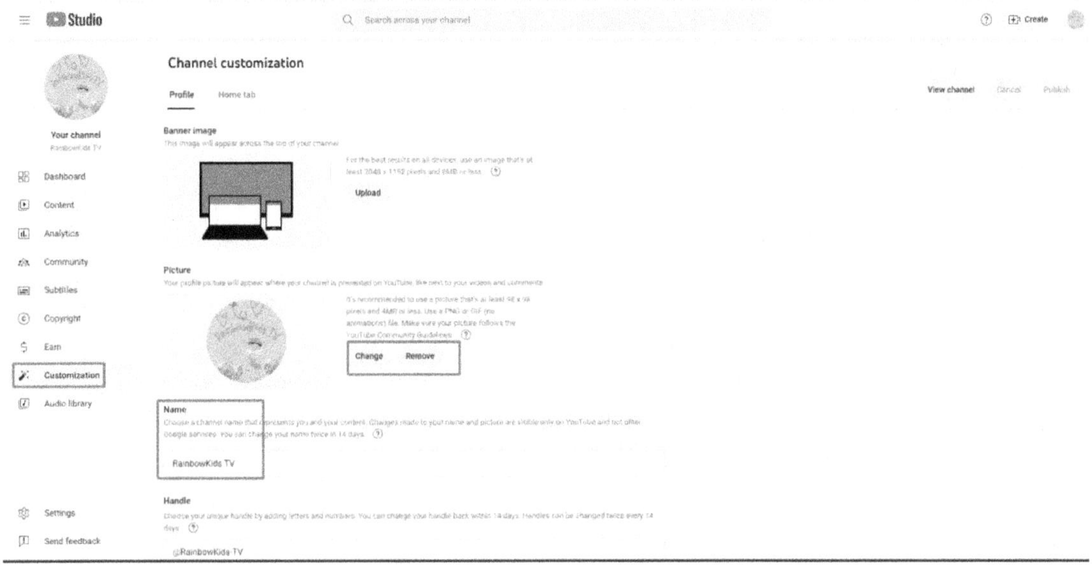

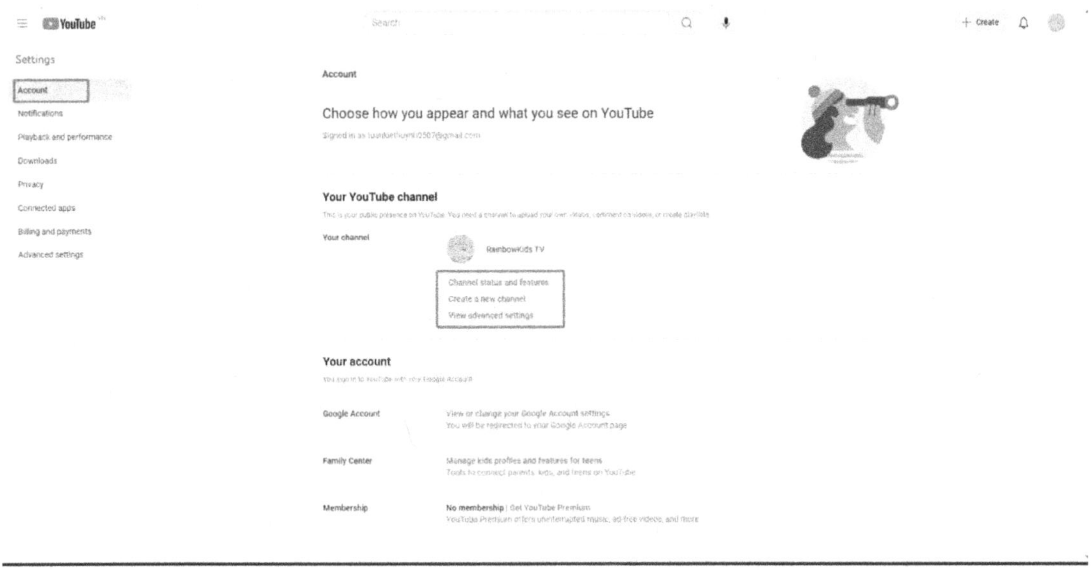

Alternatively, if you are using a personal Google Account and want to change your name across all Google services:

1. Go to **Manage Your Google Account**.

2. Under the **Personal Info** section, select **Name**.
3. Edit your first and last name as desired.
4. Click **Save** to update your changes.

Your new name should reflect within a few minutes on YouTube, but it may take longer for changes to appear across all Google services.

Best Practices for Choosing a YouTube Name

Your YouTube name is crucial, especially if you plan to create content or engage actively. Here are some tips to pick the best name:

✅ **Keep It Simple and Memorable** – A short, easy-to-remember name is more effective.
✅ **Make It Relevant** – If you have a niche (e.g., gaming, tech, or fitness), consider a name that aligns with your interests.
✅ **Avoid Special Characters and Numbers** – Names with excessive symbols or numbers can be harder to find.
✅ **Check for Availability** – Ensure your chosen name isn't already widely used by other channels.
✅ **Consider Future Growth** – Pick a name that you won't outgrow if you decide to expand your content focus.

Personal vs. Business YouTube Accounts

If you are using YouTube for personal enjoyment, your real name might be sufficient. However, if you're planning to build a brand or business presence, consider creating a **YouTube Brand Account**.

What is a YouTube Brand Account?

A **Brand Account** allows multiple people to manage the channel without giving access to your personal Google Account. This is ideal for businesses, content creators, or teams running a shared YouTube channel.

How to Create a Brand Account

1. Go to YouTube Settings. https://www.youtube.com/account

2. Under **Your Channel**, select **Create a New Channel**.

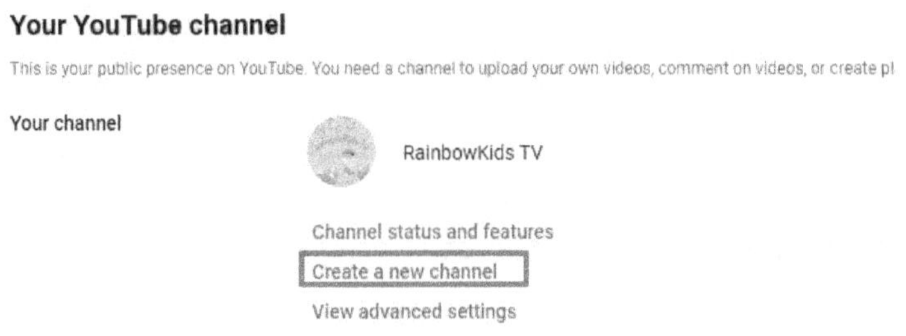

3. Enter a **Brand Name** instead of your personal name.

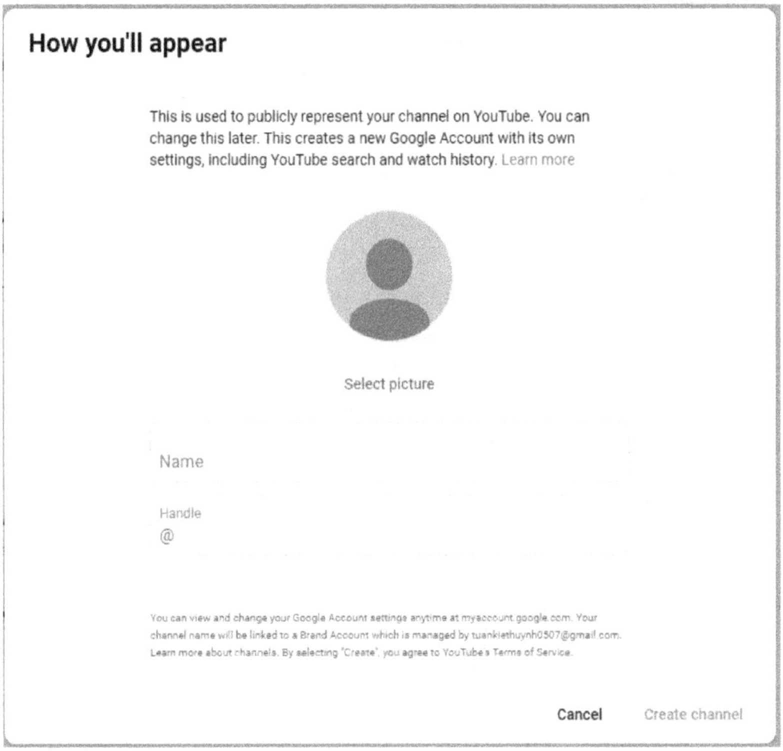

4. Click **Create** and follow the setup instructions.

Once set up, you can assign multiple managers to the account, making it easier to run a team-based YouTube channel.

Final Thoughts

Customizing your profile picture and name is an important step in making YouTube feel personal and engaging. Whether you're watching videos casually or preparing to launch your own content, a well-thought-out profile helps enhance your presence.

✅ **Your profile picture should be clear, simple, and representative of you or your brand.**
✅ **Your YouTube name should be memorable and relevant to your interests or niche.**
✅ **If you're planning to create content, consider a YouTube Brand Account for better management.**

By setting up these fundamental elements, you're now ready to fully explore and enjoy the YouTube experience. In the next section, we'll dive into understanding the YouTube dashboard, helping you navigate and customize your user experience efficiently.

1.2.2 Understanding Your YouTube Dashboard

The YouTube Dashboard is the central hub for managing your account, tracking your activity, and customizing your experience on the platform. Whether you're a casual viewer or an aspiring content creator, understanding the YouTube Dashboard will help you navigate the platform more efficiently. This section will provide an in-depth look at the YouTube Dashboard, its key features, and how you can use it to enhance your YouTube experience.

---

1. What is the YouTube Dashboard?

The YouTube Dashboard is a control panel that provides access to essential tools and insights about your YouTube activity. For regular users, it offers an overview of their watch history, subscriptions, and recommended content. For content creators, the Dashboard becomes even more powerful, offering detailed analytics, video management tools, and monetization settings.

You can access the YouTube Dashboard by clicking on your profile icon in the top-right corner of the YouTube homepage and selecting **"YouTube Studio"** (if you're a creator) or simply navigating through the menu on the left-hand side of the screen.

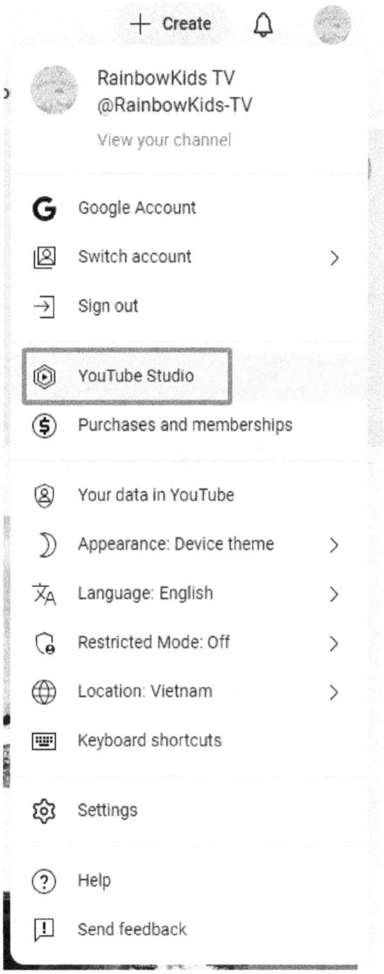

2. Key Sections of the YouTube Dashboard

The YouTube Dashboard is divided into several sections, each serving a specific purpose. Below is a breakdown of the most important sections and how to use them.

Home Section

When you log into YouTube, the **Home** section is the first thing you see. This page is personalized based on your interests, watch history, and subscriptions. Here's what you'll find on your Home page:

- **Recommended Videos** – YouTube's algorithm suggests videos based on your watch history and engagement.
- **Trending Content** – A section showcasing popular videos across different categories.
- **Shorts Feed** – A dedicated space for YouTube Shorts, which are short-form vertical videos.
- **Live Streams** – Recommended live broadcasts that match your interests.

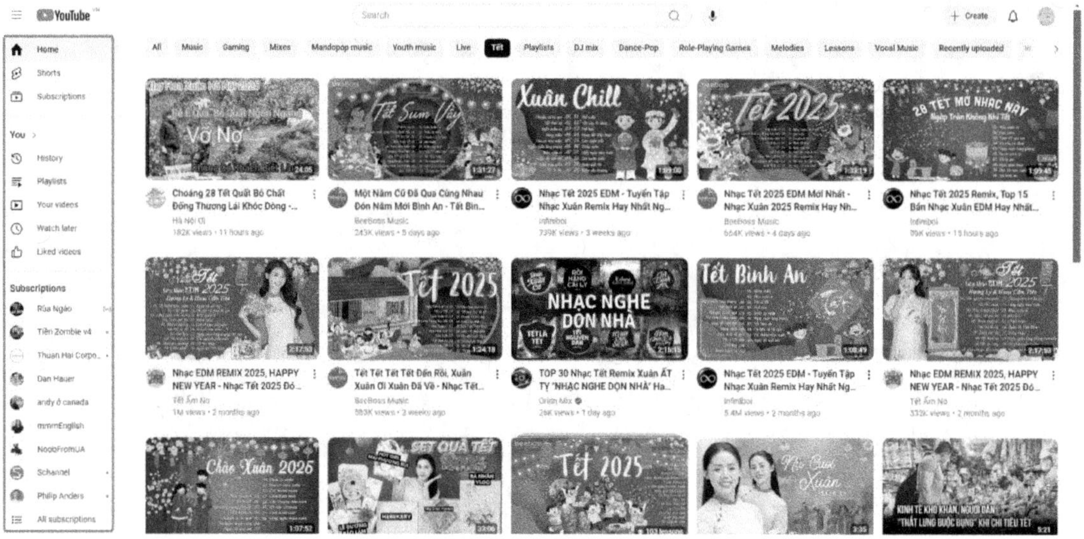

Subscriptions Section

The **Subscriptions** tab allows you to keep track of new content from channels you've subscribed to. This section is useful for staying updated with your favorite creators and never missing an upload.

Features include:

- **Recent Uploads** – A chronological feed of the latest videos from your subscribed channels.
- **Community Posts** – If a creator shares updates, polls, or images, you'll see them here.
- **Live Videos from Subscribed Channels** – If a creator you follow is live, their stream will appear here.

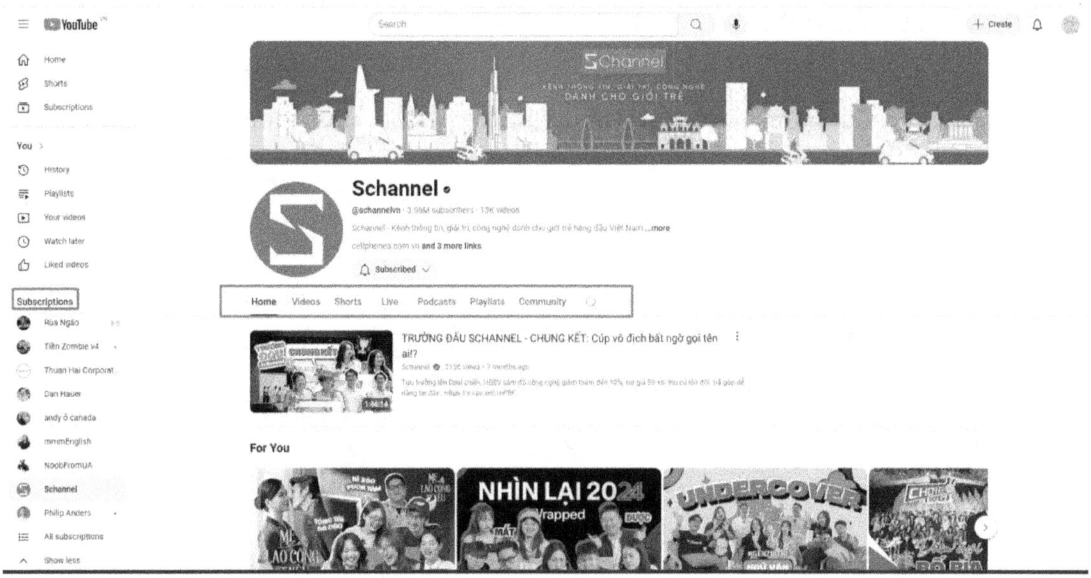

Library and History Section

The **Library** section acts as a personal archive of your YouTube activity. It includes:

- **Watch History** – A log of all the videos you've watched, making it easy to revisit content.
- **Liked Videos** – A collection of videos you've given a thumbs-up to.
- **Playlists** – Any playlists you've created or saved for later viewing.
- **Downloads** (for YouTube Premium users) – Offline videos available for viewing without an internet connection.

Watch Later and Playlists

The **Watch Later** feature allows you to save videos to view at a more convenient time. Playlists, on the other hand, enable you to organize videos into specific collections, such as "Educational Videos," "Workout Routines," or "Favorite Music Videos."

How to create a playlist:

1. Click the **Save** button below a video.
2. Select **"Create a new playlist."**
3. Name your playlist and adjust the privacy settings (Public, Unlisted, or Private).

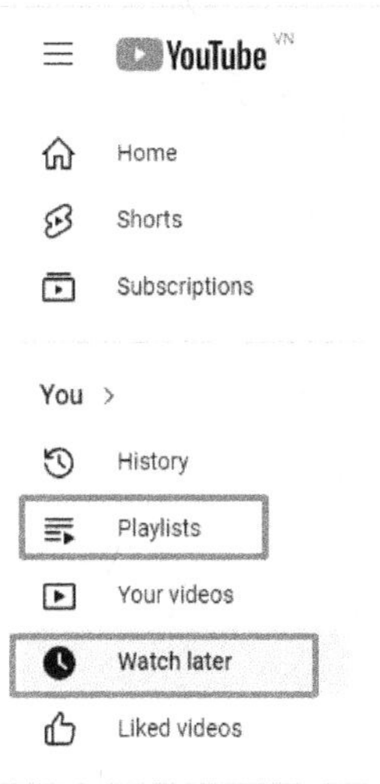

Notifications and Bell Icon

The **Bell Icon** next to your profile picture notifies you about important updates, including:

- New uploads from subscribed channels.
- Replies to your comments.
- Mentions from other users.
- Announcements from YouTube.

Clicking the bell icon allows you to customize notifications by selecting **"All," "Personalized,"** or **"None."**

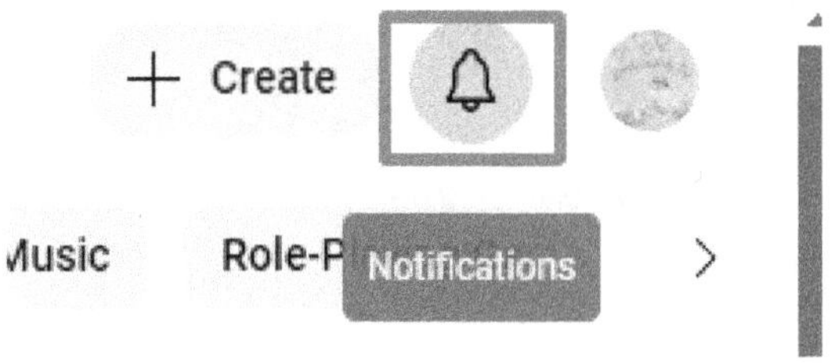

3. YouTube Dashboard for Creators

If you are a content creator, the **YouTube Studio Dashboard** provides additional tools for managing your channel.

Channel Overview

When you enter YouTube Studio, you'll see a summary of your channel's performance, including:

- **Recent video performance** – Stats on your latest uploads.
- **Subscriber count** – Your current number of subscribers.
- **News and updates** – YouTube's latest feature announcements.

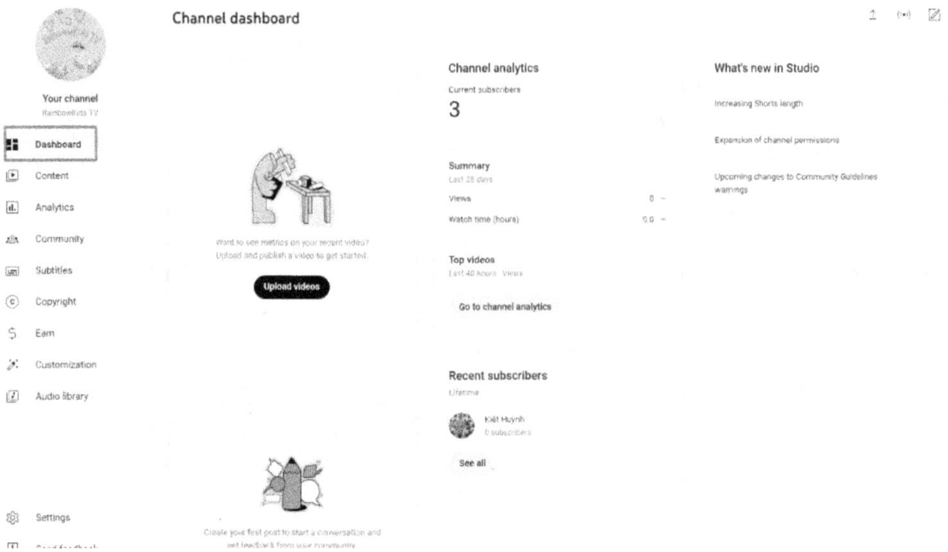

Analytics and Performance Tracking

YouTube Analytics is a powerful tool that helps creators understand their audience. It provides insights into:

- **Watch time** – The total time viewers have spent watching your videos.
- **Audience retention** – How long viewers stay engaged with your content.
- **Traffic sources** – Where your views are coming from (search, external websites, etc.).

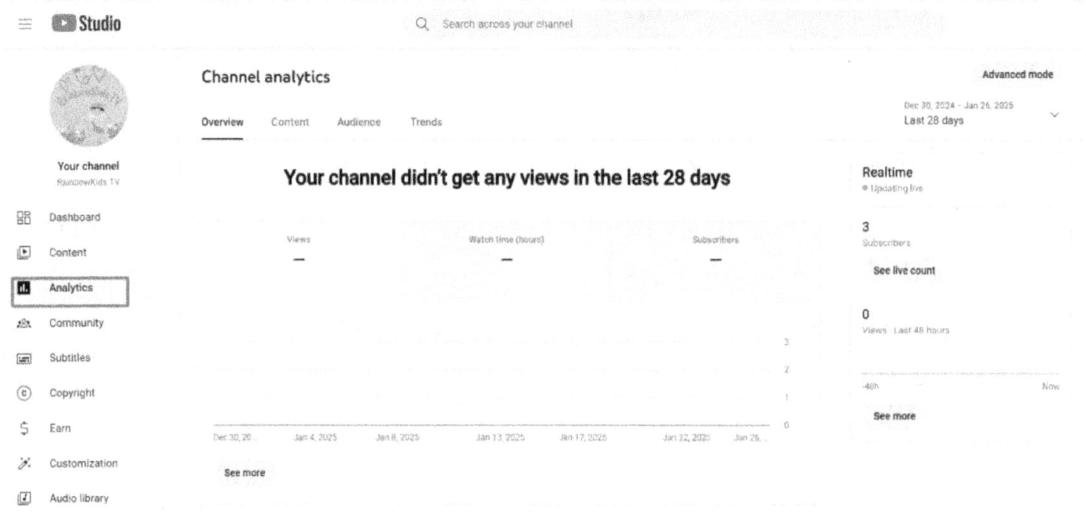

Content Management

The **Videos** tab lets you manage all your uploaded content, including:

- **Editing video details** – Title, description, and thumbnail customization.
- **Checking copyright claims** – Ensuring your videos comply with YouTube's policies.
- **Adding captions and subtitles** – Making content accessible to a wider audience.

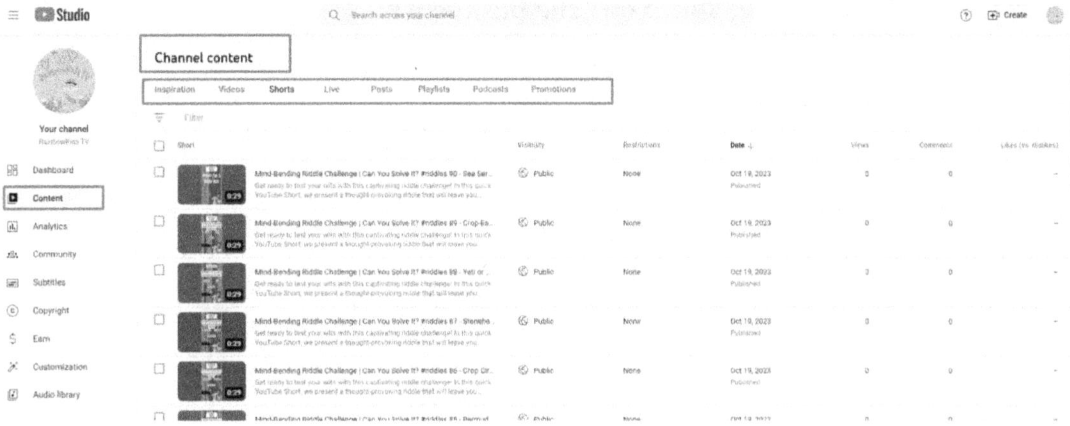

Monetization and Revenue

For creators who qualify, the **Monetization** tab allows them to:

- Enable ads on their videos.
- Join the **YouTube Partner Program (YPP).**
- Set up **Super Chats and Channel Memberships.**

Comments and Community Engagement

The **Comments** section helps creators engage with their audience by:

- Replying to comments directly.
- Filtering spam or inappropriate messages.
- Pinning top comments to highlight valuable discussions.

---

4. Customizing Your YouTube Dashboard Experience

YouTube allows users to customize their Dashboard by:

- **Adjusting recommendations** – Clicking "Not interested" on unwanted videos.
- **Managing subscriptions** – Organizing channels into custom lists.
- **Personalizing notifications** – Selecting which updates to receive.

---

5. Tips for Efficiently Using Your YouTube Dashboard

To make the most of your YouTube Dashboard:

✅ **Regularly clear your Watch History** to refresh recommendations.
✅ **Subscribe to favorite channels** for easy access to new content.
✅ **Use playlists** to keep content organized.
✅ **Customize notifications** to avoid unnecessary alerts.
✅ **Explore YouTube Studio** if you plan to create content.

Conclusion

Understanding your YouTube Dashboard is essential for maximizing your experience on the platform. Whether you're a casual viewer or an aspiring content creator, knowing how to navigate and use YouTube's features will help you stay organized, discover new content, and engage with the community effectively. By mastering the Dashboard, you can enjoy a seamless and personalized YouTube experience, making your time on the platform more enjoyable and productive.

1.2.3 Privacy Settings and Security

As a YouTube user, understanding and managing your privacy settings and security is crucial for maintaining a safe and enjoyable experience on the platform. YouTube provides various tools and options to help users control who can see their content, what personal information is shared, and how they can protect their accounts from potential security threats. This section will guide you through the essential aspects of privacy settings and security measures to help you navigate YouTube safely.

Understanding YouTube Privacy Settings

Privacy settings on YouTube determine how your activity, content, and personal information are shared with others. These settings help you control:

- Who can see your uploaded videos and playlists.
- Whether your subscriptions are public or private.
- How others interact with your content.

- The level of personalization YouTube applies based on your activity.

1. Setting Your Account Privacy Preferences

To access and adjust your privacy settings:

1. Open YouTube and sign in to your Google account.
2. Click on your profile picture in the top-right corner.
3. Select **"Settings"** from the dropdown menu.

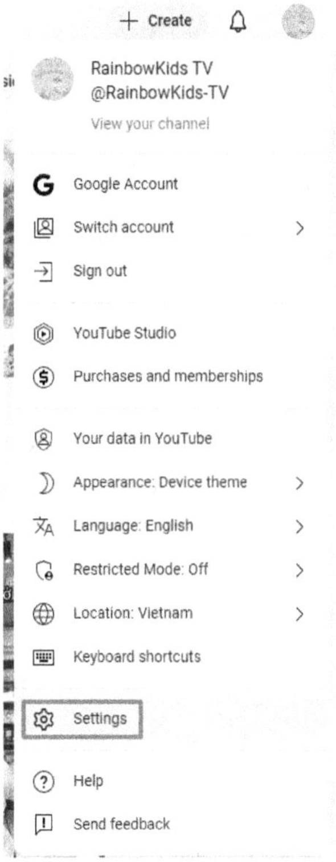

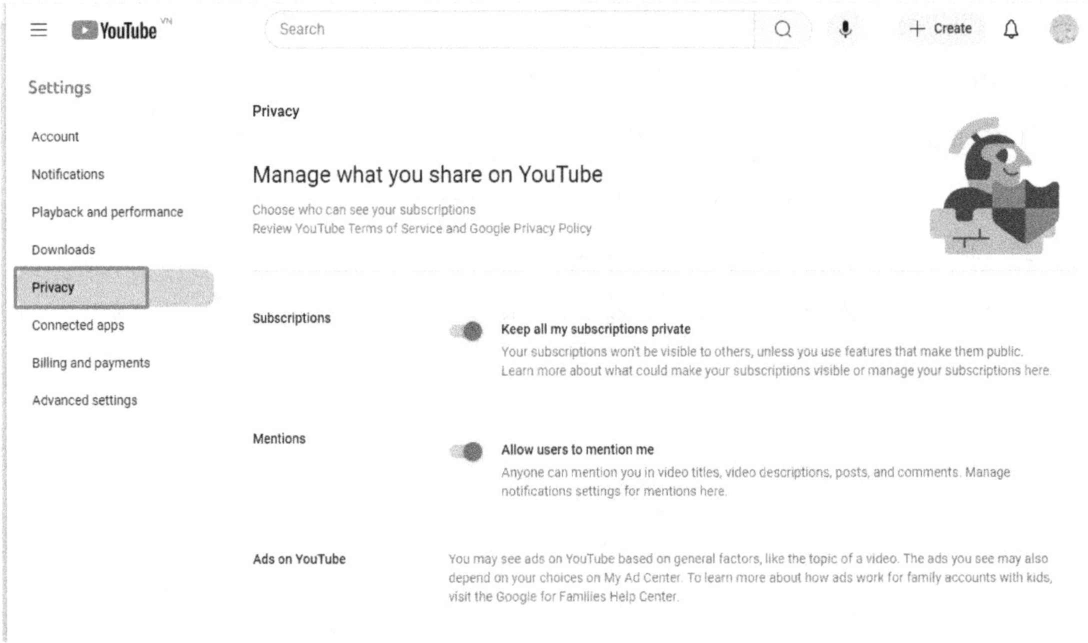

4. Navigate to the **"Privacy"** section.

Here, you can manage various privacy-related options, including your subscription visibility, playlist settings, and liked videos.

2. Managing Your Video Privacy Settings

Every time you upload a video, YouTube allows you to choose its visibility:

- **Public**: Anyone can watch your video, and it may appear in search results and recommendations.
- **Unlisted**: Only people with the direct link can watch the video, but it won't appear in search results or on your channel page.
- **Private**: Only you (and selected people you invite) can view the video.

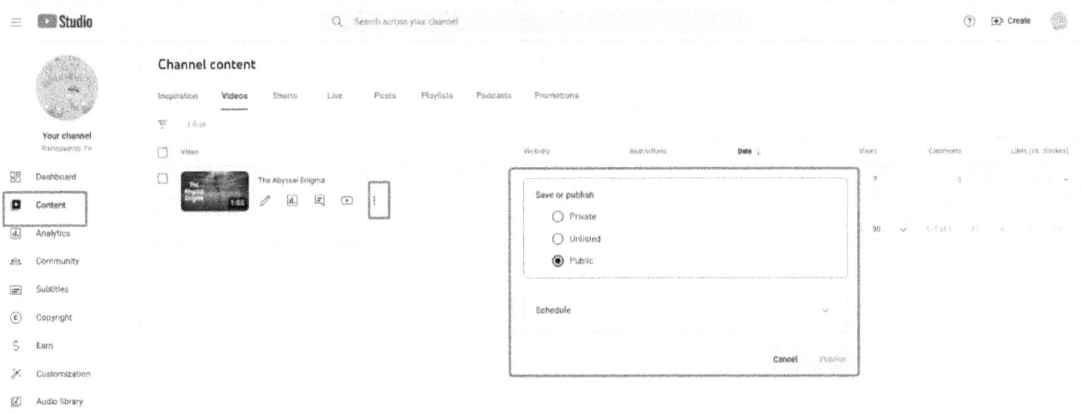

To set video privacy:

1. Go to **YouTube Studio** and click on **"Content"** in the left menu.
2. Select the video you want to manage.
3. Click **"Visibility"**, then choose **Public, Unlisted, or Private**.
4. Click **Save** to apply the changes.

If you are concerned about privacy, setting sensitive or personal videos as "Unlisted" or "Private" is a good option.

3. Controlling Your Subscriptions and Playlists

By default, your subscriptions and playlists may be visible to others. However, you can choose to keep them private:

1. Go to **"Settings"** > **"Privacy"** in YouTube.
2. Toggle on **"Keep all my subscriptions private"** if you don't want others to see which channels you follow.
3. Toggle on **"Keep all my saved playlists private"** to restrict visibility of playlists you create.

These settings ensure that your viewing preferences remain private.

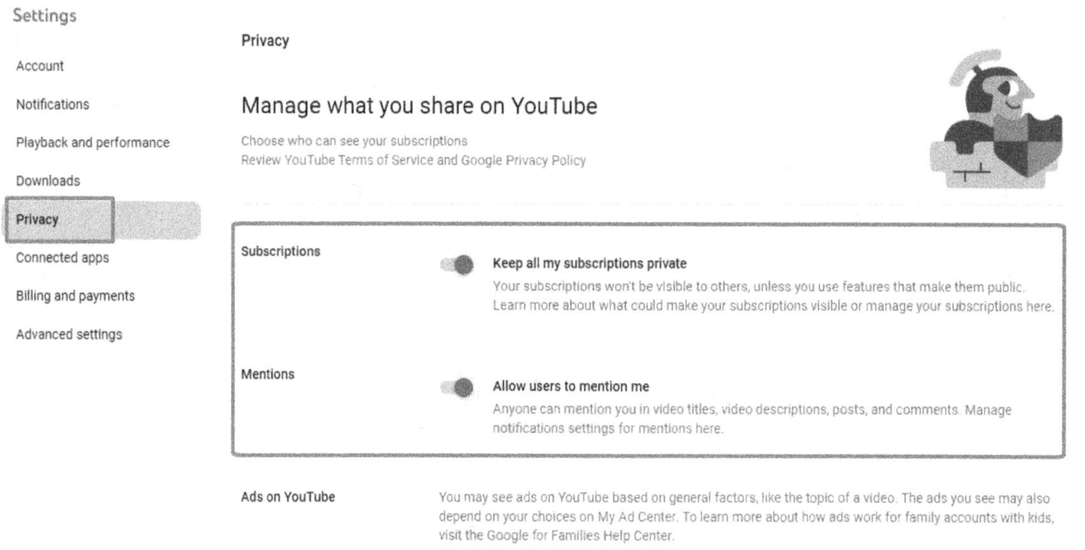

4. Managing Comments and Interactions

YouTube allows you to control how others interact with your content by managing comment settings:

- **Allow all comments**: Anyone can comment on your videos.
- **Hold potentially inappropriate comments for review**: YouTube filters out comments that may be offensive.
- **Hold all comments for review**: No comments appear unless you approve them.
- **Disable comments**: No one can comment on your videos.

To adjust these settings:

1. Open **YouTube Studio**.
2. Click **"Settings"** on the left menu.
3. Select **"Community" > "Defaults"**.
4. Choose your preferred comment settings.

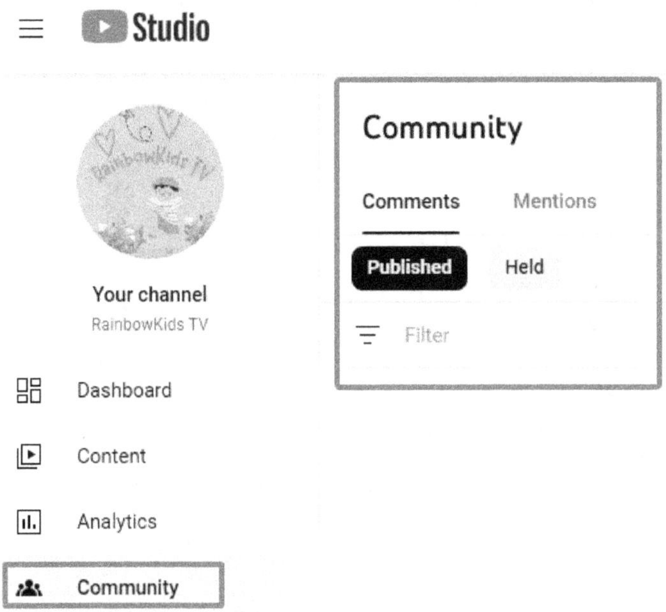

Managing comments helps maintain a positive and respectful interaction on your channel.

Enhancing Your YouTube Security

Security is just as important as privacy on YouTube. Keeping your account safe prevents unauthorized access and protects your personal information.

1. Strengthening Your Google Account Security

Since YouTube is linked to your Google account, securing your Google account is the first step to ensuring YouTube security. Follow these best practices:

Enable Two-Factor Authentication (2FA)

Two-Factor Authentication adds an extra layer of security by requiring a verification code in addition to your password.

To enable 2FA:

1. Go to your **Google Account Settings**.
2. Click **"Security"** in the left menu.
3. Find **"2-Step Verification"** and click **"Get Started"**.

4. Follow the instructions to set up authentication via your phone or an authentication app.

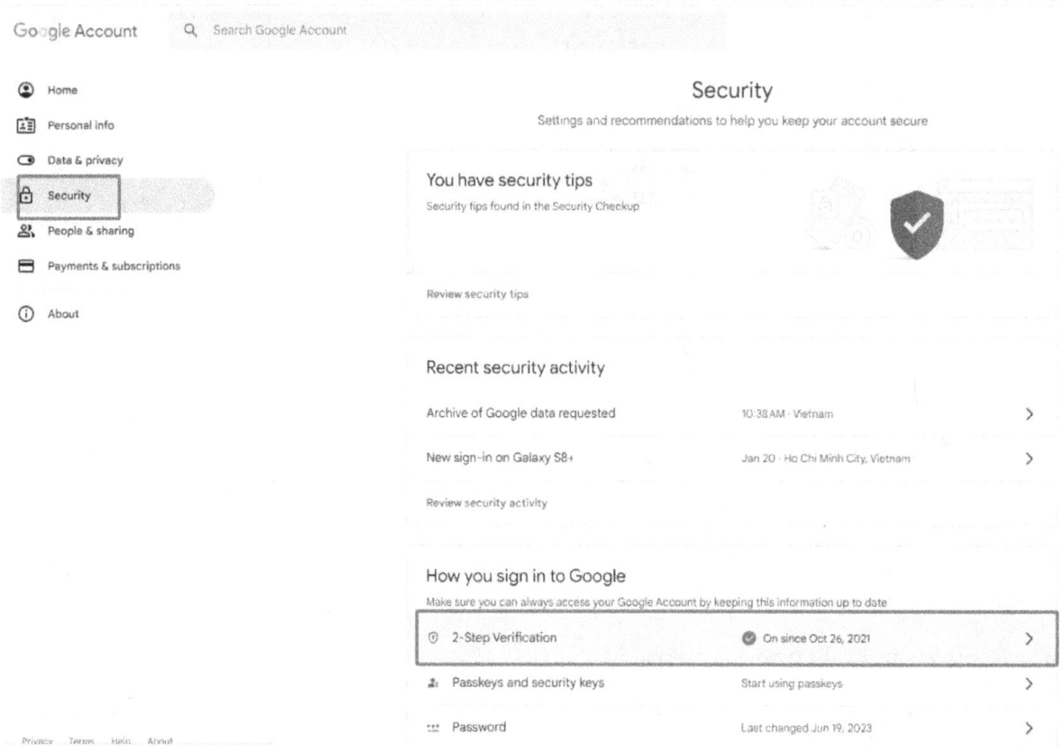

Use a Strong Password

A secure password should be:

- At least 12 characters long.
- A mix of uppercase and lowercase letters, numbers, and special symbols.
- Unique (not used for other accounts).

Consider using a password manager to store your credentials securely.

2. Recognizing and Avoiding Phishing Attempts

Phishing scams attempt to steal your login credentials by tricking you into clicking malicious links or providing your password on fake websites. To avoid phishing:

- Never click on suspicious links in emails claiming to be from YouTube or Google.

- Always check the URL before logging in (it should be **accounts.google.com** or **youtube.com**).
- Enable Google's **Advanced Protection Program** if you handle sensitive content.

3. Managing Connected Apps and Devices

You may have granted third-party apps or devices access to your Google account over time. It's essential to review and revoke unnecessary access:

1. Go to your **Google Account Settings**.
2. Click **"Security"** > **"Third-party apps with account access"**.
3. Remove any apps or devices that you no longer use or recognize.

This ensures that only trusted applications can access your YouTube data.

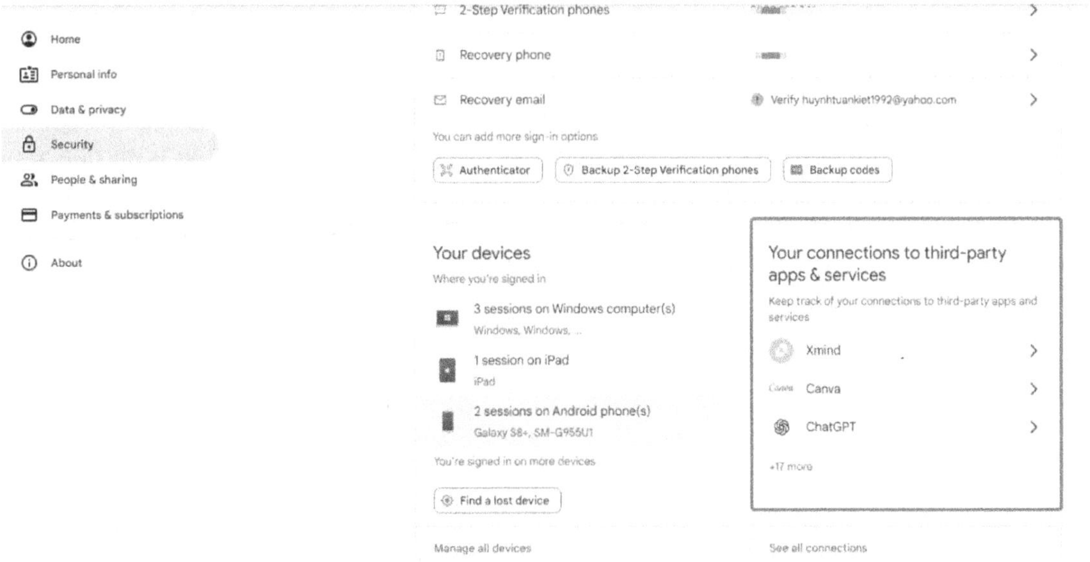

4. Reporting Suspicious Activity

If you suspect unauthorized access or see unusual activity on your account, take action immediately:

- Change your password.
- Review recent activity in **Google Account Security**.

- Use Google's **Security Checkup** to review and strengthen your security settings.
- Report hacked accounts to YouTube Support if you lose access.

5. Handling Harassment and Cyberbullying

If you experience harassment or cyberbullying on YouTube, you can:

- **Block users**: Prevent specific users from commenting or interacting with your content.
- **Report inappropriate content**: Flag videos, comments, or messages that violate YouTube's policies.
- **Adjust privacy settings**: Restrict who can comment or contact you.

These measures help ensure a safer and more positive experience.

Conclusion

Managing your privacy settings and security on YouTube is essential for protecting your account, maintaining control over your content, and ensuring a safe online experience. By understanding and applying these best practices, you can enjoy YouTube with peace of mind, knowing that your personal information and activity are safeguarded. Whether you're a casual viewer or an aspiring creator, taking the time to configure your privacy and security settings properly will enhance your overall YouTube experience.

1.3 Exploring the YouTube Interface

1.3.1 Home Tab: Discovering Recommended Videos

The YouTube **Home Tab** is the first thing you see when you open YouTube, whether on a desktop, mobile device, or smart TV. It is a personalized hub where YouTube curates a selection of videos based on your viewing habits, subscriptions, and trending content. This tab is essential for discovering new videos, engaging with your favorite creators, and exploring topics you might not have considered before.

In this section, we'll explore how the Home Tab works, how YouTube recommends videos, and how you can make the most of this feature to enhance your viewing experience.

---

1. How the YouTube Home Tab Works

The Home Tab serves as YouTube's central feed, displaying a collection of videos tailored to each user. It uses a sophisticated recommendation system that considers various factors, including:

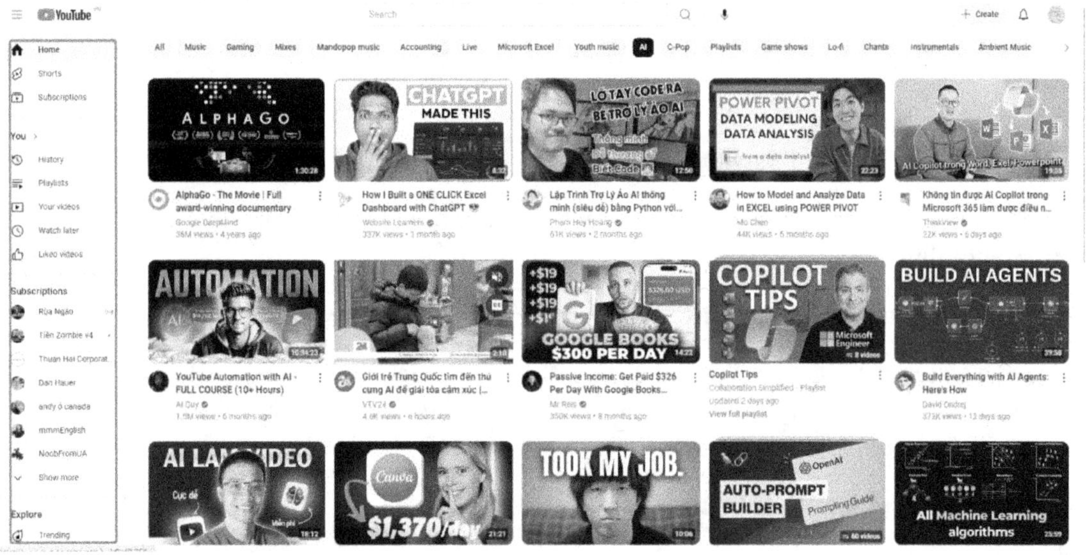

- **Your Watch History** – Videos similar to those you've previously watched will appear on your home feed.

- **Your Subscriptions** – Videos from channels you're subscribed to often show up in the Home Tab.
- **Trending Content** – Popular and trending videos in your region or globally may be recommended.
- **User Engagement** – Videos with high engagement, such as likes, comments, and shares, are more likely to appear.
- **Watch Time & Preferences** – YouTube tracks how long you watch different types of videos and adjusts recommendations accordingly.

The Home Tab refreshes dynamically, meaning the recommendations change as you watch more videos and interact with different types of content.

---

2. Understanding the Sections of the Home Tab

When you open YouTube's Home Tab, you'll typically see the following sections:

A. Top Video Recommendations

The first few rows of the Home Tab display what YouTube believes are the most relevant videos for you. These could include:

- Videos similar to what you've watched before
- New uploads from your subscriptions
- Popular or trending videos

YouTube tries to balance personalized recommendations with fresh content to keep your experience diverse.

B. "Up Next" and Suggested Videos

If you've watched videos on YouTube recently, the Home Tab may suggest similar content under an "Up Next" section. This helps you continue watching related videos without searching for them.

C. Sections Based on Your Interests

YouTube sometimes groups recommendations into categories such as:

- "Because You Watched…" – Videos related to something you recently watched

- "Trending in [Your Country]" – Popular videos among users in your region
- "Music for You" – If you frequently watch music videos, YouTube curates a personalized music playlist
- "Gaming, Tech, Cooking, Fitness, etc." – Custom categories based on topics you engage with

D. Shorts Section

With the rise of short-form content, YouTube's Home Tab now includes a **Shorts section**, displaying quick, vertical videos (under 60 seconds). This feature is inspired by platforms like TikTok and Instagram Reels.

E. Live Streams & Premieres

If there are live broadcasts or video premieres happening from your favorite channels, YouTube may feature them prominently on your Home Tab.

---

3. How YouTube's Recommendation System Works

YouTube's algorithm is one of the most advanced recommendation engines on the internet. It uses artificial intelligence (AI) and machine learning to predict what you'll want to watch next. Here's how it determines recommendations:

A. User Behavior Tracking

YouTube monitors:

- What videos you watch
- How long you watch them
- Whether you like, comment, or share them
- Which videos you skip
- How often you return to certain types of content

B. Video Metadata and Content Analysis

YouTube's algorithm also considers:

- Video titles, descriptions, and tags

- Thumbnail images
- The popularity of a video within a certain niche

C. Community Engagement Metrics

Videos with high engagement (likes, comments, shares) are more likely to be recommended. This ensures users see content that is popular and engaging.

---

4. Customizing Your Home Tab Experience

YouTube's recommendations are powerful, but they aren't perfect. If you want to refine your Home Tab to better suit your interests, here's what you can do:

A. Liking and Disliking Videos

- Clicking the **"Like" (Thumbs Up)** button tells YouTube you enjoy this type of content.
- Clicking the **"Dislike" (Thumbs Down)** button helps remove unwanted content from your recommendations.

B. Removing Unwanted Videos

- Click on the three-dot menu (⋮) next to a video and select **"Not Interested"** to stop seeing similar recommendations.

C. Managing Your Watch History

- If you watch a video that doesn't align with your usual preferences, you can remove it from your watch history to prevent similar recommendations.
- To do this, go to **YouTube Settings → History & Privacy → Manage Watch History**.

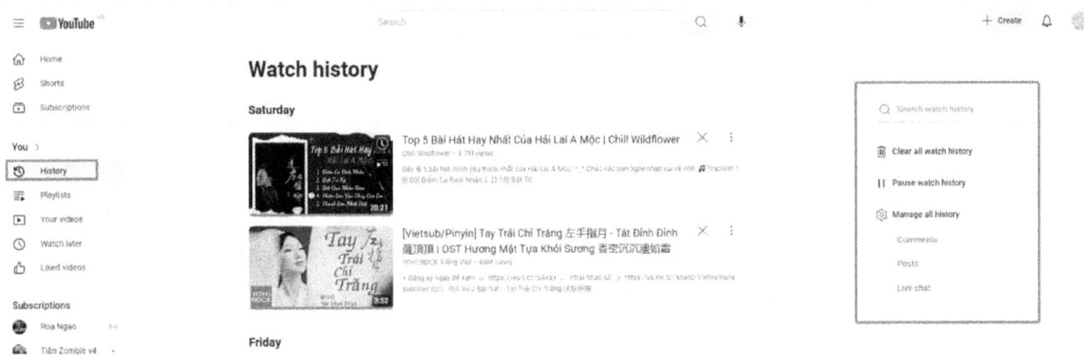

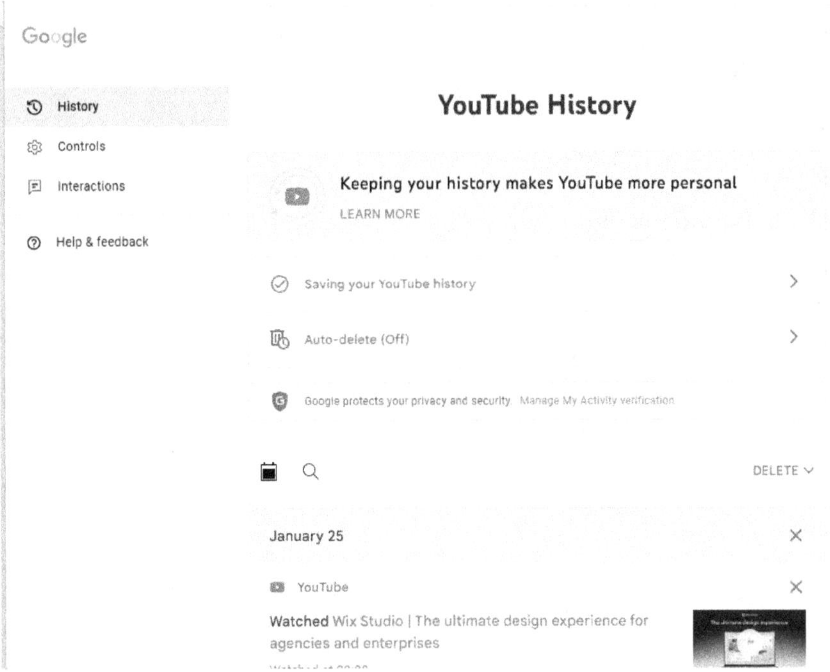

D. Subscribing to Channels

- Subscribing to channels ensures that their new videos appear in your Home Tab.
- Turning on the **notification bell** lets you receive alerts for new uploads.

E. Using Incognito Mode

- If you want to watch videos without affecting your recommendations, you can enable **Incognito Mode** in the YouTube app.

5. Making the Most of the YouTube Home Tab

To get the best experience from YouTube's Home Tab, consider these tips:

A. Explore New Content

- Check out different video categories like **Tech Reviews, Documentaries, ASMR, Travel Vlogs, Educational Talks**, and more.

B. Use Playlists

- If you find a video you like but don't have time to watch it, save it to **"Watch Later"** or create a custom playlist.

C. Balance Your Watch Time

- If you only watch one type of content (e.g., gaming), YouTube will keep recommending similar videos. Try mixing it up by watching different genres.

D. Follow Creators You Enjoy

- Engage with creators by subscribing, commenting, and liking their videos. This helps YouTube understand what you like.

E. Check Out YouTube Shorts and Live Streams

- Shorts are great for quick entertainment, while **Live Streams** let you interact with creators in real-time.

6. Conclusion

The YouTube Home Tab is an incredibly powerful tool for discovering new content. By understanding how it works and how to customize it, you can enhance your experience, find videos that interest you, and make the most of your time on YouTube.

Whether you're looking for entertainment, education, or inspiration, the Home Tab curates a feed that suits your preferences. By actively engaging with the content, fine-tuning your recommendations, and exploring new categories, you can transform your YouTube experience into something truly personalized and enjoyable.

In the next section, we'll dive deeper into the **Subscriptions Tab**, where you can follow your favorite creators and stay updated on their latest uploads.

1.3.2 Subscriptions Tab: Following Your Favorite Channels

The **Subscriptions Tab** on YouTube is a powerful feature that allows users to stay updated with their favorite content creators. It provides an organized way to track new videos from channels you follow, ensuring you never miss an update from the YouTubers, educators, entertainers, or influencers you enjoy watching. In this section, we will explore the **Subscriptions Tab**, its features, how to subscribe and manage your subscriptions, and tips to optimize your experience.

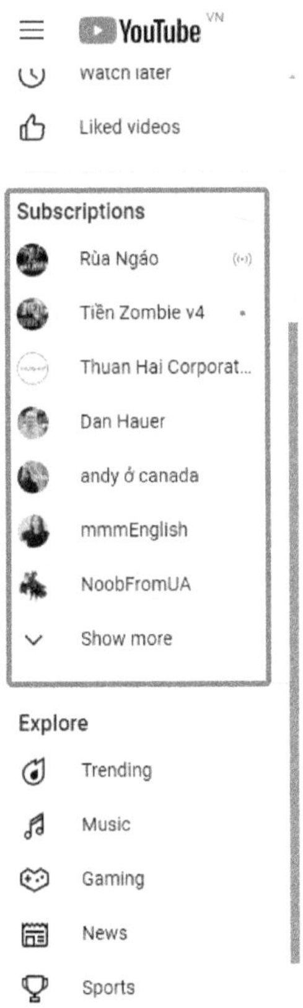

1. Understanding the Subscriptions Tab

The **Subscriptions Tab** is one of the primary sections of the YouTube interface, dedicated exclusively to showing the latest videos from the channels you follow. Unlike the **Home Tab**, which is curated by YouTube's recommendation algorithm, the **Subscriptions Tab** provides a direct feed of content from creators you have actively chosen to follow.

Where to Find the Subscriptions Tab

You can access the **Subscriptions Tab** from multiple locations in the YouTube interface:

- **On Desktop**: It is located on the left sidebar of the YouTube homepage. Clicking on "Subscriptions" will open a feed of the latest videos from your subscribed channels.
- **On Mobile (YouTube App)**: You can find the **Subscriptions Tab** at the bottom of the screen as an icon labeled **"Subscriptions."** Tapping it will take you to a dedicated section showing all new videos from your subscribed channels.
- **On Smart TVs and Gaming Consoles**: The Subscriptions Tab is accessible through the navigation menu, providing a similar experience optimized for larger screens.

What You Will See in the Subscriptions Tab

When you open the **Subscriptions Tab**, you will find:

1. **A List of New Videos** – The most recent uploads from the channels you subscribe to are displayed in chronological order.
2. **Live Streams and Premieres** – If any of your subscribed channels are live-streaming or have scheduled a premiere, they will appear at the top.
3. **Shorts from Subscribed Channels** – With the rise of short-form video content, YouTube now includes Shorts from your subscriptions.
4. **Community Posts** – Some creators use community posts to share updates, polls, or behind-the-scenes content. These posts may appear in your **Subscriptions Tab** if the creator has enabled them.

The **Subscriptions Tab** ensures that you have a **personalized, ad-free space** (except for in-video ads) where you can engage with your preferred content without interference from YouTube's recommendation system.

---

2. How to Subscribe to a YouTube Channel

Subscribing to a YouTube channel is a simple process, but understanding its benefits and features can improve your overall experience.

Steps to Subscribe to a Channel

To subscribe to a channel, follow these steps:

1. **Find a Channel** – Search for the channel using the YouTube search bar or discover it through recommendations.
2. **Click the "Subscribe" Button** – Located beneath the video player or on the channel's homepage.
3. **Enable Notifications (Optional)** – After subscribing, a **bell icon** appears next to the "Subscribed" button. Clicking this allows you to choose the type of notifications you receive.

Subscription Notification Settings

YouTube provides different levels of notifications for subscribed channels:

- **All Notifications** – You receive alerts every time the channel uploads a new video, starts a live stream, or posts an update.
- **Personalized Notifications** – YouTube's algorithm determines which updates to send based on your watch history and engagement.
- **No Notifications** – You remain subscribed but will not receive any notifications about new uploads.

Selecting the right notification setting ensures that you receive updates without being overwhelmed by unnecessary alerts.

---

3. Managing Your Subscriptions

As you subscribe to more channels over time, organizing and managing them effectively becomes essential.

Viewing Your Subscriptions List

To see all your subscribed channels:

- On **Desktop**: Click the **"Subscriptions"** tab and scroll down to view the channels.
- On **Mobile**: Open the **Subscriptions Tab** and tap **"Manage"** to see the full list.

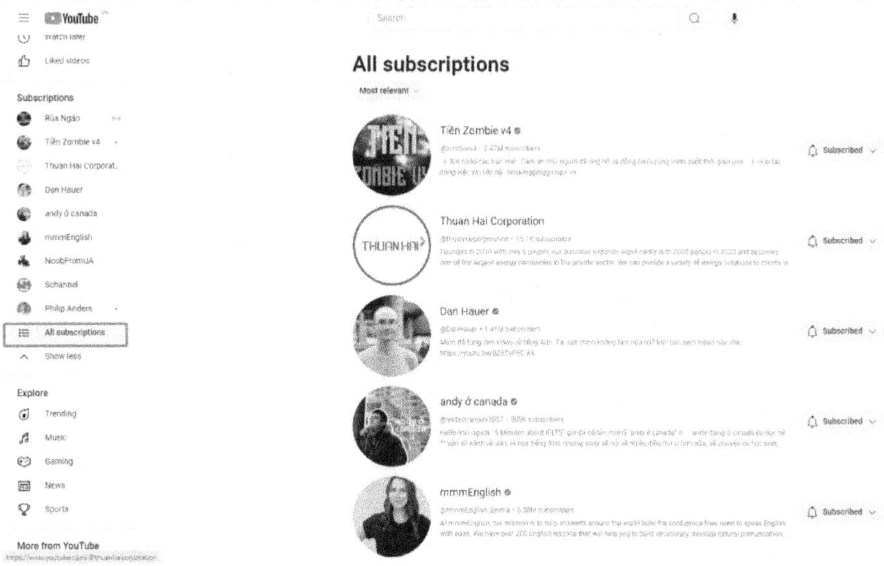

Organizing Subscriptions into Playlists

If you follow multiple types of content (e.g., educational, entertainment, music), you can organize your subscribed videos into playlists to make navigation easier.

Unsubscribing from Channels

If you no longer wish to follow a channel, unsubscribing is simple:

1. **Go to the Channel's Page**
2. **Click the "Subscribed" Button** – A pop-up will confirm the action.
3. **Confirm Unsubscribe**

This process removes the channel from your **Subscriptions Tab** but does not affect your watch history.

---

4. Benefits of Using the Subscriptions Tab

Avoiding Algorithm-Based Recommendations

Unlike the **Home Tab**, which is influenced by YouTube's algorithm, the **Subscriptions Tab** only shows content from creators you have personally chosen. This ensures a **more curated and relevant experience** without being influenced by YouTube's automated suggestions.

Staying Updated with Favorite Creators

By checking the **Subscriptions Tab** regularly, you can stay informed about new content without relying on notifications. This is especially useful if you subscribe to channels that do not upload frequently.

Discovering Exclusive Subscriber Content

Many YouTubers create content **exclusively for subscribers**, such as behind-the-scenes videos, Q&A sessions, or community polls. These updates often appear in the **Subscriptions Tab** and may not be visible in general recommendations.

---

5. Advanced Features for Subscribed Channels

YouTube offers several advanced features that enhance the subscription experience:

Memberships and Exclusive Content

Some YouTube channels offer paid memberships, allowing subscribers to access exclusive content, such as:

- **Member-only videos and live streams**
- **Early access to new uploads**
- **Custom emojis and badges in the comment section**

These features help creators generate revenue while giving subscribers extra perks.

Subscription Filters and Sorting

YouTube provides options to filter and sort subscriptions, allowing you to:

- **Sort by most recent activity**
- **View only live streams**
- **Filter by content type (videos, Shorts, community posts)**

Using these filters ensures you see the content you care about most.

---

6. Tips for an Enhanced Subscription Experience

1. **Check the Subscriptions Tab Daily** – Make it a habit to visit the tab instead of relying solely on notifications.
2. **Turn on Notifications for Important Channels** – Enable **"All Notifications"** for channels you don't want to miss.
3. **Use the "Watch Later" Playlist** – If you find videos but don't have time to watch them immediately, save them to the "Watch Later" playlist for easy access.
4. **Engage with Your Favorite Creators** – Liking, commenting, and sharing videos help creators continue making content.
5. **Balance Your Subscriptions** – Avoid subscribing to too many channels at once to prevent overwhelming your feed.

Conclusion

The **Subscriptions Tab** is an essential tool for anyone who regularly watches YouTube. It allows you to stay updated with your favorite channels, engage with content more effectively, and create a personalized viewing experience. Whether you are a casual viewer or a dedicated subscriber, understanding and utilizing the features of this tab will enhance your YouTube journey.

By following the best practices outlined in this section, you can take full advantage of the **Subscriptions Tab**, ensuring that you always stay connected with the content and creators you love.

1.3.3 Library and History: Managing Your Watched Videos

YouTube offers a powerful set of tools to help users track and manage the videos they have watched. The **Library** and **History** sections are essential features that allow you to revisit previously viewed content, organize videos for later viewing, and access playlists. Understanding how these features work will help you make the most of your YouTube experience.

---

1. Understanding the YouTube Library

The **Library** is your personal collection of YouTube activity. It provides quick access to your **watch history, saved playlists, liked videos, and downloaded content** (if applicable). This section acts as a control center where you can efficiently organize and retrieve videos.

Where to Find the Library?

The **Library** tab is located on the left-hand menu on desktop and in the bottom navigation bar on mobile devices. By tapping on this tab, you can see a summary of your recently watched videos, saved playlists, and downloads.

Key Features of the Library

The Library is divided into several sections that help you manage your viewing activity effectively:

1. **History** – Shows a chronological list of videos you have watched.

2. **Your Videos** – Displays the videos you have uploaded to YouTube (if you are a content creator).
3. **Playlists** – Allows you to access and manage your saved playlists.
4. **Liked Videos** – Stores all videos you have liked by clicking the thumbs-up button.
5. **Watch Later** – A special playlist where you can save videos you plan to watch in the future.
6. **Downloads** (For YouTube Premium users) – Stores downloaded videos for offline viewing.

Each of these sections provides valuable tools for organizing and managing your video consumption.

---

2. Managing Your Watch History

The **Watch History** feature is a record of all the videos you have watched while logged into your Google account. This feature is useful for:

- **Revisiting videos you enjoyed** without needing to search for them again.
- **Tracking content consumption** to maintain a productive viewing experience.
- **Managing recommendations**, as YouTube's algorithm uses your watch history to suggest new videos.

Viewing Your Watch History

To access your watch history:

- **On Desktop:**
    1. Click on the **Library** tab from the left-side menu.
    2. Select **History** to view a list of watched videos.
- **On Mobile:**
    1. Tap on the **Library** tab at the bottom of the screen.
    2. Select **History** to open your watched videos.

YouTube arranges your history in chronological order, making it easy to scroll through and find previously watched content.

Clearing and Managing Watch History

If you want to delete certain videos from your watch history or reset your recommendations, YouTube provides several options:

- **Removing a Single Video from History**

1. Open the **History** section.
2. Find the video you want to remove.
3. Click on the three-dot menu next to the video.
4. Select **Remove from watch history**.

- **Clearing Your Entire Watch History**

If you want to start fresh and remove all recorded history:

1. Open **History** from the Library.
2. Click on **Clear all watch history**.
3. Confirm the action when prompted.

⚠️ *Note: Clearing your watch history will reset YouTube's video recommendations since the platform uses your past views to suggest content.*

- **Pausing Watch History**

If you don't want YouTube to track your watched videos for a certain period:

1. Go to **History**.
2. Click on **Pause watch history**.
3. Confirm the action.

This is useful when you're watching videos that you don't want to influence your future recommendations.

---

3. Organizing Videos with Playlists

Playlists are a powerful tool to organize and save videos into custom categories. Instead of relying on your watch history, you can create specific playlists for different topics, such as **Cooking Tutorials, Workout Videos, Music, or Educational Content**.

How to Create a Playlist

1. Find a video you want to add to a playlist.
2. Click on the **Save** button below the video.
3. Choose an existing playlist or select **Create new playlist**.
4. Give the playlist a name and set its **privacy settings** (Public, Unlisted, or Private).
5. Click **Create** to save the playlist.

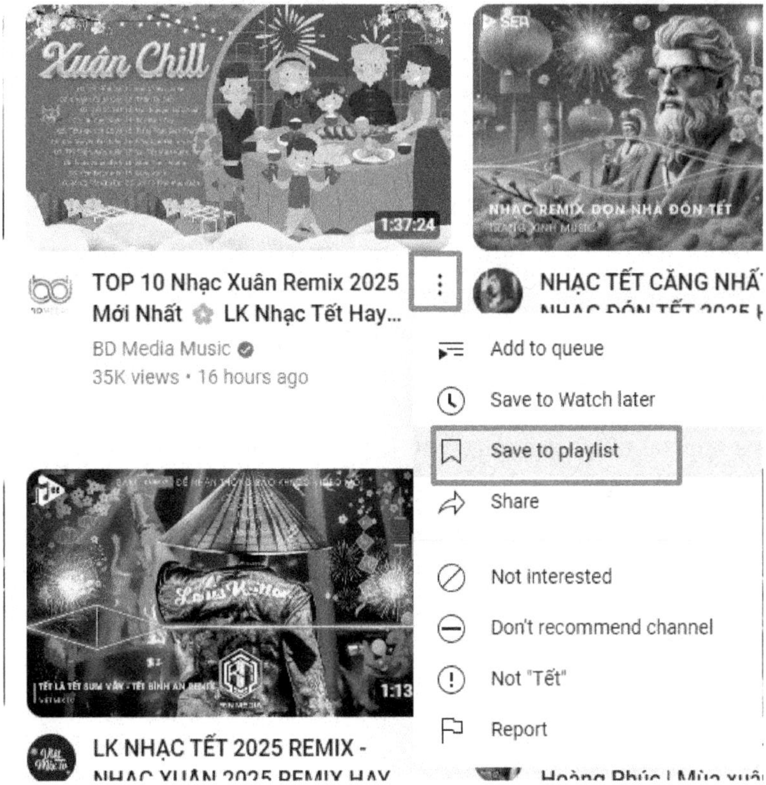

Managing Playlists

To access and edit your playlists:

- Go to the **Library** tab and scroll to the **Playlists** section.
- Click on a playlist to view its contents.
- Click the **Edit** button to rename, reorder, or remove videos.

Playlists help keep your YouTube experience more organized by categorizing videos based on your interests.

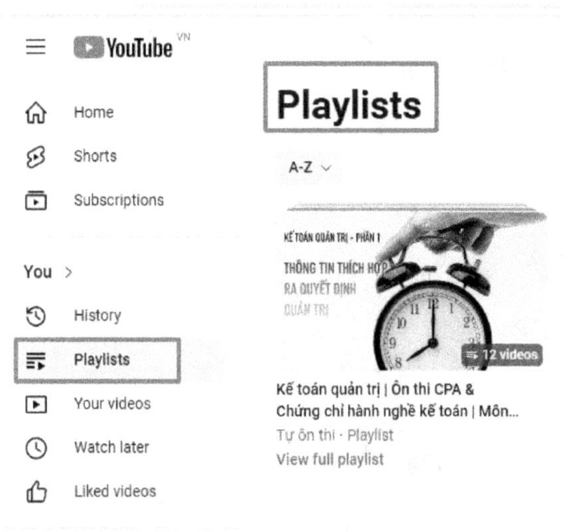

4. Using the "Watch Later" Feature

The **Watch Later** feature is a special playlist where you can save videos that you want to watch at a more convenient time. Unlike other playlists, this one is automatically created for all YouTube accounts.

Adding a Video to Watch Later

1. Find a video you want to save.
2. Click on the **Save** button below the video.
3. Select **Watch Later** from the menu.

Accessing and Managing Watch Later Videos

- Open the **Library** tab.

- Scroll to the **Watch Later** section.
- Click on the playlist to view saved videos.
- To remove a video, click on the three-dot menu and select **Remove from Watch Later**.

This feature is useful for keeping track of interesting content that you don't have time to watch immediately.

---

5. Downloading Videos for Offline Viewing (YouTube Premium Users)

If you have a **YouTube Premium** subscription, you can download videos to watch offline. This is particularly useful when traveling or when internet access is limited.

How to Download a Video

1. Find a video you want to save.
2. Click on the **Download** button below the video.

3. Select the preferred video quality.
4. The video will be saved in the **Downloads** section under the Library tab.

Managing Downloaded Videos

- Open the **Library** tab and select **Downloads**.
- Click on a video to watch it offline.
- To delete a downloaded video, tap the **three-dot menu** and choose **Remove download**.

Note: Downloaded videos will expire after a certain period unless you reconnect to the internet to renew them.

---

6. Conclusion

The **Library and History** sections of YouTube provide essential tools to manage your watched videos effectively. By using these features, you can:

✓☐ Easily find and revisit previously watched content.
✓☐ Remove or clear history to reset recommendations.
✓☐ Create and manage playlists to organize videos.
✓☐ Save videos for later viewing with the **Watch Later** feature.
✓☐ Download videos for offline viewing (if you have YouTube Premium).

Mastering these tools will help you **enhance your YouTube experience** by making it more organized, personalized, and convenient. Whether you're watching for entertainment, education, or research, understanding how to manage your watched videos will ensure you get the most out of YouTube.

CHAPTER II
Searching and Discovering Content

2.1 How to Search for Videos

The YouTube search bar is one of the most powerful tools for discovering content on the platform. Whether you're looking for entertainment, educational resources, tutorials, or specific topics, understanding how to use the search bar effectively will allow you to access a wide variety of videos with ease. In this section, we will guide you step-by-step on how to search for videos using the YouTube search bar, as well as how to refine and optimize your searches to find exactly what you're looking for.

2.1.1 Using the YouTube Search Bar Effectively

The YouTube search bar is typically located at the top of the page, and it's the first place most users go when they want to find content. It's designed to be user-friendly and versatile, capable of handling a variety of search queries, from short keywords to more complex phrases. Below, we will cover the different aspects of using the search bar effectively, helping you search like a pro.

---

1. Understanding the Search Bar Interface

The search bar on YouTube is simple yet powerful. When you type a query into the search bar, YouTube immediately starts showing search suggestions. These suggestions are often tailored to your previous search history and popular searches from other users. The suggestions can range from specific keywords to full phrases. To use this to your advantage:

- **Autocomplete**: As you start typing, YouTube will offer autocomplete suggestions based on common searches. You can click on any of these suggestions to instantly perform a search. This feature is great for finding popular or trending topics without needing to type the entire query.
- **Search Icon**: Once you've typed your search term, you can click on the magnifying glass icon to execute your search. Alternatively, you can press the "Enter" key on your keyboard.

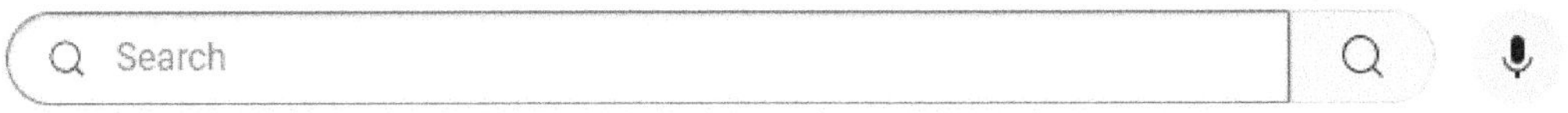

2. Using Keywords for Effective Searching

The most effective way to search for videos on YouTube is by using the right keywords. A "keyword" is simply a word or phrase that describes the content you're searching for. The more specific you are with your keywords, the more refined your search results will be. Here are some tips on using keywords effectively:

- **Use Specific Terms**: If you're looking for a video on how to bake a chocolate cake, typing "baking cake" may bring up a broad range of results. Instead, try typing more specific terms like "how to bake a chocolate cake" or "easy chocolate cake recipe." This will narrow down your results and bring up videos that are more relevant to your search.
- **Use Quotation Marks for Exact Phrases**: If you want to search for a specific phrase, use quotation marks around the phrase. For example, typing "best hiking trails in California" will search for videos that contain that exact phrase in the title or description. This is particularly useful for finding content related to specific questions, quotes, or titles.
- **Avoid Overuse of Generic Terms**: While using a single term like "cake" will bring up a large number of results, it's not always the most effective way to search. Try using more descriptive phrases that capture the essence of the video you're looking for.

3. Using Search Filters for Precision

Once you've entered your search term and the results appear, YouTube provides a set of filters to help you narrow down the content based on certain criteria. These filters are incredibly useful if you want to sort through hundreds or thousands of videos to find the most relevant ones.

Here's a breakdown of the most commonly used search filters:

- **Upload Date**: You can filter videos based on when they were uploaded. Options include past hour, past 24 hours, past week, past month, and even past year. This filter is helpful if you want the most up-to-date content on a specific topic.
- **Type**: YouTube allows you to filter results based on the type of content you're looking for. You can choose from:
  - **Videos**: The default option, showing only videos in your results.
  - **Channels**: If you're looking to find channels that upload content related to your search, use this filter.
  - **Playlists**: Use this filter to find playlists that contain a collection of videos related to your query.
  - **Movies**: If you're searching for movies, YouTube offers a filter that specifically targets full-length films.
- **Duration**: You can choose whether you want to see short videos (less than 4 minutes), long videos (more than 20 minutes), or videos of any length. This is helpful if you're looking for bite-sized tutorials or in-depth documentaries on a topic.
- **Features**: YouTube also offers filters based on video features. For example, you can filter to find videos with subtitles, live broadcasts, or 360-degree videos.

---

4. Searching with Filters for a Specific Audience

Sometimes, YouTube's search function isn't just about finding content for yourself but also targeting specific groups of people. You can use the following filters and keywords to refine your search results for particular audiences:

- **Language and Region**: If you want videos in a specific language or from a particular country, you can adjust the language and region settings on YouTube.

This allows you to view content in the desired language or from creators in a specific geographic area.

- **Age Group**: Some content may be more suited for children or adults. Use YouTube Kids for a more filtered and kid-friendly experience, or explore content suitable for a general audience or mature audiences.

---

5. Sorting Results for Better Relevance

While the YouTube search bar shows a broad array of videos by default, you can sort the results based on what's most relevant to you:

- **By Relevance**: YouTube automatically sorts search results by relevance, but you can override this to see videos that are most popular, have the most views, or are most recent.
- **By View Count**: If you're looking for the most-watched videos on a particular topic, you can use the sort feature to organize videos by the highest number of views. This is useful for discovering trending videos or finding content that has resonated with a wide audience.
- **By Rating**: This is less commonly used, but sorting by rating can help you find videos that have received the highest number of "likes" or upvotes.

---

6. Exploring Advanced Search Options

For those who want even more control over their search, YouTube offers advanced search techniques. By using specific symbols and operators in your search term, you can tailor your query to find even more targeted results. Here are a few tricks:

- **Using the Minus (-) Sign**: If you want to exclude certain terms from your search results, use the minus sign. For example, if you're looking for recipes but want to avoid chocolate cake, you can search for "cake recipe -chocolate."
- **Using the Plus (+) Sign**: If you want to ensure that a specific term appears in your search results, use the plus sign. For example, "fitness +workout" will bring up videos that focus on workouts specifically.

- **Using the Asterisk (*)**: This can be used as a wildcard to represent any word in your search query. For example, "best * for beginners" will bring up results for things like "best camera for beginners," "best guitar for beginners," and so on.

---

7. The Importance of YouTube's Search Algorithm

While the search bar on YouTube is powerful, it's important to understand that the results you get are influenced by YouTube's search algorithm. This algorithm takes into account a variety of factors to rank and display videos:

- **Relevance**: YouTube prioritizes showing videos that are most relevant to your query based on the title, description, tags, and your viewing history.
- **Engagement**: Videos with higher engagement, such as likes, comments, shares, and watch time, tend to rank higher.
- **Personalization**: Your past search history and watching habits also affect the recommendations and search results that you see.

---

8. Optimizing Your Searches with Keywords and Tags

As a user, optimizing your searches isn't just about using the search bar—it's also about how videos are tagged. Tags are keywords that creators use to make their content discoverable, so if you use the right keywords, you'll find videos more efficiently.

- **Use Keywords that Match Your Intent**: Make sure to use terms that closely match the video's content. If you're searching for a tutorial on video editing, use specific keywords like "beginner video editing tutorial" rather than just "editing."
- **Search for Popular Channels**: If you consistently enjoy content from a particular creator, searching for their name directly will bring up all their available videos.

Conclusion

The YouTube search bar is your gateway to the vast world of videos available on the platform. By using effective search techniques, such as specific keywords, filters, and advanced search options, you can find exactly what you're looking for. Whether you're searching for entertainment, learning new skills, or exploring niche topics, mastering the search bar will greatly enhance your YouTube experience. With these tips in mind, you'll be able to navigate, watch, and enjoy the content YouTube has to offer more efficiently.

2.1.2 Filtering and Sorting Search Results

YouTube hosts billions of videos, and searching for the right content can sometimes feel overwhelming. Fortunately, YouTube provides powerful filtering and sorting tools to help users refine their search results and find exactly what they need. This section will guide you through the different filtering and sorting options available on YouTube, how to use them effectively, and practical tips to enhance your search experience.

---

1. Why Use Filters and Sorting on YouTube?

Before diving into the details, it's important to understand why filtering and sorting search results on YouTube is beneficial.

- **Find Relevant Content Faster** – Instead of scrolling through hundreds of videos, filters help you narrow down results based on upload date, duration, type, and other criteria.
- **Improve Search Accuracy** – Sorting helps prioritize results based on popularity, relevance, or the latest uploads, ensuring you get the most up-to-date or engaging content.
- **Discover High-Quality Content** – Filters allow you to exclude irrelevant or low-quality videos and focus on authoritative sources.
- **Customize Your Viewing Experience** – Different filters let you find videos based on your preferences, such as short clips, long-form content, or even live streams.

Now, let's explore how to use YouTube's search filters and sorting options effectively.

---

2. Accessing Filters and Sorting Options

Step 1: Perform a Search

1. Open YouTube and locate the search bar at the top of the homepage.

2. Type your desired keywords. For example, if you're searching for "digital marketing tips," enter those words into the search bar.

3. Press **Enter** or click the **magnifying glass** icon to see the search results.

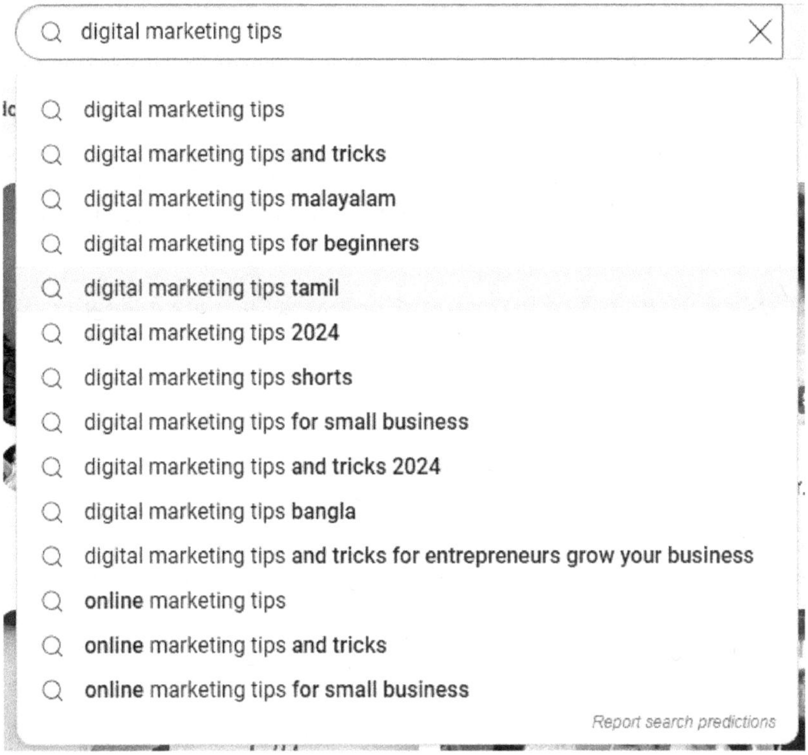

Step 2: Locate the Filter Button

Once the search results appear, you'll see a button labeled **"Filters"** below the search bar (on desktop) or within the options menu (on mobile). Clicking this button will reveal a list of available filters.

---

3. Understanding YouTube's Filtering Options

YouTube offers several filters to refine search results. These are divided into different categories:

A. Upload Date Filters

This filter helps you find videos based on when they were uploaded. This is useful if you are looking for the latest content on a specific topic.

- **Last Hour** – Shows videos uploaded within the past hour. Useful for breaking news or trending events.
- **Today** – Displays videos uploaded within the last 24 hours. Great for daily updates.
- **This Week** – Filters videos uploaded in the past seven days. Ideal for finding recent tutorials or discussions.
- **This Month** – Shows videos uploaded within the past 30 days. Useful for tracking new content over a longer period.
- **This Year** – Displays videos uploaded in the past 12 months. Best for reviewing the latest trends and updates in a field.

B. Type Filters

This filter allows you to specify the type of content you want to see.

- **Video** – Displays standard video content.
- **Channel** – Shows YouTube channels related to your search. Ideal for finding content creators.
- **Playlist** – Filters results to only display playlists. Great for finding structured learning materials or music compilations.
- **Movie** – Displays full-length movies available for rental or purchase.
- **Show** – Filters TV shows and series.

C. Duration Filters

If you prefer short or long videos, this filter helps narrow down your options.

- **Short (<4 minutes)** – Ideal for quick tutorials, summaries, or highlights.
- **Long (>20 minutes)** – Best for in-depth discussions, documentaries, and educational content.

D. Features Filters

This filter allows you to search for videos with specific features.

- **Live** – Displays only live-streaming videos. Useful for webinars, gaming streams, and live events.
- **4K / HD** – Filters results to only show high-definition videos. Great for high-quality viewing experiences.
- **Subtitles/CC** – Shows videos with subtitles or closed captions. Ideal for accessibility and learning new languages.
- **Creative Commons** – Displays videos licensed under Creative Commons, allowing for legal reuse.
- **360° / VR** – Filters results to show immersive, virtual reality videos.
- **Purchased** – Displays videos you have bought or rented on YouTube.

---

4. Sorting Search Results on YouTube

In addition to filtering, YouTube allows users to **sort** search results to prioritize them based on different criteria. Sorting options can be found directly within the **Filters** menu.

Sorting Options Available on YouTube

1. **Relevance (Default)** – YouTube automatically sorts results based on a combination of factors, including keywords, video engagement, and popularity.
2. **Upload Date** – Displays the most recently uploaded videos first. Useful for staying updated with the latest content.
3. **View Count** – Shows videos with the highest number of views first. Ideal for finding viral or widely watched content.
4. **Rating** – Sorts videos based on user ratings (likes vs. dislikes). This helps identify well-received content.

---

5. How to Combine Filters and Sorting for the Best Results

For an optimal search experience, try combining multiple filters and sorting options. Here are some practical examples:

- **Example 1:** You want to find **the latest digital marketing trends** from reliable sources.
    - Search for: "digital marketing trends"
    - Apply filters: **Upload Date → This Month, Type → Video**
    - Sort by: **View Count** (to find the most popular recent videos)
- **Example 2:** You need **a tutorial on Photoshop basics**, but only high-quality, well-received videos.
    - Search for: "Photoshop beginner tutorial"
    - Apply filters: **Duration → Long, Features → HD**
    - Sort by: **Rating** (to find the most liked videos)
- **Example 3:** You are looking for **free stock footage under Creative Commons licenses.**
    - Search for: "free stock footage"
    - Apply filters: **Features → Creative Commons**
    - Sort by: **Relevance**

---

6. Common Issues with Filters and Sorting (and How to Solve Them)

While filters and sorting can greatly improve your search experience, there are some common issues users encounter:

1. **Not Enough Results Appear** – If you apply too many filters, YouTube may not show many results. Try removing one or two filters.
2. **Irrelevant Videos Still Show Up** – Some older videos may still appear due to keyword optimization. Adjusting the **Upload Date** filter can help.
3. **Sorting by Rating May Not Show the Best Content** – Since not all users rate videos, sorting by **View Count** may provide more reliable results.
4. **Live Videos Don't Appear Even When Selected** – If no live videos exist on a topic, YouTube won't display any results. Try searching with broader keywords.

7. Final Tips for Effective Searching on YouTube

- **Use Quotation Marks ("")** – Searching for "digital marketing" ensures only exact matches appear.
- **Exclude Words with Minus (-)** – Searching **"fitness workout -yoga"** removes yoga-related videos.
- **Use 'OR' for Multiple Searches** – Searching **"iPhone OR Samsung review"** shows results for both brands.
- **Experiment with Different Filters** – Sometimes, switching filters can lead to discovering better videos.

By mastering YouTube's filtering and sorting options, you can quickly find the content you need, avoid irrelevant results, and enhance your overall viewing experience. Happy searching!

2.1.3 Understanding Video Titles, Thumbnails, and Descriptions

When searching for videos on YouTube, users are presented with a list of results that include a **title, thumbnail, and description** for each video. These three elements play a crucial role in helping viewers determine which video is most relevant to their search query. Understanding how to interpret these components will enhance your ability to find the best content quickly and efficiently.

---

1. The Role of Video Titles

What Makes a Good YouTube Video Title?

A video title is the first piece of information that viewers notice in search results. It serves as a brief summary of what the video is about and should be **clear, concise, and engaging**. Here are the key characteristics of an effective YouTube video title:

- **Descriptive** – The title should accurately reflect the content of the video. Misleading titles (clickbait) can lead to disappointment and distrust among viewers.

- **Concise** – YouTube allows up to **100 characters** for a title, but only about **50–60 characters** are visible in search results. Keeping titles short and to the point increases readability.
- **Keyword-Rich** – Titles should contain relevant keywords to improve searchability. For example, a cooking tutorial titled **"How to Bake a Chocolate Cake - Easy Recipe"** is more effective than simply **"Chocolate Cake"**.
- **Engaging and Interesting** – Viewers are more likely to click on a title that sparks curiosity or provides a solution to their problem. Titles that include words like **"How to," "Best," "Ultimate Guide," or "Tips"** tend to attract more attention.

Common Types of Video Titles

Understanding the different types of video titles can help you predict the type of content you are about to watch:

- **How-To Titles** – These indicate tutorial-style videos (e.g., *"How to Edit Videos on YouTube – Beginner's Guide"*).
- **List Titles** – These suggest videos that provide multiple points or recommendations (e.g., *"Top 10 Travel Destinations in 2024"*).
- **Question Titles** – These indicate that the video will answer a specific question (e.g., *"What is the Best Budget Laptop for Students?"*).
- **Challenge Titles** – These are common for entertainment-based content (e.g., *"24-Hour No Phone Challenge – Can I Survive?"*).
- **News or Trending Titles** – These are used for breaking news or trending topics (e.g., *"iPhone 16 Review – Is It Worth Upgrading?"*).

Identifying Clickbait Titles

Clickbait titles exaggerate or mislead viewers to increase clicks. While they may be attention-grabbing, they often result in disappointment. Signs of clickbait titles include:

- Overuse of capital letters and emojis (e.g., *"YOU WON'T BELIEVE WHAT HAPPENED 😨!!!"*)
- Vague or exaggerated claims (e.g., *"This One Trick Will Make You a Millionaire!"*)
- Sensational phrases like **"Shocking," "Insane," "Unbelievable"**

Clickbait videos often have a high **click-through rate (CTR)** but a low **watch time**, meaning viewers click on the video but leave quickly after realizing it is misleading.

---

2. Understanding YouTube Thumbnails

What Are Thumbnails?

A **thumbnail** is a small preview image that represents the video. Thumbnails are often the first thing viewers notice before reading the title or description. A well-designed thumbnail can **increase clicks and engagement**, while a poor-quality thumbnail may deter viewers.

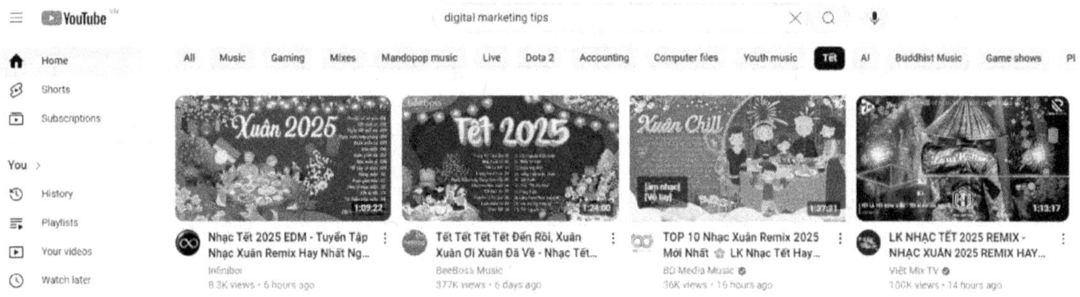

Types of Thumbnails

YouTube offers two types of thumbnails:

- **Auto-Generated Thumbnails** – YouTube automatically selects a random frame from the video. These are often blurry or unappealing.
- **Custom Thumbnails** – Creators upload a specially designed image for the video. These are usually more engaging and professional.

Characteristics of an Effective Thumbnail

Good thumbnails attract attention and provide a **visual summary** of the video. Key characteristics include:

- **High Resolution** – The recommended size for YouTube thumbnails is **1280 x 720 pixels**, with a **16:9 aspect ratio**.
- **Bright and Contrasting Colors** – Vibrant colors stand out in search results and recommendations.

- **Minimal Text** – Too much text can make the thumbnail difficult to read. A short phrase or keyword (e.g., *"5 Easy Tips"*) is ideal.
- **Clear Images and Faces** – Close-up images of people's faces with expressive reactions tend to perform well.
- **Branding Elements** – Some YouTubers use logos or consistent design styles to make their thumbnails recognizable.

Identifying Misleading Thumbnails

Some creators use deceptive thumbnails to attract clicks. These can include:

- **Fake Images** – Thumbnails that do not reflect the video content.
- **Overly Edited Faces** – Extreme reactions or expressions that do not appear in the video.
- **Unrelated Celebrities or Characters** – Using images of famous people who are not actually in the video.

Misleading thumbnails can lead to frustration and a poor viewing experience.

---

3. The Importance of Video Descriptions

What Is a Video Description?

A **video description** is the text below the video that provides additional information about the content. It can include **a summary, timestamps, links, and hashtags**.

How to Read a YouTube Video Description

When watching a video, the description can be useful for:

- **Understanding the Video Content** – The first few lines usually summarize what the video is about.
- **Finding Important Links** – Creators often include links to related content, social media, and recommended products.
- **Using Timestamps** – Some descriptions include **timestamp links** to specific sections of the video, making it easier to jump to relevant parts.

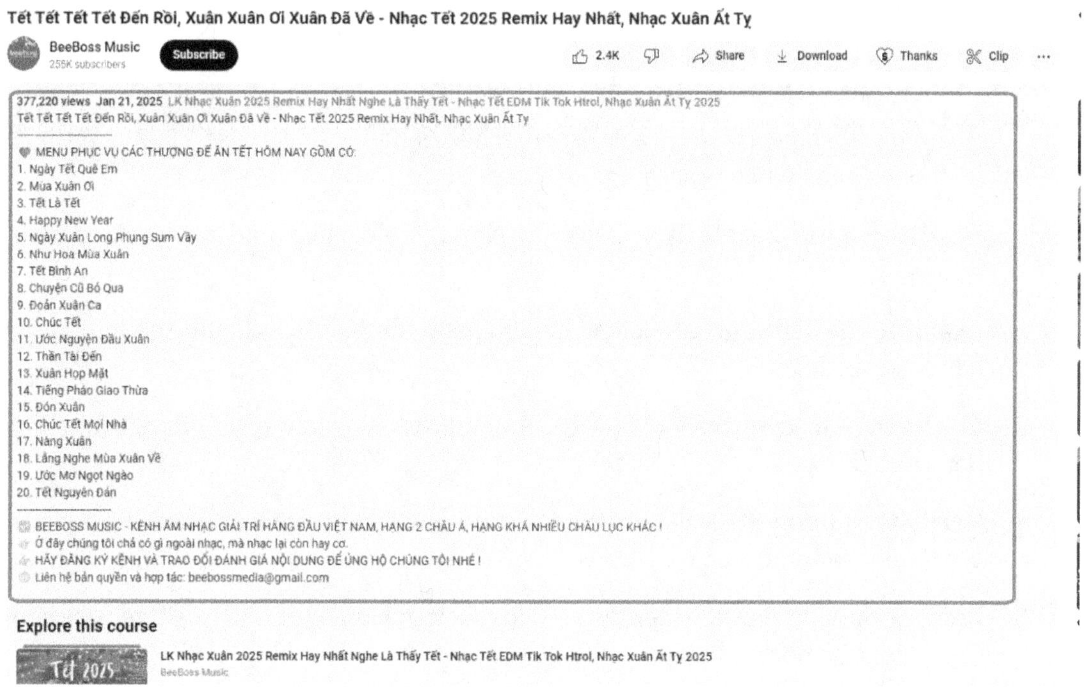

Common Elements in a YouTube Description

A well-structured video description typically includes:

- **Introduction (First Two Lines)** – A brief summary of the video.
- **Timestamps** – Clickable time markers that help navigate the video.
- **Relevant Links** – Links to sources, social media, or affiliate products.
- **Hashtags** – Keywords that categorize the video (e.g., #Travel #Food #DIY).

Recognizing Misleading Descriptions

Some descriptions are written to **manipulate the viewer** or trick the YouTube algorithm. Common misleading tactics include:

- **Keyword Stuffing** – Repeating the same keyword multiple times to rank higher in search results.
- **False Claims** – Promising information that is not actually covered in the video.
- **Clickbait Links** – Redirecting users to unrelated websites.

4. How to Use Titles, Thumbnails, and Descriptions to Choose the Best Videos

Now that you understand these three elements, here's how you can use them together to **select the best videos** when searching:

1. **Read the Title Carefully** – Look for clarity, relevance, and avoid exaggerated claims.
2. **Examine the Thumbnail** – Check if it aligns with the title and doesn't look overly edited or misleading.
3. **Check the Description** – Look for summaries, timestamps, and relevant links before clicking.
4. **Verify the Channel** – Trustworthy creators usually have a clear branding style and consistent content.
5. **Look at the Engagement Metrics** – Videos with high likes and positive comments are generally more reliable.

By mastering these elements, you can **improve your YouTube experience, avoid clickbait, and find the most valuable content** quickly.

2.2 Exploring YouTube Recommendations

2.2.1 How YouTube's Algorithm Suggests Videos

YouTube's recommendation algorithm is a powerful system designed to help users discover videos that match their interests. Whether you're watching cat videos, educational tutorials, or the latest music releases, YouTube's AI-driven engine carefully curates recommendations based on a variety of factors. Understanding how this system works can help you get better video suggestions and tailor your YouTube experience to your preferences.

In this section, we'll explore the mechanics behind YouTube's recommendation engine, including the key factors that influence video suggestions, how the algorithm evolves over time, and how you can take control of your recommendations.

---

1. What is the YouTube Recommendation Algorithm?

At its core, YouTube's recommendation algorithm is an artificial intelligence (AI) system that analyzes vast amounts of data to suggest videos that users are likely to watch. The algorithm considers user behavior, video performance, and content relevance to curate personalized recommendations.

YouTube's goal is to keep users engaged by showing them videos they will find interesting and valuable. To achieve this, the platform constantly refines its algorithm based on user interactions, feedback, and testing.

The recommendation system operates in two primary areas:

1. **The Home Page** – When you first open YouTube, the platform presents a curated feed of videos based on your viewing history, subscriptions, and engagement.
2. **The Suggested Videos Section** – When you watch a video, YouTube suggests additional content in the sidebar (or below the video on mobile devices) that aligns with your interests.

The system also influences recommendations in the "Up Next" queue, autoplay selections, and even notifications.

2. Key Factors Influencing YouTube's Recommendations

The YouTube algorithm takes multiple factors into account when determining which videos to recommend. These factors can be categorized into user behavior, video-specific data, and platform-wide trends.

User Behavior

Your interactions with videos and the platform play a significant role in shaping your recommendations. Here are some key behaviors that YouTube tracks:

- **Watch History:** The videos you watch frequently influence your future recommendations. If you watch many cooking tutorials, YouTube will suggest more cooking-related content.
- **Watch Time:** The amount of time you spend on a video is a crucial signal. If you watch a video from start to finish, YouTube assumes you found it engaging and may recommend similar content.
- **Likes and Dislikes:** Videos you like or dislike affect what gets recommended to you. Liking a video signals that you enjoy that type of content, while disliking helps YouTube understand your preferences.
- **Comments and Engagement:** Engaging with videos through comments or shares tells YouTube that you find the content valuable.
- **Subscriptions:** Subscribing to a channel informs YouTube that you want more content from that creator, which can influence your recommendations.
- **Search History:** The terms you search for impact your recommendations. If you often search for workout videos, YouTube will prioritize fitness-related content.

Video-Specific Data

Apart from user behavior, YouTube evaluates specific data related to individual videos:

- **Click-Through Rate (CTR):** This measures how often users click on a video after seeing its thumbnail and title. Higher CTR videos are more likely to be recommended.
- **Engagement Metrics:** Comments, shares, and likes indicate that a video is valuable, making it more likely to be recommended.

- **Retention Rate:** If a video keeps viewers engaged for a long duration, YouTube sees it as high-quality content and promotes it in recommendations.
- **Relevance to Other Videos:** YouTube compares videos to see if they are related to content you've watched before, leading to topic-based recommendations.

Platform-Wide Trends

Beyond personal user behavior and video performance, YouTube's recommendations also consider broader trends:

- **Popular and Trending Videos:** Viral videos and popular trends get boosted in recommendations, even if you haven't watched similar content before.
- **Seasonal and Event-Based Content:** YouTube may promote videos related to holidays, major events, or cultural moments based on their relevance.
- **Emerging Creators and Topics:** YouTube's algorithm often experiments by recommending videos from smaller creators or new trending topics to diversify content exposure.

---

3. How the Algorithm Learns and Adapts Over Time

The YouTube recommendation system is not static—it continuously evolves based on user behavior and feedback. Here's how it adapts:

Machine Learning and AI

YouTube uses deep learning and AI models to improve recommendations dynamically. These models analyze vast amounts of data, identifying patterns in user behavior and content engagement. The AI then refines recommendations in real time based on new data.

Personalized Learning

The more you use YouTube, the better the algorithm understands your preferences. If you start watching a new genre of videos, such as photography tutorials, YouTube will gradually shift recommendations to include more of that content.

Feedback Loops

User feedback directly impacts recommendations. If many users stop watching a video quickly, YouTube may reduce its recommendation frequency. Conversely, if a video receives high engagement, the algorithm promotes it more aggressively.

---

4. How to Improve Your YouTube Recommendations

If you feel like your recommendations don't match your interests, you can take control of the algorithm in several ways:

Clearing or Managing Your Watch History

- Go to **YouTube Settings > History & Privacy** and clear watch history to reset recommendations.
- Alternatively, remove specific videos from your history instead of clearing everything.

Interacting More with Desired Content

- Like, comment, and subscribe to channels that align with your interests.
- Watch videos fully to show YouTube that you enjoy the content.

Using the "Not Interested" Option

- If a recommended video is irrelevant, click the **three-dot menu** next to it and select **"Not Interested"** to refine your recommendations.

Exploring New Topics Intentionally

- If you want to diversify your recommendations, actively search for new topics and watch videos related to them.

---

5. The Future of YouTube's Recommendation Algorithm

YouTube continues to improve its recommendation system to enhance user experience. Future developments may include:

- **Better Content Moderation:** Addressing misinformation and harmful content while still providing personalized recommendations.

- **Increased Transparency:** YouTube is working on explaining why certain videos are recommended.
- **AI-Powered Personalization:** Enhancing AI capabilities to make recommendations even more tailored to user interests.

Conclusion

YouTube's recommendation algorithm plays a central role in shaping the videos you see on the platform. By understanding how it works, you can make better use of YouTube's features, refine your recommendations, and enjoy a more tailored viewing experience. Whether you're a casual viewer or someone who spends hours exploring content, taking control of your recommendations will help you discover the best videos for your interests.

Would you like to optimize your YouTube experience? Start by actively engaging with content you enjoy, managing your watch history, and using feedback tools to shape your recommendations.

2.2.2 Customizing Your Recommendations

YouTube's recommendation system is a powerful tool designed to help you discover videos that match your interests. However, if left unchecked, it may sometimes suggest content that doesn't align with your preferences. Fortunately, YouTube allows you to customize your recommendations by interacting with videos, managing your watch history, and adjusting your account settings. In this section, we will explore various ways to take control of your recommendations, ensuring that your YouTube experience remains enjoyable and relevant.

Understanding YouTube's Recommendation Algorithm

Before diving into customization, it is helpful to understand how YouTube generates recommendations. YouTube's algorithm considers multiple factors, including:

- **Your watch history:** Videos you watch influence what gets recommended to you.

- **Your search history:** Your past searches affect the types of videos YouTube suggests.
- **Your engagement with videos:** Likes, dislikes, comments, and shares play a role in shaping recommendations.
- **Your subscriptions:** Channels you subscribe to influence what appears on your homepage.
- **Trending and popular content:** YouTube sometimes suggests viral or trending videos based on your region and interests.

By recognizing these factors, you can take deliberate actions to refine and personalize your YouTube feed.

Steps to Customize Your YouTube Recommendations

1. Managing Your Watch History

One of the most effective ways to influence your recommendations is by managing your watch history. If you frequently watch videos from a particular genre, YouTube will assume you are interested in similar content.

Viewing and Deleting Your Watch History

To manage your watch history:

1. Open YouTube and click on your profile picture.
2. Select **"Your data in YouTube"** from the menu.
3. Click **"Manage your YouTube Watch History"** to view a list of all the videos you have watched.
4. To delete a specific video from your history, click the **three-dot menu** next to the video and select **"Delete"**.
5. To clear your entire watch history, click **"Delete all time"** under the history settings.

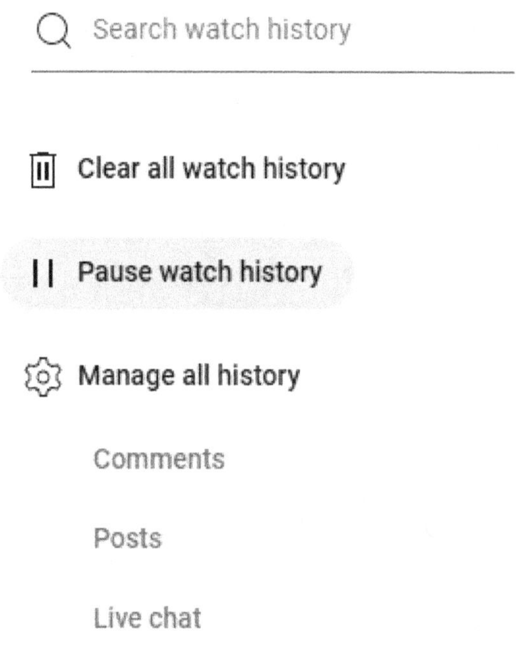

Pausing Watch History

If you don't want certain videos to affect your recommendations, you can pause your watch history:

1. Go to **"Manage your YouTube Watch History"** as mentioned above.
2. Click **"Turn off"** under the watch history settings.

When watch history is paused, YouTube will stop using your viewing activity to suggest new videos, making it a useful feature when exploring different topics temporarily.

---

2. Managing Your Search History

Just like your watch history, your search history plays a key role in determining what YouTube recommends. If you search for a specific topic frequently, YouTube will assume you're interested in that content.

Clearing Your Search History

To remove irrelevant searches:

1. Open YouTube and go to **"Your data in YouTube"**.
2. Click on **"Manage your YouTube Search History"**.
3. Browse through your search history and delete specific entries by clicking the **three-dot menu** and selecting **"Delete"**.
4. You can also clear your entire search history by selecting **"Delete all time"**.

Pausing Search History

To prevent YouTube from tracking your searches:

1. Go to **"Manage your YouTube Search History"**.
2. Click **"Turn off"** to stop YouTube from recording your searches.

Pausing search history is useful when you are researching a temporary topic and do not want recommendations to be affected.

---

3. Using the 'Not Interested' and 'Don't Recommend Channel' Options

If YouTube recommends videos that do not interest you, you can manually refine your recommendations by marking them as **"Not Interested"** or **"Don't Recommend Channel"**.

Marking a Video as 'Not Interested'

1. On your YouTube homepage or recommended feed, find a video you don't want to see.
2. Click the **three-dot menu** next to the video.
3. Select **"Not Interested"**.
4. YouTube will prompt you with an additional question asking why—choosing a reason helps improve future recommendations.

Blocking an Entire Channel

If you do not want videos from a particular channel appearing in your recommendations:

1. Click the **three-dot menu** next to a video from that channel.

2. Select **"Don't Recommend Channel"**.
3. YouTube will remove videos from that channel from your recommendations.

This feature is particularly helpful if you find certain creators or content genres unappealing.

---

4. Liking and Disliking Videos

Engaging with content by liking or disliking videos sends a strong signal to YouTube's algorithm.

- **Liking a video** increases the chances of seeing similar content.
- **Disliking a video** decreases the likelihood of similar videos appearing in your feed.

While YouTube no longer displays public dislike counts, the dislike button still helps refine recommendations for individual users.

To like or dislike a video:

1. Open the video you're watching.
2. Click the **thumbs-up (Like)** or **thumbs-down (Dislike)** button below the video.

Consistently interacting with videos in this way helps tailor your YouTube experience.

---

5. Subscribing to and Unsubscribing from Channels

Your subscriptions significantly impact your recommendations. YouTube assumes that if you subscribe to a channel, you want to see more content from that creator.

Subscribing to Channels You Enjoy

To ensure you receive recommendations from your favorite creators:

1. Click the **"Subscribe"** button below any video.
2. Enable the notification bell to receive updates about new uploads.

Unsubscribing from Channels You No Longer Watch

If a channel no longer interests you:

1. Visit the channel's homepage.
2. Click the **"Subscribed"** button.
3. Select **"Unsubscribe"** to stop receiving recommendations from that channel.

Unsubscribing is an effective way to refine your feed if your interests have changed over time.

---

6. Exploring and Resetting Your Recommendations

Checking Your Recommendations History

To see how YouTube has shaped your recommendations:

1. Open **YouTube Settings**.
2. Click **"Your data in YouTube"**.
3. Scroll to **"Manage YouTube Recommendations"** to review how YouTube generates your suggestions.

Resetting Your Recommendations

If your recommendations no longer align with your interests, you can reset them:

1. **Clear both your watch and search history** (as explained earlier).
2. **Unsubscribe from unwanted channels**.
3. **Start fresh by watching new content** that aligns with your current preferences.

This method allows YouTube to rebuild recommendations based on your most recent activity.

Conclusion

Customizing your YouTube recommendations ensures that your homepage and suggested videos align with your interests. By managing your watch and search history, engaging with videos through likes and dislikes, marking unwanted content as "Not Interested," and refining your subscriptions, you can take control of your YouTube experience.

YouTube's recommendation system is dynamic, meaning small changes in your activity can quickly shift what appears in your feed. By applying these strategies consistently, you can create a tailored, enjoyable, and distraction-free viewing experience.

2.2.3 Managing Your Watch History for Better Suggestions

YouTube's recommendation system is designed to provide users with personalized video suggestions based on their viewing history. The more you watch, the better YouTube understands your interests and tailors content accordingly. However, without proper management, your watch history can lead to irrelevant recommendations, cluttered suggestions, or even privacy concerns. This section will guide you on how to manage your watch history effectively to enhance your viewing experience and maintain control over the recommendations you receive.

Understanding YouTube's Watch History

Your watch history on YouTube is a record of all the videos you have watched while logged into your Google account. This data is stored by YouTube and used by its algorithm to refine video recommendations on your home page, search results, and even in the "Up Next" section after each video.

Watch history affects:

- **Personalized Recommendations:** YouTube suggests videos based on what you've previously watched.
- **Search Predictions:** When you type in the search bar, YouTube may suggest queries based on your past searches and watched videos.
- **Ad Personalization:** Advertisements on YouTube are often influenced by the type of content you engage with.
- **Playlists and Suggested Videos:** Your history affects the auto-generated "Mix" playlists and "Up Next" suggestions.

Managing your watch history ensures that your recommendations align with your actual interests rather than being distorted by random or one-time video views.

How to View and Access Your Watch History

To access and review your YouTube watch history:

1. **On Desktop:**
    - Click on the three-line **menu (☰)** on the top left corner of the YouTube homepage.
    - Select **"History"** from the sidebar.
    - You will see a chronological list of all the videos you have watched.
2. **On Mobile (YouTube App):**
    - Open the **YouTube app** on your device.
    - Tap on your **profile picture** in the top right corner.
    - Select **"Your data in YouTube"** → Scroll down to **"YouTube Watch History."**
3. **On YouTube TV (Smart TV or Console):**
    - Go to the **Library tab.**
    - Navigate to **"History"** and browse your watched content.

You can scroll through your history and take actions such as deleting individual videos, pausing history tracking, or clearing all data.

Clearing and Deleting Videos from Watch History

If your recommendations have become irrelevant due to one-time searches or accidental clicks, you can delete specific videos from your history.

How to Delete Individual Videos

1. Go to **YouTube History** (using the steps mentioned above).
2. Find the video you want to remove.
3. Click the **three-dot menu** next to the video.

4. Select **"Remove from watch history."**

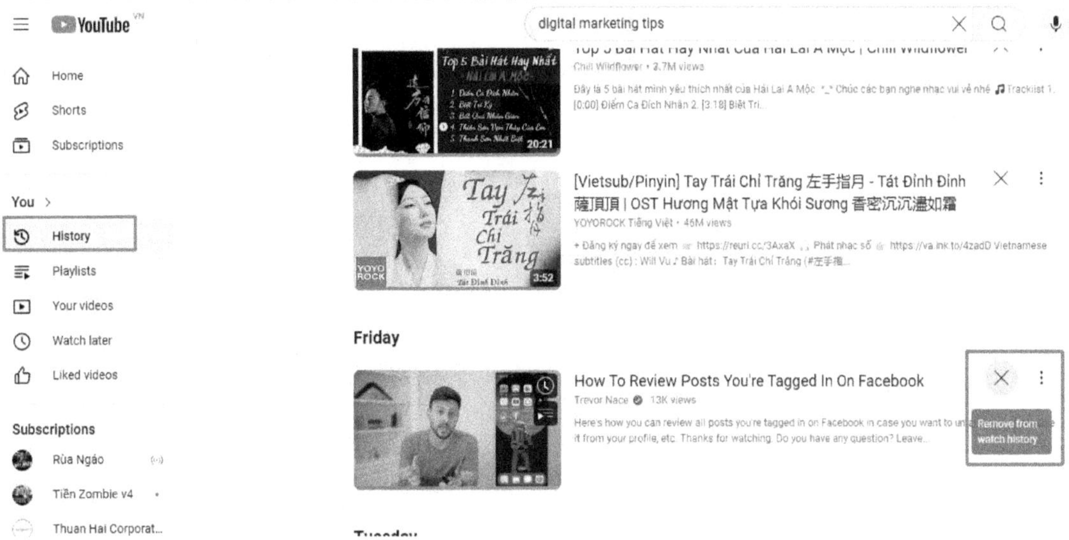

This action will prevent the video from influencing your recommendations in the future.

How to Clear Your Entire Watch History

If you want to reset your YouTube recommendations completely, you can erase all watched videos:

1. Open **YouTube History.**
2. Click on **"Clear all watch history."**
3. Confirm the action.

Keep in mind that clearing all watch history will temporarily disrupt YouTube's ability to recommend personalized content. However, it can be a good option if your recommendations have become completely irrelevant.

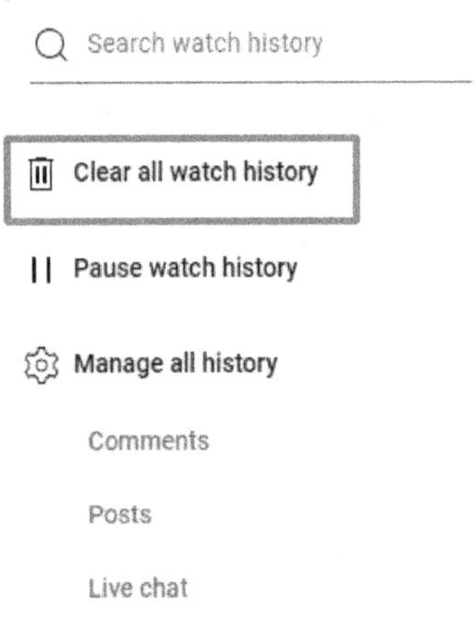

Pausing Your Watch History

YouTube provides an option to **pause watch history**, which means YouTube will not track or record the videos you watch during this period. This is useful if you want to explore a new topic without affecting your regular recommendations.

How to Pause Watch History

1. Go to **YouTube History.**
2. Click **"Manage all history."**
3. Find the **"Saving YouTube History"** section.
4. Toggle **"Pause watch history."**

While paused, new videos you watch will not appear in your history or affect recommendations. However, previously watched videos will still influence recommendations until you clear them.

Using Incognito Mode for Private Viewing

If you want to watch videos without them being recorded in your history, YouTube offers an **Incognito Mode** on mobile devices.

How to Enable Incognito Mode

1. Open the **YouTube app** on your phone.
2. Tap on your **profile picture** in the top right.
3. Select **"Turn on Incognito."**

While in **Incognito Mode**, YouTube will not track your watch history. Once you turn it off, your activity will resume tracking.

Best Uses for Incognito Mode:

- Watching one-time content without affecting recommendations.
- Searching for sensitive topics privately.
- Exploring new topics without altering your regular feed.

Managing Your Watch History Across Devices

Since YouTube syncs your history across all devices linked to your Google account, changes made on one device (e.g., deleting history) will reflect everywhere.

Steps to Manage Across Devices:

1. If you clear history on **desktop**, it will also be erased from your phone and smart TV.
2. If you pause watch history on **mobile**, it applies to all devices.
3. If you watch a video on **YouTube TV**, it will appear in your phone's history as well.

This synchronization ensures that you can manage and refine your recommendations consistently, no matter which device you use.

Customizing Your Recommendations with History Edits

If you notice that certain recommendations dominate your feed, you can actively **modify your watch history** to better shape future suggestions.

Tips for Refining Recommendations:

- Regularly remove **irrelevant** videos.
- Watch more of what **genuinely interests** you.
- Use the **"Not Interested"** feature on videos that don't match your preferences.

How to Mark a Video as "Not Interested"

1. On your YouTube **homepage**, find a recommended video you dislike.
2. Click the **three-dot menu (⋮)** next to the video.
3. Select **"Not Interested."**

YouTube will immediately remove the video from your recommendations and learn to avoid similar content in the future.

Conclusion

Effectively managing your watch history is key to maintaining a relevant and enjoyable YouTube experience. By deleting unnecessary videos, pausing history when needed, using incognito mode for private viewing, and customizing recommendations, you can ensure that your feed aligns with your interests.

Regularly reviewing and refining your watch history will help YouTube's algorithm work for you, not against you. Whether you're using YouTube for entertainment, education, or discovery, taking control of your viewing data will significantly improve your overall experience.

Would you like to explore a completely fresh start? Consider **resetting your history and strategically rebuilding it** by watching only high-quality, relevant content—this will ensure that YouTube suggests videos that truly matter to you.

2.3 Discovering New Channels and Playlists

2.3.1 Subscribing to Channels

Introduction to YouTube Subscriptions

One of the best ways to personalize your YouTube experience is by subscribing to channels that interest you. Subscriptions allow you to keep up with your favorite creators, get notified about new uploads, and build a curated feed of content tailored to your preferences. Whether you enjoy educational videos, entertainment, technology updates, or vlogs, subscribing helps you stay connected without manually searching for content each time.

This section will cover everything you need to know about subscribing to channels, including how to find and subscribe to creators, the benefits of subscriptions, managing your subscriptions effectively, and customizing your subscription notifications.

How to Subscribe to a YouTube Channel

Subscribing to a channel on YouTube is a simple process that allows you to receive updates whenever the channel uploads new content. Follow these steps to subscribe to a channel:

1. Searching for a Channel to Subscribe To

If you already know the name of the channel you want to subscribe to, you can use the **YouTube search bar** to find it:

- Click on the **search bar** at the top of the YouTube homepage.
- Type the name of the channel or related keywords.
- Press **Enter** or click the **search icon** (🔍).
- In the search results, look for the channel name (usually accompanied by a circular profile image).
- Click on the **channel name** to visit the channel's homepage.

2. Subscribing from a Channel Page

Once you are on the channel's homepage, you will see a **red "Subscribe" button** on the right side of the page, near the channel name and logo.

- Click the **"Subscribe"** button.
- If you are not logged in, YouTube will prompt you to sign in to your Google account.
- After subscribing, the button will change to **"Subscribed"** with a notification bell icon next to it.

3. Subscribing from a Video Page

You can also subscribe directly from a video you are watching:

- Scroll below the video player.
- Find the **channel name** displayed next to the profile picture of the creator.
- Click on the **"Subscribe"** button located next to the channel name.
- The button will change to **"Subscribed"**, confirming your subscription.

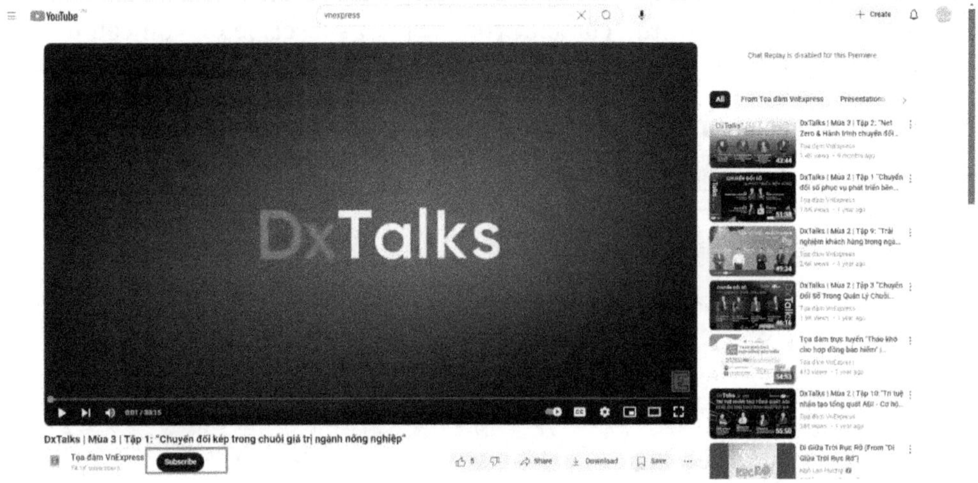

Benefits of Subscribing to Channels

1. Easy Access to New Content

Subscribing ensures that new videos from your favorite channels appear in your **Subscriptions tab**. You don't have to search for new content manually—it will be delivered directly to your YouTube feed.

2. Customizing Your Feed

The more channels you subscribe to, the more tailored your **YouTube homepage** will be. YouTube's algorithm prioritizes content from subscribed channels, making your browsing experience more relevant to your interests.

3. Supporting Content Creators

Subscribing to a channel helps content creators grow. It signals to YouTube that the channel is popular, which may increase its visibility to other users. Many creators rely on subscriptions to build a loyal audience and continue producing content.

4. Access to Exclusive Content

Some channels offer exclusive content to subscribers, such as **community posts, members-only videos, and live streams**. By subscribing, you can engage with the creator in a more interactive way.

Managing Your Subscriptions

If you subscribe to multiple channels, your **Subscriptions tab** can become cluttered. Fortunately, YouTube provides tools to manage and organize your subscriptions effectively.

1. Viewing Your Subscriptions List

To see all your subscribed channels:

- Click on the **Subscriptions** tab on the left sidebar of YouTube.
- Here, you will find the latest videos from channels you have subscribed to.

Alternatively, you can access a full list of your subscriptions:

- Click on your **profile icon** in the top right corner.
- Select **"Your Channel"** > **"Subscriptions"**.
- You will see all the channels you have subscribed to, along with their latest uploads.

2. Organizing Your Subscriptions

To keep your subscriptions organized, consider the following strategies:

a) Using Playlists

Instead of manually searching for videos, you can create **playlists** based on topics or creators. This helps you categorize content and watch it later.

b) Removing Inactive Subscriptions

Over time, you may find that some channels no longer post content you enjoy. To unsubscribe:

- Go to the **channel page**.
- Click on the **"Subscribed"** button.
- Select **"Unsubscribe"** from the dropdown menu.

c) Prioritizing Certain Channels

If you follow many channels but want to prioritize a few, enable **notifications** (explained in the next section) for selected creators.

Customizing Your Subscription Notifications

When you subscribe to a channel, YouTube provides different **notification settings** to keep you updated.

1. Understanding Notification Options

After subscribing, you will see a **bell icon** next to the "Subscribed" button. Clicking this bell allows you to choose from three notification settings:

- **All Notifications (🔔)** – You will receive updates for every new video, live stream, and post from the channel.

- **Personalized Notifications** (default setting) – YouTube's algorithm decides which updates you receive based on your watch history and interaction with the channel.
- **No Notifications** – You will remain subscribed but won't receive any alerts.

2. Enabling or Disabling Notifications

To change your notifications for a specific channel:

- Visit the **channel page**.
- Click the **bell icon** next to the "Subscribed" button.
- Select your preferred notification setting.

3. Managing All Subscription Notifications

To adjust notifications for all your subscriptions:

- Click on your **profile icon** in the top right corner.
- Select **"Settings"** > **"Notifications"**.
- Here, you can enable or disable general notifications for subscriptions, comments, and recommendations.

Best Practices for Managing Subscriptions

To get the most out of your YouTube subscriptions, consider the following tips:

1. **Only subscribe to channels you genuinely enjoy.** This keeps your feed relevant and prevents unnecessary clutter.
2. **Review your subscriptions periodically.** Unsubscribe from inactive channels or those that no longer match your interests.
3. **Use the "Watch Later" feature.** If you don't have time to watch a video immediately, add it to your **Watch Later** playlist.
4. **Balance your subscriptions.** Mix educational, entertainment, and personal interest channels to create a well-rounded YouTube experience.
5. **Engage with creators.** Liking, commenting, and sharing videos from your subscribed channels helps boost their content and fosters a sense of community.

Conclusion

Subscribing to YouTube channels is a powerful way to personalize your video-watching experience. Whether you're following educational content, entertainment, or niche interests, subscriptions ensure that you stay updated with the latest uploads from your favorite creators.

By managing your subscriptions effectively and customizing notifications, you can optimize your YouTube feed, making it a more enjoyable and useful tool for learning and entertainment.

In the next section, we will explore how to **browse trending videos and find curated playlists**, helping you discover even more great content on YouTube.

2.3.2 Browsing Trending Videos

YouTube is a dynamic platform where new videos go viral every day, reflecting the latest trends in entertainment, news, music, and culture. Browsing trending videos allows you to stay updated with what's popular and discover new creators and content that align with your interests. In this section, we'll explore how the **Trending** section works, what factors influence which videos appear, and how you can make the most of this feature to enhance your YouTube experience.

Understanding the YouTube Trending Tab

The **Trending** tab on YouTube showcases a curated selection of videos that are currently gaining widespread attention. This section helps users quickly find popular content without having to search manually.

Where to Find the Trending Tab

- On **desktop**, you can find the Trending section by clicking the **Explore** tab on the left sidebar and selecting **Trending**.
- On **mobile**, open the YouTube app, tap the **Explore** button at the bottom, and then select **Trending**.

- On **smart TVs**, Trending content may be featured on the homepage or under a specific category in the YouTube app.

What You'll See in the Trending Tab

The Trending section displays a mix of video categories, including:

1. **General trending videos** – A mix of the most popular content across various genres.
2. **Music** – Trending songs and official music videos.
3. **Gaming** – Popular gaming content, including playthroughs, reviews, and e-sports.
4. **Movies & Shows** – Trailers, behind-the-scenes clips, and film-related content.

This structure ensures that users with different interests can quickly find something they'll enjoy.

How YouTube Determines Trending Videos

YouTube uses a sophisticated algorithm to decide which videos appear in the Trending section. Unlike **Recommended Videos**, which are personalized based on your watch history, Trending videos are **not customized**—everyone in a specific country sees the same Trending tab.

Here are the key factors that determine what appears in the Trending section:

1. Views and Watch Time

- A video needs a significant number of views within a short period to be considered trending.
- **Watch time (how long people watch the video)** matters more than just clicks. A video with millions of short views might not trend, whereas a video with high watch duration can.

2. Growth Rate of Views

- A video doesn't need to have the highest number of views overall—it needs to be growing **rapidly** compared to others.
- If a video suddenly gains traction within hours, it is more likely to be featured.

3. Engagement Metrics

- Likes, shares, and comments indicate that users are actively engaging with the content.
- High engagement rates increase the chances of a video trending.

4. Video Age

- Older videos rarely appear in the Trending section.
- YouTube prioritizes **fresh content**, often featuring videos that are less than 48 hours old.

5. Channel Influence

- While smaller channels can trend, videos from **popular creators** with large followings tend to appear more frequently.
- Well-known YouTubers often have an advantage in getting their videos trending.

6. Content Quality and Compliance

- YouTube ensures that trending videos adhere to community guidelines.
- Clickbait, misleading thumbnails, or videos with harmful content will not trend.

Understanding these factors helps viewers interpret why certain videos appear in Trending and allows content creators to optimize their uploads for better visibility.

How to Browse Trending Videos Effectively

With thousands of videos trending globally, you may want to refine your exploration. Here are some strategies to find the most relevant trending videos for you:

1. Filter by Category

Since the Trending tab includes various types of videos, you can focus on specific categories:

- **Interested in music?** Check the Music section for new releases.
- **Love gaming?** Explore the Gaming section to find popular content.

- **Looking for the latest movie trailers?** The Movies & Shows category is perfect for that.

2. Check Regional Trends

YouTube Trending is location-based, meaning users in different countries see different trending videos.

- If you want to explore trends from another country, use a **VPN** or change your location in **YouTube's settings**.
- This is especially useful for language learners, international news followers, or those interested in foreign entertainment.

3. Identify Patterns in Trending Videos

- Do you notice similar **themes, challenges, or hashtags**?
- Are certain creators appearing more often?
- Are new formats (shorts, live streams, etc.) dominating the Trending tab?

Recognizing patterns can help you predict upcoming trends before they become mainstream.

4. Follow Trending News & Events

Many trending videos are tied to real-world events, viral challenges, or breaking news.

- If a major event happens, YouTube's Trending section often reflects that.
- Stay updated on **social media platforms like Twitter or Reddit** to see what's gaining traction online.

5. Use YouTube Shorts for Quick Trends

- YouTube Shorts (short-form videos) often go viral quickly.
- The Trending tab sometimes highlights Shorts separately.
- These videos are **under 60 seconds**, making them an easy way to explore trends quickly.

How to Save and Engage with Trending Videos

1. Save Videos for Later

- If you find an interesting trending video but don't have time to watch it, **add it to your Watch Later playlist**.
- You can also **create a separate playlist** for trending videos you want to revisit.

2. Interact with Trending Content

- **Like and comment** to engage with creators.
- **Share videos** with friends or on social media to spread awareness.
- If you enjoy a particular creator, consider **subscribing** and turning on notifications.

3. Compare Trends Across Platforms

- Check what's trending on **TikTok, Instagram, and Twitter** to see if the same topics are popular.
- Many viral challenges start on one platform before spreading to YouTube.

Potential Drawbacks of the Trending Section

While browsing trending videos is a great way to stay updated, there are a few things to keep in mind:

1. Trending Videos Are Not Always High-Quality

- Just because a video is trending doesn't mean it's the best content available.
- Some trending videos may be **clickbait or low-effort** content.

2. Trends May Not Align with Your Interests

- Since Trending is **not personalized**, you may see videos that don't match your preferences.
- The **Recommended** section is often better for content that suits your tastes.

3. Fake Virality and Manipulation

- Some videos trend due to **artificial engagement (bots, paid views, etc.)**.
- Be mindful of videos with **exaggerated claims or misleading thumbnails**.

Final Thoughts on Browsing Trending Videos

The YouTube Trending section is a powerful tool for discovering the latest viral content, staying informed about current events, and identifying new creators. By understanding how it works and using strategic browsing techniques, you can make the most of this feature and enhance your YouTube experience.

If you want **a curated, personalized experience**, combining the Trending tab with **subscriptions, recommended videos, and playlists** is the best approach.

So, the next time you open YouTube, take a moment to explore what's trending—you might just discover your new favorite creator or video!

2.3.3 Finding Curated Playlists and Series

Introduction

YouTube is more than just a collection of random videos; it is a platform that allows users to organize and curate content into structured playlists and series. These curated playlists and series help viewers enjoy videos in a logical sequence, whether for entertainment, learning, or keeping up with specific topics. Understanding how to find and use these curated collections can enhance your YouTube experience, making it easier to follow long-form content without manually searching for individual videos.

In this section, we will explore the concept of curated playlists and video series, how to find them, and how to use them effectively for an improved viewing experience.

Understanding Curated Playlists and Video Series

What Are Curated Playlists?

A **curated playlist** is a collection of videos grouped together by a creator or YouTube's algorithm based on a common theme, subject, or purpose. Playlists can be created by individual users, YouTube channels, or even YouTube itself. They serve multiple purposes, such as:

- Organizing educational courses or tutorials

- Grouping episodes of a web series
- Collecting music videos from a particular artist or genre
- Compiling highlights from a gaming channel
- Gathering interviews, documentaries, or news coverage on a specific topic

Curated playlists allow users to watch videos in a sequence without manually searching for the next one, making the experience seamless and convenient.

What Are Video Series on YouTube?

A **video series** on YouTube is similar to a TV show, where episodes are uploaded in a specific order. Unlike regular playlists, some YouTube series are designed with a structured narrative or progression, making them ideal for:

- Episodic storytelling
- Long-form documentaries
- Step-by-step tutorial guides
- Multi-part vlogs or travel diaries
- Educational lectures

YouTube even allows creators to mark a playlist as an **"Official Series"**, ensuring that videos play in the correct order and are recommended as a cohesive unit.

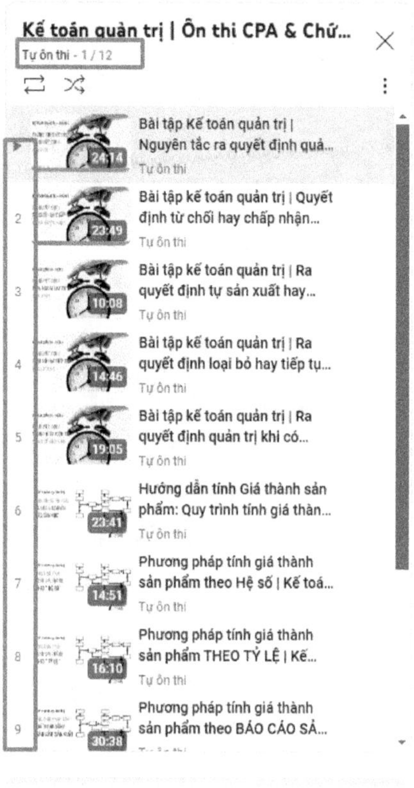

How to Find Curated Playlists and Video Series

1. Searching for Playlists Using the YouTube Search Bar

One of the easiest ways to find curated playlists and series is by using YouTube's search bar. Instead of searching for individual videos, you can refine your search to specifically look for playlists.

Steps to Search for Playlists:

1. Open YouTube and type your keyword in the search bar.
2. After searching, click on the **Filters** option.
3. Under the **Type** category, select **Playlist** to filter results.
4. Browse the available playlists and select the one that best suits your needs.

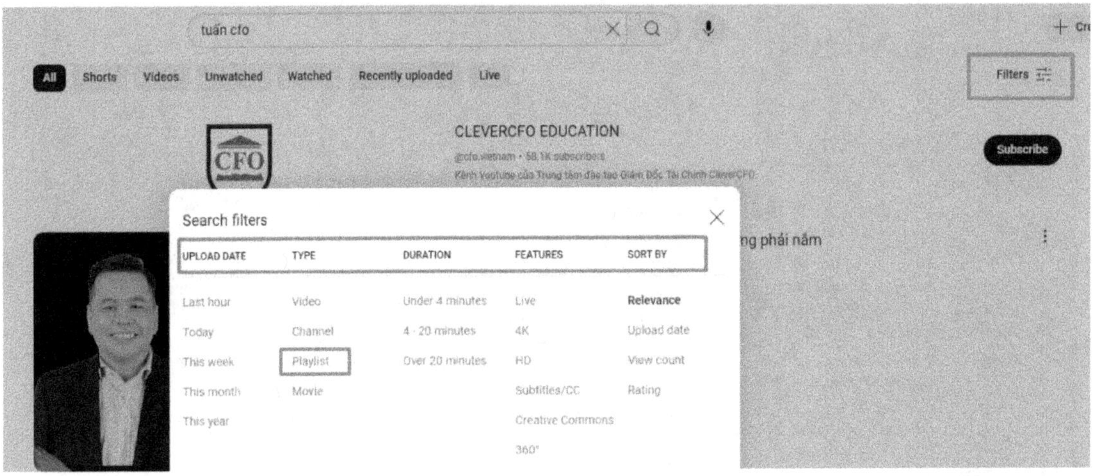

For example, if you search for **"Beginner Guitar Lessons"** and filter by playlists, you will see a collection of videos grouped together, often by an instructor who has organized them in a progressive learning order.

2. Finding Playlists on a Channel's Page

Many YouTube creators organize their content into playlists to help viewers navigate their videos more easily. If you have a favorite channel, you can check if they have created any playlists.

Steps to Find Playlists on a Channel:

1. Visit a YouTube channel by clicking on the creator's name.
2. Navigate to the **Playlists** tab on their channel page.
3. Browse through the available playlists to find structured content.
4. Click on a playlist to start watching in sequence.

For example, an educational channel like **Khan Academy** or **TED-Ed** often has playlists grouped by subject, such as "Algebra Basics" or "Science Explained."

3. Discovering YouTube's Curated Playlists and Series

YouTube itself curates playlists and video series based on trending topics, popular searches, and personalized recommendations. You can find these in several places:

- **The YouTube Homepage:** Based on your watch history, YouTube suggests curated playlists that align with your interests.

- **YouTube's Explore Section:** You can browse curated playlists in categories like Music, Gaming, News, Learning, and more.
- **YouTube Mix:** A dynamically generated playlist based on your listening history, particularly useful for music lovers.
- **YouTube Learning Playlists:** Educational content grouped together to help users learn new skills.

For instance, if you frequently watch fitness videos, YouTube may suggest a curated playlist called **"30 Days of Home Workouts."**

Benefits of Watching Curated Playlists and Series

1. Continuous and Seamless Viewing Experience

Curated playlists allow for **autoplay**, meaning you don't have to manually select the next video. This is especially useful when watching:

- TV show episodes
- Learning modules
- Multi-part documentary series

With a playlist, you can sit back and enjoy without interruptions.

2. Structured Learning and Skill Development

Many educational and tutorial-based YouTube channels create playlists to help viewers follow a structured learning path. This is beneficial for:

- Language learning (e.g., **"Spanish for Beginners"**)
- Software tutorials (e.g., **"Mastering Photoshop"**)
- Cooking series (e.g., **"How to Cook Italian Dishes"**)

By following a curated playlist, you ensure that you learn topics in the correct order rather than watching random, unorganized videos.

3. Discovering New Content Easily

When you watch a playlist, YouTube often recommends similar content, helping you discover:

- New channels with related content
- Additional videos that expand on a topic you're interested in
- Different perspectives or explanations of the same concept

For example, if you're watching a **"History of World War II"** playlist, YouTube may recommend another playlist from a different creator covering a similar topic in more detail.

4. Saving Time with Pre-Organized Content

Instead of searching for individual videos every time you want to continue learning or watching, playlists provide a **one-click solution** to access multiple related videos in sequence.

How to Save and Manage Playlists for Future Viewing

1. Saving a Playlist to Your Library

If you find a playlist you like, you can save it to your **Library** to access it later.

Steps to Save a Playlist:

1. Open the playlist.
2. Click on the **Save Playlist** button.
3. Choose to add it to **Watch Later** or create a new playlist folder.

Now, you can easily return to the playlist without searching for it again.

2. Creating Your Own Playlists

YouTube also allows you to create personal playlists to organize your favorite videos.

Steps to Create a Playlist:

1. Click on a video you want to add to a playlist.
2. Click the **Save** button below the video.
3. Select **Create new playlist** and name it accordingly.

4. Set the privacy settings (Public, Unlisted, or Private).

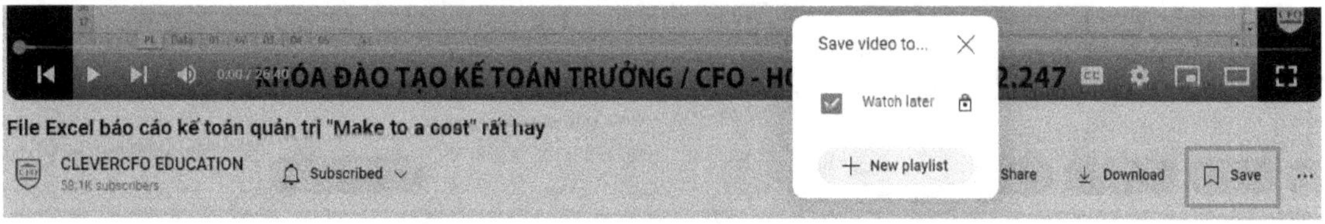

For example, you might create a **"Weekend Relaxation"** playlist with your favorite calming music or a **"DIY Home Projects"** playlist for future reference.

Conclusion

Curated playlists and video series on YouTube provide an organized and efficient way to enjoy content, whether for entertainment, education, or skill-building. By learning how to find and use these playlists effectively, you can enhance your YouTube experience, save time, and enjoy a seamless viewing journey.

Now that you understand how to discover and utilize playlists, you can explore YouTube more efficiently and make the most out of your video-watching experience!

CHAPTER III
Watching and Interacting with Videos

3.1 Understanding Video Player Controls

YouTube's video player is the core of the platform, allowing users to watch content with ease. Whether you're streaming a tutorial, a music video, or a documentary, understanding how to control playback ensures the best viewing experience. This section will cover the fundamental controls, including playing and pausing videos, adjusting volume, and making minor tweaks to enhance your viewing.

3.1.1 Play, Pause, and Adjusting Volume

The most basic function of the YouTube video player is playing and pausing videos. To start a video, simply click on the play button, usually represented by a triangular "▶" icon in the center of the video screen or on the bottom-left corner of the control bar. If a video is already playing, clicking the same button will pause it.

Alternatively, you can use the spacebar or the "K" key on your keyboard to play or pause videos instantly. This shortcut is particularly useful when you are watching a long video and need to stop momentarily without moving your mouse.

Another way to control playback is by tapping directly on the video screen if you are using a mobile device. A single tap brings up the play/pause button, allowing you to pause or resume the video with ease.

Pausing a video stops playback but retains your position so that you can resume exactly where you left off. This is useful if you need to take notes, answer a phone call, or step away momentarily.

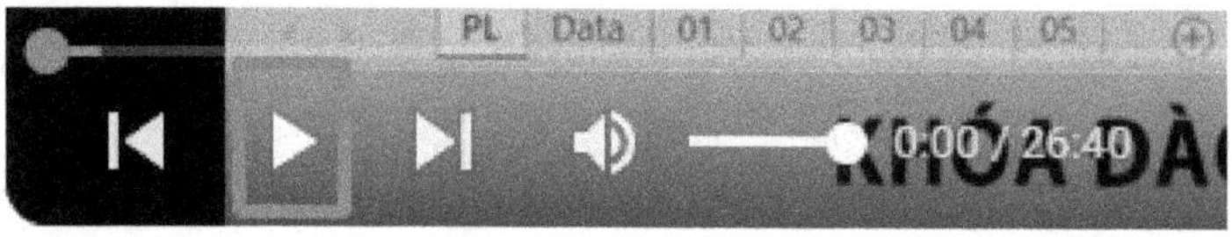

Using the Seek Bar for Precise Playback Control

YouTube provides a seek bar at the bottom of the video player, allowing users to skip forward or rewind to a specific part of the video. You can do this by dragging the red progress bar to a different timestamp.

Keyboard shortcuts also help in navigating through the video:

- **Left arrow (←)**: Rewinds the video by 5 seconds.
- **Right arrow (→)**: Skips forward by 5 seconds.
- **J key**: Moves the video back 10 seconds.
- **L key**: Moves the video forward 10 seconds.
- **0-9 keys**: Jumps to a percentage of the video. Pressing "5" will take you to the 50% mark, and "9" to 90%.

These shortcuts enhance your control over playback and make navigation more efficient.

Adjusting Video Volume

Controlling volume ensures a comfortable listening experience, whether you are using headphones, speakers, or watching in a quiet environment.

Using On-Screen Controls

- The volume slider is located at the bottom-left of the video player, next to the play button.
- Clicking the speaker icon mutes or unmutes the sound.
- Dragging the slider up or down adjusts the volume accordingly.

Using Keyboard Shortcuts

- **Up arrow**: Increases the volume by 5%.
- **Down arrow**: Decreases the volume by 5%.
- **"M" key**: Mutes or unmutes the video instantly.

Using these shortcuts can be handy if you need to quickly adjust volume levels without moving your mouse.

Adjusting Volume on Mobile Devices

On smartphones and tablets, volume control is linked to the device's hardware buttons. Simply press the volume up or down buttons on the side of your phone to control sound levels. You can also mute by using the on-screen controls or the mute switch on your device.

Muting and Unmuting Videos

There are instances where you may want to mute a video entirely, such as when you're in a quiet place but still want to watch content.

- On **desktop**, clicking the speaker icon on the bottom-left of the video player mutes the audio. Clicking it again unmutes it.
- On **mobile**, muting a video can be done using the on-screen controls or by lowering the device volume completely.

YouTube automatically remembers the last volume setting used, so if you mute a video and later play another one, it may start muted unless you adjust the volume again.

Enhancing the Audio Experience

For an improved listening experience, consider adjusting additional settings:

1. **Using Headphones or External Speakers** – This can enhance audio quality, especially for music videos or educational content.
2. **Enabling Captions** – If a video has low audio quality or background noise, turning on subtitles (closed captions) can help you follow along.
3. **Using YouTube's Audio Enhancements** – Some YouTube videos support spatial audio, which improves sound depth when using headphones.

For videos with very low volume, you can also adjust the system volume from your computer's audio settings or increase the speaker's output manually.

Common Issues and Troubleshooting

If you experience issues with video playback or volume, here are some common problems and solutions:

Video Not Playing or Pausing Properly

- Ensure your internet connection is stable. Slow connections can cause lag.
- Try refreshing the page or restarting your device.
- Clear your browser's cache if the problem persists.

Volume is Too Low or Not Working

- Check if the video is muted and unmute it.
- Increase the system volume on your computer or device.
- Test the video on another browser or device to see if the issue persists.

Audio is Out of Sync with Video

- Try adjusting the video quality (covered in the next section) to see if it resolves the lag.
- Restart your browser or YouTube app.
- Ensure your device's audio drivers are updated.

Conclusion

Mastering the basic controls of YouTube's video player enhances your overall experience, allowing you to seamlessly play, pause, and adjust volume. Whether you are using keyboard shortcuts, on-screen buttons, or mobile gestures, these features provide flexibility in managing video playback.

In the next section, we will explore how to **change video quality and captions** to further optimize your YouTube experience.

3.1.2 Changing Video Quality and Captions

YouTube provides users with extensive control over their viewing experience, allowing them to adjust video quality and enable captions based on their preferences. Whether you're watching videos in high definition (HD) for clarity or reducing quality to save data, YouTube offers various options to ensure an optimal viewing experience. Additionally, captions make videos more accessible by providing on-screen text for dialogue, sound effects, and other audio cues.

This section will guide you through the process of adjusting video quality and captions, explaining how they work, when to use them, and the best practices for an enhanced YouTube experience.

---

1. Understanding Video Quality on YouTube

YouTube offers multiple video quality options ranging from low resolution (144p) to ultra-high definition (4K and beyond). The available options depend on the original video's resolution and your internet connection.

1.1 Video Quality Resolutions on YouTube

YouTube provides the following resolution options:

- **144p** – Lowest quality, primarily for slow internet connections.
- **240p** – Slightly better but still low quality.
- **360p** – Standard resolution for mobile viewing.
- **480p** – Better quality, suitable for small screens.
- **720p (HD)** – High Definition, good for most devices.
- **1080p (Full HD)** – Full High Definition, ideal for large screens.
- **1440p (2K)** – Higher quality than Full HD, but requires more bandwidth.
- **2160p (4K)** – Ultra High Definition (UHD), best for large screens and fast internet connections.

YouTube automatically selects a resolution based on your internet speed and device capabilities, but you can manually change it according to your preferences.

2. How to Change Video Quality on YouTube

2.1 Changing Video Quality on Desktop

1. **Start playing a video** – Open YouTube and select the video you want to watch.
2. **Click the settings icon** – It looks like a small gear ⚙️ in the bottom-right corner of the video player.
3. **Select "Quality"** – A list of available resolutions will appear.

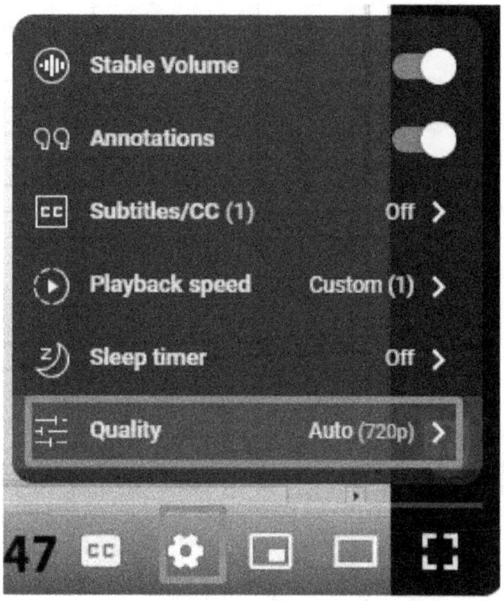

4. **Choose your preferred resolution** – Higher resolutions provide better clarity but require a stronger internet connection.

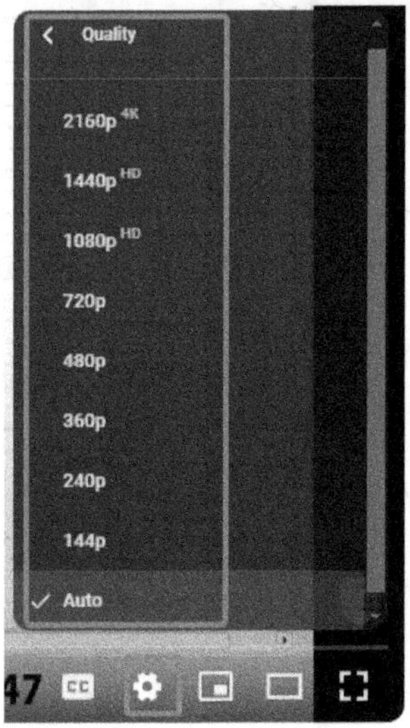

2.2 Changing Video Quality on Mobile Devices

1. **Open the YouTube app** and play a video.
2. **Tap on the video to bring up controls** and then tap the three-dot menu (⋮) in the top-right corner.
3. **Select "Quality"** – A menu with resolution options will appear.
4. **Choose from "Higher picture quality," "Data saver," or "Advanced" settings.**
    - **Higher picture quality:** Automatically selects the best resolution.
    - **Data saver:** Lowers quality to reduce data usage.
    - **Advanced:** Allows manual selection of a resolution.

2.3 Automatic vs. Manual Quality Selection

By default, YouTube adjusts video quality automatically based on your internet speed. However, if you experience buffering or slow playback, you can manually lower the quality for a smoother experience.

Tips for Choosing the Right Quality Setting:

- **Use 144p or 240p** when on a slow or limited mobile data connection.
- **Use 360p or 480p** for standard-quality viewing.

- **Use 720p or higher** for an HD experience if you have a strong internet connection.
- **Use 1080p, 2K, or 4K** for a premium experience on large screens or smart TVs.

---

3. Understanding YouTube Captions

Captions, also known as subtitles, provide on-screen text that represents the spoken words and sounds in a video. They enhance accessibility for people who are deaf or hard of hearing and help viewers understand content in different languages.

Types of Captions on YouTube

1. **Auto-Generated Captions** – YouTube uses AI to automatically generate captions for videos. Accuracy may vary.
2. **Creator-Uploaded Captions** – Video creators can manually add captions to improve accuracy.
3. **Community-Contributed Captions** – In some cases, users can submit captions for review.
4. **Translated Subtitles** – Some videos provide translated captions for multilingual audiences.

---

4. How to Enable and Customize Captions

Enabling Captions on Desktop

1. **Start playing a video** – Open YouTube and select a video.
2. **Click the "CC" button** – This enables captions if available.
3. **To customize, click the settings icon (⚙️)**
4. **Select "Subtitles/CC"** – Choose from available languages or auto-generated captions.

Enabling Captions on Mobile Devices

1. **Open the YouTube app** and play a video.
2. **Tap on the video screen** to bring up controls.
3. **Tap the "CC" icon** – This turns captions on.
4. **To change language, tap the three-dot menu > Subtitles/CC** and choose a preferred language.

---

5. Customizing Captions for Better Readability

Adjusting Caption Settings on Desktop

1. **Click the settings icon (⚙️)** in the video player.
2. **Select "Subtitles/CC" > "Options."**
3. **Customize text appearance:**
    - Change font size
    - Adjust background opacity
    - Modify text color

Adjusting Caption Settings on Mobile

1. **Go to YouTube Settings (Profile > Settings).**
2. **Tap on "Captions."**
3. **Customize text size, background, and style.**

---

6. Common Issues and Troubleshooting

Video Quality Issues

- **Buffering?** Lower the quality to improve playback.
- **Blurry video?** Increase the resolution if your internet supports it.
- **Can't change quality?** The video may have been uploaded in a lower resolution.

Caption Problems

- **No captions available?** The creator may not have enabled them.
- **Incorrect auto-generated captions?** Try using manual captions if available.
- **Can't find translated subtitles?** Not all videos support multilingual captions.

---

7. Best Practices for an Optimal Viewing Experience

Choosing the Right Settings for Different Situations

- **Use low-quality settings when on limited mobile data.**
- **Use auto-generated captions for videos in foreign languages.**
- **Enable high-quality settings when watching on large screens.**

Accessibility Considerations

- Captions make content accessible for people with hearing impairments.
- Customizing text and background improves readability for all users.

Conclusion

Changing video quality and enabling captions on YouTube can greatly enhance your viewing experience. Whether you need better resolution for clarity or captions for accessibility, YouTube offers plenty of options to customize your experience. By understanding how to adjust these settings, you can make the most out of YouTube's features while enjoying content seamlessly.

3.1.3 Using Full-Screen and Theater Modes

YouTube provides multiple viewing modes to enhance the user experience, with **Full-Screen Mode** and **Theater Mode** being two of the most commonly used options. These modes allow you to adjust the way videos are displayed based on your preference and the type of content you are watching. Understanding how to use these modes effectively can greatly improve your viewing experience, whether you are watching a short video clip, a movie, or a live stream.

In this section, we will explore what Full-Screen and Theater Modes are, their differences, how to enable them, and when to use each mode for the best experience.

---

1. What is Full-Screen Mode?

Full-Screen Mode allows the video to occupy the entire display, hiding all distractions such as YouTube's interface elements, navigation bars, and video recommendations. When activated, the video expands to cover your entire screen, providing a more immersive experience.

Benefits of Full-Screen Mode

- **Immersive Viewing Experience** – With no distractions, you can focus entirely on the video.
- **Better for Large Screens** – On bigger displays, full-screen mode ensures the best use of available screen space.
- **Ideal for High-Resolution Content** – Watching videos in 1080p, 4K, or even 8K is best enjoyed in full-screen mode.
- **Enhanced Gaming or Sports Viewing** – Full-screen mode is especially useful for watching gameplay videos, live streams, or sports events where you need to see details clearly.

How to Enable Full-Screen Mode

1. **Using the Video Player Controls**
    - Click the **full-screen button** (a square icon with four arrows pointing outward) in the bottom-right corner of the video player.
    - The video will expand to cover your entire screen.

2. **Using Keyboard Shortcuts**
    - Press the **F key** on your keyboard (for desktops and laptops) to toggle full-screen mode on or off.
3. **On Mobile Devices**
    - Rotate your smartphone or tablet to **landscape mode**, and the video will often switch to full-screen automatically.
    - If it doesn't, tap the full-screen icon.

How to Exit Full-Screen Mode

- Click the **full-screen button** again.
- Press the **Esc key** on your keyboard (on desktops/laptops).
- On mobile devices, rotate the device back to **portrait mode** or tap the full-screen button again.

---

2. What is Theater Mode?

Theater Mode is an alternative viewing mode that enlarges the video player while keeping some YouTube interface elements visible, such as the video title, comments, and recommendations. Unlike full-screen mode, which removes everything except the video itself, theater mode provides a wider, cinema-like experience while still allowing users to interact with other elements on the page.

Benefits of Theater Mode

- **Wider Display for Better Viewing** – The video expands horizontally, making it larger than the default player.
- **Easier Access to Comments and Related Videos** – You can still scroll down to read comments or explore recommended videos.
- **Better for Multitasking** – If you want to watch a video while checking the description, interacting with comments, or browsing related content, theater mode is ideal.
- **Great for Educational Videos** – If you need to take notes or follow along with a tutorial while keeping the video large, theater mode is a good choice.

How to Enable Theater Mode

1. **Using the Video Player Controls**
    - Click the **Theater Mode button** (a rectangle with two arrows pointing outward) located next to the full-screen button.
    - The video player will expand horizontally, while keeping YouTube's interface visible.

2. **Using Keyboard Shortcuts**
    - Press the **T key** on your keyboard (on desktops and laptops) to toggle theater mode on or off.

How to Exit Theater Mode

- Click the **Theater Mode button** again.
- Press the **T key** on your keyboard.
- Refresh the page, and the video will return to the default mode.

---

3. Full-Screen vs. Theater Mode: Key Differences

Feature	Full-Screen Mode	Theater Mode
Video Size	Covers the entire screen	Expands width but not height
YouTube Interface Visibility	Hidden	Visible
Best for	Movies, immersive videos, gaming	Tutorials, multitasking, browsing comments
Keyboard Shortcut	F key	T key
Mobile Compatibility	Yes	No

---

4. When to Use Each Mode

When to Use Full-Screen Mode

- Watching **movies or TV shows** for an immersive experience.
- Enjoying **high-definition videos** without distractions.
- Watching **sports, gaming, or action-packed content** where details matter.
- Viewing **live streams** that you want to focus on without reading comments.

When to Use Theater Mode

- Watching **educational content or tutorials** where you might need to read instructions or comments.
- **Browsing and multitasking**, such as searching for related videos while watching.
- Following along with **video descriptions**, timestamps, or links.
- Engaging with **comment sections and discussions** while watching the video.

---

5. Common Issues and Troubleshooting

Full-Screen Mode Not Working

Possible Causes:

- Browser settings may be blocking full-screen mode.
- Extensions or plugins (such as ad blockers) could interfere.
- Your device's display settings might be restricting full-screen functionality.

Solutions:

- Try switching to a different browser.
- Disable browser extensions temporarily.
- Check YouTube's settings and permissions.

Theater Mode Resets After Refresh

Possible Causes:

- YouTube does not save theater mode settings permanently.

- Browser cache might be preventing changes from sticking.

Solutions:

- Manually activate theater mode each time.
- Use browser extensions that remember video player settings.

---

6. Tips for a Better Viewing Experience

1. **Use Keyboard Shortcuts** – The F key (Full-Screen Mode) and T key (Theater Mode) help switch quickly.
2. **Adjust Video Quality** – In full-screen mode, make sure to **increase resolution** for a clearer picture.
3. **Enable Subtitles** – If watching tutorials or foreign-language content, captions can enhance understanding.
4. **Use Dark Mode** – Combining theater mode with YouTube's **dark mode** reduces eye strain.
5. **Disable Auto-Play** – Prevent distractions by turning off auto-play when watching in full-screen or theater mode.

---

7. Conclusion

Both **Full-Screen Mode** and **Theater Mode** offer unique ways to enjoy YouTube videos based on your needs. Full-screen mode is perfect for immersive viewing, while theater mode balances a larger player with access to other YouTube features. By mastering these modes and using the right shortcuts, you can optimize your experience and make watching YouTube videos more enjoyable.

Now that you know how to use these viewing modes, the next section will explore **how to engage with YouTube videos**, including **liking, commenting, and sharing** content!

3.2 Engaging with Videos

Engaging with videos on YouTube goes beyond just watching content. Interaction features like liking, disliking, commenting, and sharing help users express their opinions, support creators, and discover more personalized recommendations. Engaging with videos also influences YouTube's recommendation system, shaping the type of content that appears in your feed.

In this section, we will explore the different ways to interact with videos, starting with the **Like and Dislike** functions, which are fundamental tools for providing feedback on YouTube.

3.2.1 Liking and Disliking Videos

The **Like and Dislike** buttons are among the simplest yet most powerful interaction tools on YouTube. They allow viewers to quickly express their opinions on a video and help shape the overall viewer feedback on a particular piece of content.

1. What Are the Like and Dislike Buttons?

- The **Like (👍) button** is used to show appreciation for a video. Clicking this button indicates that you found the content enjoyable, informative, or valuable.
- The **Dislike (👎) button** is used to express discontent or dissatisfaction with a video. This could be due to poor content quality, misleading information, or simply because the video did not meet your expectations.

Although both buttons exist, only the number of **Likes** is publicly visible. YouTube removed the public dislike count to reduce harassment and targeted attacks on creators. However, dislikes still contribute to YouTube's recommendation system and help fine-tune the content that appears in your feed.

---

2. How to Like and Dislike a Video

Using the Like and Dislike buttons is incredibly easy:

1. **On Desktop (Web Browser):**

- Open YouTube and play any video.
- Below the video, you'll see a **thumbs-up (👍) and thumbs-down (👎) button** next to each other.
- Click the **thumbs-up** button to like the video. The icon will turn blue, indicating that you have liked it.
- Click the **thumbs-down** button to dislike the video. The icon will turn darker, but the total number of dislikes will not be visible to the public.

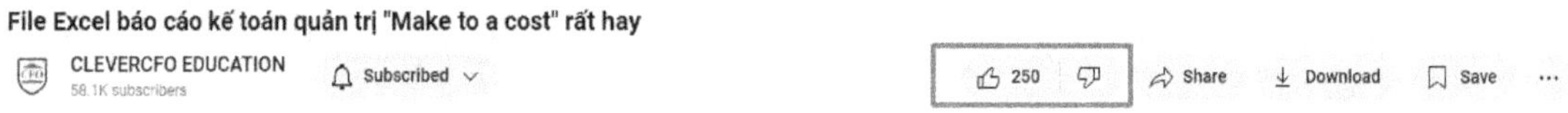
File Excel báo cáo kế toán quản trị "Make to a cost" rất hay
CLEVERCFO EDUCATION
58.1K subscribers
Subscribed
250
Share
Download
Save

2. **On Mobile (YouTube App):**
    - Open the YouTube app and start watching a video.
    - Tap on the **thumbs-up** button to like or the **thumbs-down** button to dislike.
    - If you tap a button by mistake, you can tap it again to undo your action.

---

3. The Impact of Liking and Disliking Videos

Liking and disliking videos influence both **your personal recommendations** and **the creator's content visibility** on YouTube.

A. How Likes Affect Your YouTube Experience

1. **YouTube's Algorithm Adjusts Your Recommendations**
    - When you like a video, YouTube assumes that you enjoy that type of content and will recommend similar videos.
    - If you dislike a video, YouTube will take note and show fewer videos of that kind in your future recommendations.
2. **Your YouTube Library Records Your Likes**
    - Every video you like is automatically saved in your **"Liked Videos" playlist**, which can be accessed from your YouTube Library.

- This makes it easy to revisit videos you found helpful or entertaining.

3. **Creators See Your Engagement**
    - Content creators can see the number of likes and dislikes they receive in their **YouTube Studio Analytics** dashboard.
    - More likes signal positive engagement and can boost a video's ranking in search results.

B. How Likes and Dislikes Affect Content Creators

1. **Engagement Signals Boost Video Visibility**
    - YouTube prioritizes videos with higher engagement (likes, comments, and watch time) in search results and recommendations.
    - Videos with a high number of likes are more likely to appear on **YouTube's Trending page** or in suggested video sections.
2. **Dislikes Provide Constructive Feedback**
    - Although dislikes do not affect a video's visibility as much as likes, they still provide feedback to creators.
    - A large number of dislikes might indicate that the video contains misleading information, poor quality content, or controversial material.
3. **Creators Can Use Like/Dislike Ratios to Improve Content**
    - By analyzing the like-to-dislike ratio, content creators can adjust their content strategies to meet audience expectations.
    - Some creators use **polls and community posts** to understand why viewers liked or disliked a particular video.

---

4. Can You See Who Liked or Disliked Your Video?

No, YouTube does not show individual likes or dislikes to users or creators. You can only see the total number of likes, while the dislike count is hidden from public view. However, creators can track overall engagement statistics in their **YouTube Studio Analytics**.

---

5. Best Practices for Using Likes and Dislikes Effectively

1. **Like Videos to Support Your Favorite Creators**
   - If you enjoy a creator's content, liking their video helps them gain more visibility and encourages them to create more videos.
2. **Use Dislikes Thoughtfully**
   - If a video is misleading or contains false information, disliking it is a good way to provide feedback.
   - However, avoid disliking videos just because you don't personally agree with the creator's opinion.
3. **Engage Beyond Just Liking or Disliking**
   - If you want to give detailed feedback, consider **leaving a comment** instead of just disliking a video.
   - Sharing videos you like can help spread valuable content to others.

---

6. Common Questions About Liking and Disliking Videos

Q1: Can I Undo a Like or Dislike?

Yes, you can undo a like or dislike at any time by clicking the same button again.

Q2: Do Likes and Dislikes Affect Monetization?

Not directly. However, videos with high engagement (likes, comments, shares) tend to perform better, leading to more views and potential monetization opportunities.

Q3: Can Creators Disable Likes and Dislikes?

No, YouTube does not allow creators to disable the Like and Dislike buttons. However, they can choose to **disable comments** if they want to limit audience interaction.

Q4: Why Did YouTube Remove the Public Dislike Count?

YouTube removed public dislikes to **prevent harassment and targeted attacks** against creators, especially smaller channels. However, dislikes still influence YouTube's algorithm.

7. Conclusion

The **Like and Dislike** buttons arc simple yet powerful tools that allow users to engage with content and influence their viewing experience. By using these features wisely, you can help shape the content you see, support your favorite creators, and contribute to the overall YouTube community.

Now that you understand the importance of liking and disliking videos, let's explore **commenting on videos** in the next section. Comments allow for more in-depth interactions and discussions with other viewers and creators.

3.2.2 Commenting on Videos

YouTube is not just a video streaming platform—it is also a vast social network where users can engage with content and creators through likes, shares, and comments. Commenting on videos is one of the most interactive ways to participate in the YouTube community. Whether you want to express appreciation for a video, ask a question, share an opinion, or interact with other viewers, the comment section provides a space for meaningful discussions.

In this section, we will explore everything you need to know about commenting on YouTube videos, including how to post, edit, and delete comments, best practices for engaging in discussions, and how to handle potential negativity in the comment section.

1. Why Commenting on Videos Matters

Commenting is a powerful way to engage with video content. Here's why it matters:

- **Supporting Creators**: A thoughtful comment can show appreciation and encouragement to content creators, motivating them to continue making videos.
- **Sharing Opinions**: Viewers can express their thoughts about a video, whether they agree or disagree with the content.
- **Asking Questions**: Many people use the comment section to ask for clarifications, request additional content, or seek help.

- **Building a Community**: Commenting allows viewers to engage in discussions, meet like-minded individuals, and become part of an online community.
- **Increasing Visibility**: A well-written comment can get many likes and replies, making it more visible to other viewers.

---

2. How to Comment on a YouTube Video

Posting a comment on YouTube is simple and can be done from both desktop and mobile devices.

Commenting on Desktop

1. **Open a Video**: Navigate to a YouTube video that you want to comment on.
2. **Scroll Down to the Comment Section**: Below the video description, you will see a text box that says **"Add a comment..."**
3. **Type Your Comment**: Enter your message in the text box. You can express an opinion, ask a question, or share feedback.
4. **Post the Comment**: Click the **"Comment"** button (or press **Enter**) to submit your comment. It will now be visible to other users.

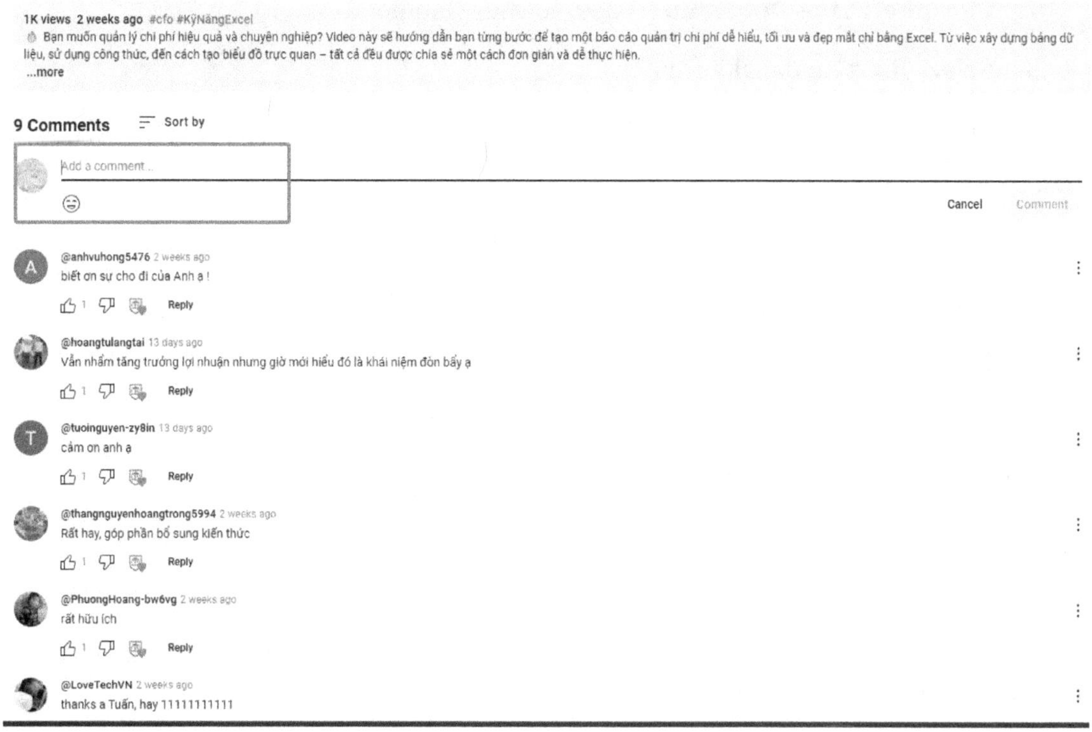

Commenting on Mobile Devices

1. **Open the YouTube App** and select a video.
2. **Scroll Below the Video** until you see the comment section.
3. **Tap on "Add a comment..."** and enter your message.
4. **Press the Send Icon** (usually a small arrow) to post your comment.

---

3. Editing and Deleting Comments

Sometimes, you may want to edit or delete a comment after posting it. YouTube allows users to modify or remove their own comments.

Editing a Comment

If you made a typo or want to reword your comment:

1. **Find Your Comment**: Scroll to your comment on the video.

2. **Click the Three-Dot Menu** (⋮) next to your comment.
3. **Select "Edit"** and make your changes.
4. **Click "Save"** to update your comment.

Deleting a Comment

If you want to remove a comment permanently:

1. **Locate Your Comment** on the video.
2. **Click the Three-Dot Menu** (⋮) next to your comment.
3. **Select "Delete"** and confirm the action.

Once deleted, a comment cannot be recovered.

---

4. Engaging in Conversations

YouTube comments allow for direct interaction with other users. You can reply to comments, mention users, and like or dislike comments.

Replying to Comments

- Click or tap the **"Reply"** button under a comment.
- Type your response and press **Enter** or tap **Send**.
- Your reply will appear indented under the original comment.

Mentioning Other Users

- To tag another user in a comment or reply, type **"@"** followed by their username.
- The mentioned user may receive a notification, depending on their settings.

Liking and Disliking Comments

- Click the **thumbs up (👍) icon** to like a comment.
- Click the **thumbs down (👎) icon** to dislike a comment.
- Highly liked comments appear at the top of the section.

---

5. Best Practices for Commenting on YouTube

To make your comments meaningful and well-received, consider these best practices:

Be Respectful and Positive

- Keep comments constructive and respectful.
- Avoid insults, hate speech, or offensive language.
- If you disagree with a video or comment, express your opinion politely.

Stay Relevant to the Video Topic

- Comments should relate to the video content.
- Avoid spamming unrelated promotions or links.

Avoid Spam and Self-Promotion

- YouTube discourages excessive self-promotion in comments.
- Comments that repeatedly promote external links or personal content may be flagged as spam.

Use Humor and Creativity

- Witty or insightful comments often get more engagement.
- Funny, clever, or unique comments can get many likes.

---

6. Managing Negative Comments and Trolls

While YouTube comments can be engaging and positive, they can also attract negativity. Here's how to handle it:

Dealing with Negative Feedback

- If someone criticizes your opinion, consider whether the feedback is constructive.
- Engage in healthy discussions, but avoid escalating conflicts.

Recognizing and Ignoring Trolls

- Some users post inflammatory comments just to provoke reactions.

- The best response to trolls is often **no response**.

Reporting Abusive Comments

- If you come across offensive, spammy, or harmful comments:
    1. Click the **three-dot menu** next to the comment.
    2. Select **"Report"** and choose the reason.
    3. YouTube will review reported comments for violations.

---

7. Conclusion

Commenting on YouTube videos is a great way to engage with content, express opinions, and connect with other viewers. By following best practices and maintaining respectful interactions, you can have a positive experience in the YouTube community.

Now that you understand how to comment effectively, let's explore how to **share videos on social media** in the next section!

3.2.3 Sharing Videos on Social Media

Sharing videos on social media is one of the best ways to spread content, engage with your network, and make sure your favorite creators get more views. YouTube makes it incredibly easy to share videos across different platforms, whether you want to post them on Facebook, Twitter (X), Instagram, LinkedIn, or even through direct messaging apps like WhatsApp and Telegram.

In this section, we'll explore the various ways you can share YouTube videos, the benefits of sharing, best practices for effective sharing, and how to integrate YouTube videos into your social media strategy.

---

1. Why Share YouTube Videos on Social Media?

Social media is a powerful tool that connects millions of people worldwide. Sharing YouTube videos on social platforms comes with several benefits:

Expanding Video Reach

Every time you share a YouTube video, you're introducing it to a new audience. Your friends, family, and followers may not have seen that content otherwise, and by sharing, you help increase its reach.

Supporting Your Favorite Creators

When you share a video, you're helping its creator gain more views and engagement. This is especially valuable for small or independent creators trying to grow their audience.

Saving and Organizing Content

Sometimes, you may want to save a video for later viewing or reference. Sharing it on your social media profile can serve as a reminder or a collection of interesting videos you've watched.

Starting Conversations and Engagement

Videos are a great way to spark discussions. Whether it's a tutorial, a funny clip, or an important news update, sharing videos can encourage interaction among your friends and followers.

---

2. How to Share YouTube Videos on Social Media

YouTube provides multiple ways to share videos easily across different platforms.

- Using the YouTube "Share" Button

One of the simplest ways to share a video is by using the **Share** button located beneath the video player.

Step-by-Step Guide:

1. Open the YouTube video you want to share.
2. Click on the **Share** button below the video.

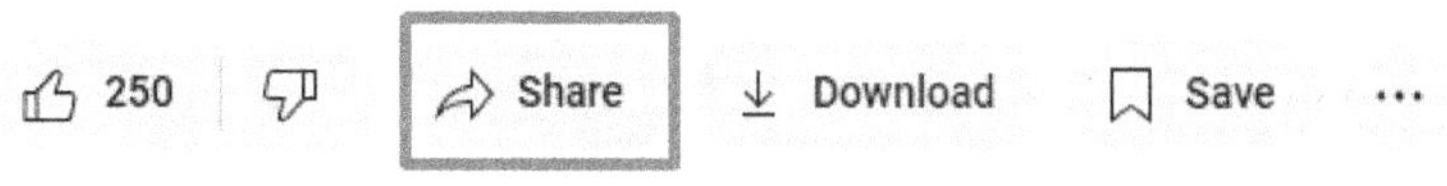

3. Choose your preferred social media platform (Facebook, Twitter, WhatsApp, etc.).

4. A new window will open where you can add a caption or comment before posting.
5. Click **Post** or **Send** to share the video.

- Copying and Sharing the Video Link

If your preferred platform isn't listed in YouTube's share options, you can manually copy the video's URL and paste it wherever you want.

Step-by-Step Guide:

1. Click on the **Share** button below the video.
2. Select **Copy link** to copy the URL to your clipboard.
3. Open your social media platform or messaging app.
4. Paste the link in a post, message, or story.
5. Add any comments or hashtags to provide context before sharing.

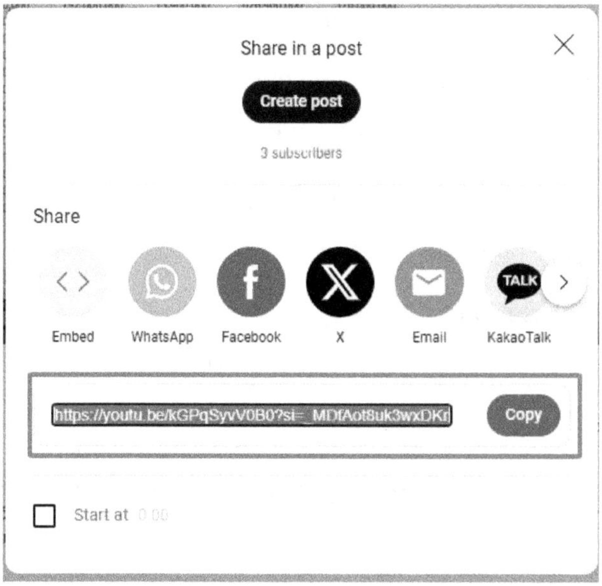

- **Sharing via Mobile Apps**

On mobile devices, YouTube integrates with various apps for easy sharing.

Step-by-Step Guide:

1. Open the YouTube app and find the video.
2. Tap the **Share** button.
3. Select the app where you want to share the video (Instagram, Snapchat, Twitter, etc.).
4. Customize your post and tap **Send** or **Post**.

---

3. Platform-Specific Sharing Tips

Each social media platform has its own best practices for sharing YouTube videos effectively.

Facebook

Facebook is one of the best platforms for video sharing.

- Instead of just posting a link, add a short description of why the video is interesting.

- Use relevant hashtags to make the post discoverable.
- Share the video in relevant Facebook groups where people may be interested.
- Consider posting the video as a "story" for more visibility.

Twitter (X)

Twitter has a character limit, so keep your message concise.

- Add engaging captions that grab attention.
- Use trending hashtags to increase visibility.
- Tag the video creator if applicable.
- Use Twitter threads if you want to provide additional context or discuss different parts of the video.

Instagram and Instagram Stories

Instagram doesn't allow direct YouTube video sharing, but you can work around this.

- Use **Instagram Stories** to post a screenshot of the video with a call-to-action like "Check out this amazing video!"
- For users with over 10,000 followers, use the **Swipe-Up Link** feature in Instagram Stories to directly link to the video.
- Use **Instagram bio links** to direct people to longer YouTube videos.

LinkedIn

If the video is educational or work-related, LinkedIn is a great place to share it.

- Provide a brief explanation of how the video is relevant to your industry.
- Use hashtags like #Learning, #Education, or #BusinessTips to reach professionals.
- Engage with comments and start a discussion.

WhatsApp and Telegram

For private sharing, messaging apps are excellent.

- Send videos directly to friends, family, or groups.

- Use the status feature to post video links that disappear after 24 hours.
- Create a list of friends interested in a specific topic and share related videos regularly.

---

4. Best Practices for Sharing YouTube Videos

Add Personal Insights

Instead of just posting a link, write a short explanation of why you're sharing the video. It makes your post more engaging.

Use Hashtags and Mentions

Hashtags increase visibility, and tagging the video creator can lead to more engagement.

Post at the Right Time

Different platforms have peak activity times. For example:

- **Facebook:** Best time is early afternoon.
- **Twitter:** Mornings and evenings get higher engagement.
- **LinkedIn:** Weekday mornings work best.

Avoid Over-Sharing

Posting too many videos too frequently can annoy your audience. Be selective about what you share.

Engage with Comments

When people react to your shared video, reply to comments to keep the conversation going.

---

5. Alternatives to Direct Sharing

If you want to share YouTube videos in a more unique way, consider these options:

- Embedding Videos in Blogs or Websites

Many bloggers and website owners embed YouTube videos in their content.

How to Embed a Video:

1. Click the **Share** button.
2. Select **Embed** and copy the HTML code.
3. Paste the code into your website's blog post or page.

- Creating Reaction or Commentary Videos

Instead of just sharing a video, create your own reaction or commentary video discussing the content.

- Using Email Newsletters

If you manage a newsletter, including YouTube videos can enhance engagement.

---

6. Conclusion

Sharing YouTube videos on social media is an excellent way to spread knowledge, entertain your audience, and support content creators. Whether you're sharing for fun, education, or engagement, using the right strategies can maximize your reach and interaction.

By understanding the different platforms, best practices, and alternative sharing methods, you can make the most of YouTube's vast content and bring value to your online community.

3.3 Creating and Managing Playlists

3.3.1 Saving Videos to Watch Later

YouTube is a vast platform with millions of videos covering a wide range of topics. Often, you may come across an interesting video that you don't have time to watch immediately. Instead of searching for it later or risking losing track of it, YouTube provides a convenient feature called **"Watch Later."** This feature allows users to save videos to a special playlist that can be accessed anytime.

In this section, we'll explore how to save videos to the **Watch Later** playlist, manage saved videos, remove videos after watching them, and organize your playlist efficiently.

---

1. What is the "Watch Later" Playlist?

The **Watch Later** playlist is a built-in YouTube feature that enables users to bookmark videos for future viewing. Unlike custom playlists, which you can create and name yourself, the Watch Later playlist is automatically provided by YouTube.

Key Features of the "Watch Later" Playlist:

- **Quick access** to saved videos.
- **Automatic synchronization** across devices (desktop, mobile, tablet).
- **Videos remain saved** until you manually remove them.
- **Easier video management** compared to searching for videos again.

This feature is especially useful if:

- You find an interesting video but don't have time to watch it immediately.
- You want to collect multiple videos to watch in a dedicated session.
- You need to save videos for research or learning purposes.

---

2. How to Save Videos to "Watch Later"

You can add videos to the **Watch Later** playlist using different methods depending on the device you're using.

Saving Videos on Desktop (PC or Mac)

1. **While Watching a Video:**
    - Click on the **"Save"** button located below the video.
    - Select **"Watch Later"** from the menu.
2. **From the Video Thumbnail:**
    - Hover over the video thumbnail in your YouTube feed or search results.
    - Click on the three-dot menu (⁝) in the bottom-right corner.
    - Select **"Save to Watch Later."**

Saving Videos on Mobile (Android & iOS)

1. **While Watching a Video:**
    - Tap the **"Save"** button below the video.
    - Choose **"Watch Later"** from the options.
2. **From the Video List or Search Results:**
    - Tap the three-dot menu (⁝) next to the video title.
    - Select **"Save to Watch Later."**

Saving Videos from Shared Links

- If someone shares a video link via a messaging app, you can open the video and follow the same steps above to save it for later.

---

3. Accessing and Managing Your "Watch Later" Playlist

Once you have saved videos, you can access them easily and manage them based on your preferences.

How to Find the "Watch Later" Playlist

- **On Desktop:**
    1. Go to **YouTube Homepage**.
    2. Click on **"Library"** in the left sidebar.
    3. Scroll down to find **"Watch Later."**
- **On Mobile App:**
    1. Tap the **"Library"** tab at the bottom.
    2. Scroll down and select **"Watch Later."**

---

4. Organizing Your "Watch Later" Playlist

Since videos are saved in the order they were added, your **Watch Later** playlist can become cluttered over time. Here are some tips to manage and organize your saved videos effectively.

Rearrange Videos in "Watch Later"

- YouTube allows you to reorder videos manually on desktop:
    1. Open the **Watch Later** playlist.
    2. Click and drag videos up or down to change the order.

Removing Watched or Unwanted Videos

Once you finish watching a video, you might want to remove it from your Watch Later playlist to keep it tidy.

- **On Desktop:**
    - Click the three-dot menu (⋮) next to the video title.
    - Select **"Remove from Watch Later."**
- **On Mobile:**
    - Tap the three-dot menu (⋮) next to the video.
    - Choose **"Remove from Watch Later."**

- **Bulk Removal:**
    - If you have watched multiple videos and want to clear them quickly, YouTube offers a **"Remove Watched Videos"** option in the playlist settings.

---

5. Alternatives to "Watch Later"

Although **Watch Later** is convenient, you might prefer other ways to save and organize videos based on your needs.

Creating Custom Playlists

If you have many videos on specific topics, you can create **custom playlists** instead of using Watch Later.

- Benefits of Custom Playlists:
    - Organize videos by category (e.g., "Cooking Recipes," "Tech Reviews").
    - Share playlists with friends or on social media.
    - Add descriptions to explain the playlist's purpose.

Using the "Save to Queue" Feature

- If you don't want to save videos permanently, **YouTube's Queue** feature allows you to create a temporary playlist while browsing.
- However, once you close your YouTube session, the Queue disappears.

Bookmarking Videos in a Web Browser

- If you prefer external organization, you can bookmark YouTube videos in your browser's **Bookmarks** folder.
- This method is useful if you watch videos across multiple accounts.

---

6. Common Issues and Troubleshooting

Issue 1: Videos Disappearing from Watch Later

- Sometimes, a saved video may no longer be available due to:

  - The uploader deleting the video.
  - YouTube removing the video for policy violations.
  - The video being set to **private** by the creator.

Issue 2: Unable to Add Videos to Watch Later

- Ensure you are **logged into your YouTube account** before saving videos.
- If you reach the limit (5,000 videos), you need to remove some videos before adding more.

Issue 3: Syncing Issues Across Devices

- If saved videos don't appear on another device:
  - Check if you're using the **same Google account**.
  - Refresh the YouTube app or browser page.
  - Clear YouTube cache and data (on mobile).

---

7. Tips for Using "Watch Later" Effectively

1. **Use "Watch Later" for Short-Term Viewing** – Don't let it become a messy backlog.
2. **Regularly Review and Remove Videos** – Keep your playlist fresh and relevant.
3. **Combine "Watch Later" with Custom Playlists** – Separate entertainment, education, and other content.
4. **Enable Offline Viewing (YouTube Premium Users)** – Download Watch Later videos for travel or areas with limited internet access.
5. **Use Browser Extensions (for Desktop Users)** – Some Chrome extensions allow bulk actions for Watch Later management.

Conclusion

The **"Watch Later"** feature is a simple yet powerful tool that enhances your YouTube experience by allowing you to save and organize videos efficiently. Whether you're using it for entertainment, learning, or research, managing your **Watch Later** playlist properly ensures a smoother and more enjoyable viewing experience.

By following the steps and best practices outlined in this chapter, you can **take full advantage of YouTube's video-saving features** and make the most of your time on the platform.

3.3.2 Creating and Organizing Playlists

WelcomeCreating and organizing playlists on YouTube is a fantastic way to curate content that aligns with your interests or needs. Playlists allow users to group videos together in a specific order or based on a particular theme, making it easier to manage, revisit, and share their favorite videos. Whether you're a casual viewer or someone who spends a lot of time on YouTube, understanding how to create and organize playlists can significantly enhance your experience on the platform.

In this section, we'll dive deep into the process of creating and organizing playlists, offering step-by-step instructions, best practices, and tips for making your playlists more engaging and effective.

What Are Playlists on YouTube?

A YouTube playlist is essentially a collection of videos that play in a set order or on shuffle. You can create playlists around themes, topics, or even moods, allowing you to enjoy uninterrupted viewing of your favorite content. Playlists can be either public (anyone can see and access them) or private (only you can view them), giving you full control over who sees your curated lists.

For creators, playlists are an excellent tool for structuring content and guiding viewers through a sequence of videos. This is particularly useful for tutorials, vlogs, or a series of related content. Playlists can also boost engagement, as users are more likely to watch a video to completion if it's part of a playlist.

Why Create Playlists?

Before we get into the "how-to" aspect, let's explore why playlists are so useful on YouTube:

1. **Better Organization:** Playlists allow you to organize your videos into categories based on your interests. Instead of scrolling through a cluttered library, you can easily find related content in a few clicks.
2. **Improved Discovery:** Playlists help with video discovery. YouTube's algorithm favors playlists when suggesting videos, meaning your playlist may show up in recommendations to other users, leading to increased visibility for your videos.
3. **Improved Viewer Retention:** By adding multiple videos to a playlist, you keep viewers engaged for longer periods. The continuous play feature means they won't have to manually click on each video, which encourages them to keep watching.
4. **Efficient Content Sharing:** Playlists are easy to share. Whether you're sharing a single video or a series, you can send a link to your entire playlist, making it a convenient way to share a cohesive collection of content.
5. **Personalization:** Playlists can be tailored to different moods, genres, or topics. You can create a playlist for relaxation, workout music, educational videos, tutorials, or even a mix of videos from different creators.

Creating a Playlist on YouTube

Now, let's explore the process of creating a playlist on YouTube. Whether you're using the website or the mobile app, the process is simple and easy to follow.

Creating a Playlist on Desktop

1. **Sign in to Your Account:** Make sure you're logged into your YouTube account. Without logging in, you won't be able to save or manage playlists.
2. **Choose a Video:** Start by navigating to a video you'd like to add to a playlist. You can search for the video or choose one from your homepage, subscriptions, or a specific channel.
3. **Click the "Save" Button:** Below the video player, you'll see a "Save" button next to the thumbs-up (like) and thumbs-down (dislike) icons. Click on the "Save" button.
4. **Select "Create New Playlist":** A menu will pop up, showing you your existing playlists (if any). To create a new playlist, click on the "Create New Playlist" button.

5. **Name Your Playlist:** Choose a descriptive name for your playlist. Make it specific to the theme of the videos you're adding, such as "Top Travel Vlogs" or "Funny Cat Videos."
6. **Set Privacy Settings:** Choose whether your playlist will be public, unlisted, or private. Public playlists can be seen by anyone, unlisted playlists can only be shared with a link, and private playlists are only visible to you.
7. **Click "Create":** Once you've named your playlist and set the privacy level, click "Create." Your playlist is now live, and you can add more videos to it!
8. **Add More Videos:** As you continue watching videos, repeat the process and add them to your playlist by clicking the "Save" button and selecting your newly created playlist.

Creating a Playlist on Mobile

1. **Open the YouTube App:** Launch the YouTube app on your mobile device and make sure you're signed in.
2. **Choose a Video to Add:** Navigate to the video you want to add to a playlist.
3. **Tap the "Save" Icon:** Below the video, tap the "Save" icon (the icon with a playlist symbol).
4. **Create a New Playlist:** Tap "Create new playlist." If you don't see this option, you may need to scroll through your existing playlists first.
5. **Name Your Playlist and Set Privacy:** Enter a name for your playlist and select its privacy settings (Public, Unlisted, or Private).
6. **Tap "Create":** After naming your playlist, tap "Create." The video will be added to your new playlist.

Organizing Your Playlist

Once you've created your playlist and started adding videos, the next step is organizing it. A well-organized playlist makes it easier for viewers (and yourself) to navigate through the content. Here's how you can organize your playlists effectively.

Reordering Videos in a Playlist

YouTube allows you to reorder the videos in your playlist, so you can choose the exact sequence in which they'll play.

1. **Go to Your Playlist:** From your YouTube homepage, click on your profile picture, then go to "Your Channel" and select "Playlists." Choose the playlist you want to organize.
2. **Click the "Edit Playlist" Button:** Once you're in your playlist, click on the three dots (More Options) and select "Edit Playlist."
3. **Reorder Videos:** You'll see a list of all the videos in the playlist. To reorder them, simply drag and drop the videos into the desired position.
4. **Save Your Changes:** After reordering your videos, click the "Save" button to lock in your changes.

Adding or Removing Videos from a Playlist

To keep your playlist up-to-date or adjust the selection of videos:

1. **Edit Playlist:** Go to your playlist and click the "Edit Playlist" option.
2. **Add New Videos:** To add new videos, click the "Add Videos" button and search for or paste the URL of the videos you want to add.
3. **Remove Videos:** If you want to remove a video, click the "X" next to the video title in the playlist. This will remove it from the playlist, but it won't delete the video itself from YouTube.

Best Practices for Organizing Playlists

Creating a playlist is just the beginning; keeping it organized is key to making it more enjoyable for your viewers (and yourself). Here are some tips for maintaining organized playlists:

1. **Group Similar Videos:** Keep videos in the same playlist that are related to the same theme or topic. For example, if you have a playlist about cooking tutorials, make sure all the videos are related to food preparation and recipes.
2. **Use Descriptive Titles:** Choose clear, specific names for your playlists. A playlist titled "Music Videos" is vague, while "Top 10 Relaxing Instrumental Tracks" is specific and helpful.

3. **Regularly Update Your Playlist:** As you discover new videos, keep your playlists fresh by adding them. Similarly, if some videos become outdated, remove them to ensure the playlist remains relevant.
4. **Create Multiple Playlists for Different Interests:** Instead of stuffing all your favorite videos into one playlist, consider creating separate playlists for different interests, like "Workout Videos," "Travel Vlogs," and "Educational Content."
5. **Public vs. Private Playlists:** Consider making thematic playlists public so your followers can enjoy them too. You can also keep certain playlists private for personal use or for sharing with specific people.

Sharing and Promoting Your Playlists

Once your playlist is organized and ready to go, it's time to share it with others. Playlists can be a great way to build a community or share content you love. Here's how to share your playlist:

1. **Copy the Playlist URL:** From your playlist page, click the "Share" button and copy the URL to share it with others.
2. **Embed Playlists on Websites or Blogs:** You can also embed playlists on your website or blog by copying the embed code.
3. **Promote on Social Media:** Post your playlist link on social media platforms like Facebook, Twitter, or Instagram, or use it in your videos to encourage your followers to check out the playlist.
4. **Send Playlists to Friends:** Directly share playlists with friends by sending them a link via email, text, or messaging apps.

Conclusion

Creating and organizing playlists is an essential part of the YouTube experience, both for personal use and for content creators. Playlists make your video-watching experience more enjoyable and organized while giving you control over the order and grouping of videos. By following the steps outlined in this guide, you can easily create, organize, and share playlists that will keep your content easy to access and fun to watch.

Remember, playlists are a powerful tool to keep viewers engaged, whether you're watching for personal enjoyment or curating content for your audience.

3.3.3 Sharing Playlists with Others

Playlists are an excellent way to organize and curate videos on YouTube, whether for personal enjoyment, educational purposes, or entertainment. However, a playlist becomes even more useful when shared with others. Sharing playlists allows you to introduce friends, family, or colleagues to a collection of videos that you find interesting, informative, or entertaining. In this section, we will explore how to share playlists effectively, discuss different sharing options, and provide tips for making your playlists more engaging and accessible to others.

---

1. Why Share YouTube Playlists?

Before diving into the technical steps of sharing, it's important to understand why you might want to share a YouTube playlist. Here are some common reasons:

- **Entertainment** – Share a collection of your favorite music videos, funny clips, or movie trailers with friends.
- **Education** – Organize tutorial videos or lectures and share them with students, colleagues, or fellow learners.
- **Collaboration** – Work on a project or event that requires video references, and share a curated playlist with team members.
- **Inspiration** – Share motivational talks, workout routines, or DIY videos with people who might benefit from them.

By sharing playlists, you make it easier for others to access multiple videos in an organized manner without searching for them individually.

---

2. How to Share a YouTube Playlist

Sharing a playlist on YouTube is a straightforward process. Below are step-by-step instructions for sharing playlists using different devices.

2.1 Sharing a Playlist on Desktop (PC/Mac)

1. **Open YouTube** and log in to your account.
2. Click on the **Library** tab in the left-hand menu.
3. Scroll down to the **Playlists** section and select the playlist you want to share.
4. Once the playlist opens, look for the **Share** button below the playlist title.
5. Click on **Share**, and a pop-up window will appear with different sharing options.
6. Copy the provided **link** or select a specific social media platform (such as Facebook, Twitter, or WhatsApp) to share directly.

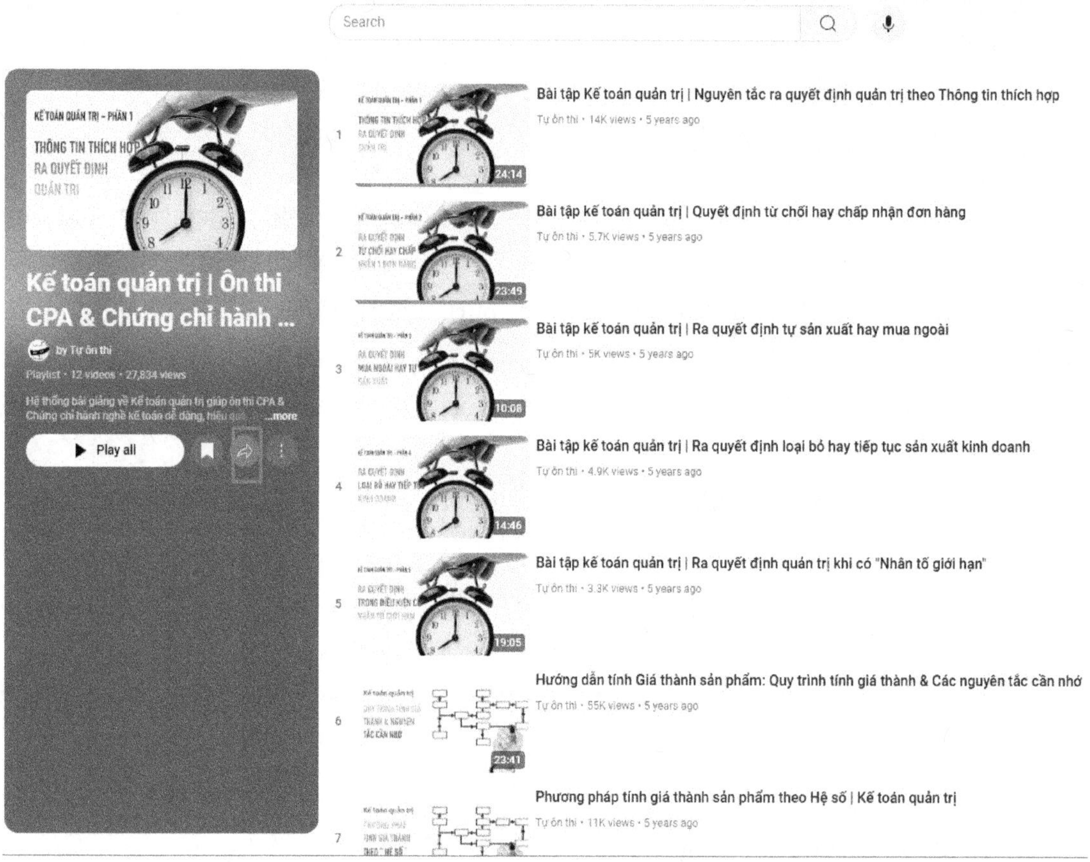

2.2 Sharing a Playlist on Mobile (Android/iOS)

1. Open the **YouTube app** and sign in to your account.
2. Tap on the **Library** tab at the bottom of the screen.
3. Under **Playlists**, select the playlist you want to share.
4. Tap on the **Share** button (represented by an arrow or three dots, depending on your device).
5. Choose a sharing option, such as copying the link, sending it via messaging apps, or posting it on social media.

2.3 Sharing via Email

- If you want to share a playlist via email, copy the playlist link and paste it into an email message.
- Add a short description explaining why you are sharing the playlist and what the recipient can expect from the videos.

---

3. Understanding Playlist Privacy Settings

Before sharing a playlist, it's essential to check its privacy settings to ensure that others can view it. YouTube offers three privacy settings for playlists:

3.1 Public Playlists

- Anyone can view the playlist.
- It appears in YouTube search results and on your channel page.
- Recommended if you want to share your playlist with a broad audience.

3.2 Unlisted Playlists

- Only people with the link can view the playlist.
- It does not appear in search results or on your channel page.
- Best for sharing with specific groups without making it public.

3.3 Private Playlists

- Only you can view the playlist.

- If you want to share it, you must change the setting to **Unlisted** or **Public**.
- Suitable for personal collections that are not meant for sharing.

To change privacy settings:

1. Open the playlist on YouTube.
2. Click the **Edit** button (pencil icon).
3. Select **Playlist Settings** > **Privacy** > Choose **Public** or **Unlisted** if you want to share it.
4. Click **Save**.

---

4. Different Ways to Share Playlists

4.1 Sharing on Social Media

YouTube makes it easy to share playlists directly on platforms like:

- **Facebook** – Post the playlist link on your timeline or in a group.
- **Twitter** – Tweet the playlist link along with a short description.
- **Reddit** – Share in relevant communities, especially if the playlist contains useful content.
- **Instagram** – Share the link in your bio or through Instagram Stories.

4.2 Embedding a Playlist on a Website or Blog

If you run a website or blog, embedding a YouTube playlist can be a great way to provide content to your visitors. To embed a playlist:

1. Open the playlist and click **Share**.
2. Select **Embed** from the options.
3. Copy the provided **HTML code**.
4. Paste the code into your website's HTML editor.

This is useful for educators, bloggers, and businesses that want to integrate video content into their platforms.

4.3 Creating a QR Code for Playlist Sharing

For offline sharing, you can generate a QR code linked to your playlist:

1. Copy the playlist URL.
2. Use a free QR code generator online (such as QR Code Monkey or QRStuff).
3. Generate and download the QR code.
4. Print it on flyers, posters, or share it in presentations.

This is especially helpful for events, conferences, or educational purposes.

---

5. Managing and Updating Shared Playlists

Once a playlist is shared, you might want to **add, remove, or reorder videos** while keeping it relevant for viewers. Here's how:

5.1 Adding New Videos to a Shared Playlist

- Search for a new video.
- Click **Save to Playlist** and select the shared playlist.
- The video will be automatically updated in the shared link.

5.2 Removing Videos from a Shared Playlist

- Open the playlist.
- Click the three-dot menu next to the video.
- Select **Remove from Playlist**.

5.3 Reordering Videos for Better Flow

- Drag and drop videos in the playlist order.
- Prioritize important or introductory videos at the beginning.

These updates will reflect automatically for anyone using the shared playlist link.

---

6. Best Practices for Playlist Sharing

To maximize engagement when sharing playlists, keep these best practices in mind:

- **Use a Clear Playlist Title** – Make it descriptive and engaging.
- **Write a Good Playlist Description** – Explain what viewers can expect.
- **Organize Videos Logically** – Arrange videos in a meaningful order.
- **Update Playlists Regularly** – Remove outdated content and add fresh videos.
- **Encourage Interaction** – Ask viewers to comment, like, and share.

---

7. Conclusion

Sharing playlists is a powerful way to curate and distribute YouTube content efficiently. Whether you're sharing for fun, education, or collaboration, knowing how to use YouTube's playlist-sharing features effectively can enhance the experience for both you and your audience. By mastering different sharing methods and optimizing your playlists for engagement, you can make your YouTube content more accessible and enjoyable for everyone.

Would you like to try sharing a playlist now? Give it a shot and see how others react to your curated videos!

CHAPTER IV
Managing Your YouTube Experience

4.1 Adjusting YouTube Settings

4.1.1 Managing Playback Preferences

YouTube offers a variety of playback settings that allow users to control how videos are played, ensuring a seamless and personalized viewing experience. Whether you want to adjust video quality, enable captions, or manage autoplay, YouTube provides a range of customization options. In this section, we will explore the different playback preferences available and how you can optimize them to enhance your viewing experience.

Understanding Playback Preferences

Playback preferences refer to the settings that control how videos are displayed and played on YouTube. These preferences impact aspects such as video resolution, subtitles, autoplay functionality, and playback speed. Adjusting these settings can improve video performance, save data, and make content more accessible.

You can manage playback settings on different devices, including desktop, mobile, and smart TVs. Some settings are available only for logged-in users, while others can be adjusted even without an account.

Adjusting Video Quality Settings

What is Video Quality?

Video quality refers to the resolution at which a video is played. YouTube offers multiple resolution options ranging from low-quality 144p to high-definition 1080p, 4K, and even 8K for supported videos. The available resolutions depend on the original quality of the uploaded video and your internet speed.

How to Change Video Quality on Desktop

1. Open YouTube and play any video.
2. Click the **Settings (gear icon)** at the bottom-right corner of the video player.
3. Select **Quality** from the menu.
4. Choose from the available resolution options (e.g., 144p, 360p, 720p, 1080p, etc.).
5. If you want YouTube to automatically adjust based on your internet speed, select **Auto**.

How to Change Video Quality on Mobile

1. Open the YouTube app and start playing a video.
2. Tap the video to reveal controls, then tap the **More options (three dots)** in the upper-right corner.
3. Select **Quality**.
4. Choose a resolution or select **Auto** for automatic adjustment.
5. On mobile, you can also set a default quality preference by going to **Settings > Video Quality Preferences**.

Impact of Video Quality on Data Usage

Higher resolutions consume more data. For instance:

- **144p:** ~100MB per hour
- **360p:** ~300MB per hour
- **720p HD:** ~1.5GB per hour
- **1080p Full HD:** ~3GB per hour
- **4K Ultra HD:** ~7GB per hour

If you have limited data, consider selecting **Data Saver mode**, which prioritizes lower resolutions while maintaining acceptable video quality.

Enabling and Customizing Captions (Subtitles)

Why Use Captions?

Captions enhance accessibility, making videos understandable for viewers who are deaf, hard of hearing, or watching in a noisy environment. Many videos on YouTube have automatic captions, while others include manually added subtitles.

How to Turn On Captions on Desktop

1. Play a YouTube video.
2. Click the **CC (Closed Captions)** button at the bottom of the video player.
3. To change the language, click **Settings (gear icon) > Subtitles/CC**, then select your preferred language.

How to Turn On Captions on Mobile

1. Open the YouTube app and play a video.
2. Tap the **More options (three dots)** in the upper-right corner.
3. Select **Captions** and choose your preferred language.

Customizing Caption Appearance

You can change the font style, size, and background opacity of captions:

1. On desktop, go to **YouTube Settings > Playback & Performance > Subtitles/CC**.
2. Select **Options** to adjust the text color, size, and background.

Managing Autoplay Settings

What is Autoplay?

Autoplay allows YouTube to automatically play the next recommended video after the current one finishes. This feature can be useful for continuous watching but may also consume unnecessary data and play videos you don't intend to watch.

How to Enable/Disable Autoplay on Desktop

1. Play a video on YouTube.
2. Toggle the **Autoplay switch** (located at the top-right corner of the video player).
3. If the switch is **blue**, autoplay is enabled. If it is **gray**, autoplay is disabled.

How to Enable/Disable Autoplay on Mobile

1. Open the YouTube app and go to **Settings > Autoplay**.
2. Toggle **Autoplay Next Video** on or off.
3. If you are on mobile data, you can enable **Autoplay only on Wi-Fi** to save data.

How to Disable Autoplay on YouTube Homepage

YouTube automatically plays a preview of videos on the homepage. To turn this off:

1. Go to **YouTube Settings > General**.
2. Select **Muted Playback in Feeds**.
3. Choose **Off** to disable autoplay previews.

Adjusting Playback Speed

Why Change Playback Speed?

Playback speed controls allow you to watch videos faster or slower based on your preference. Speeding up videos saves time, while slowing down videos can help with comprehension.

How to Adjust Playback Speed on Desktop

1. Play a YouTube video.
2. Click the **Settings (gear icon)** in the video player.
3. Select **Playback Speed**.
4. Choose a speed (e.g., **0.25x, 0.5x, 1.5x, 2x**).

How to Adjust Playback Speed on Mobile

1. Open the YouTube app and play a video.
2. Tap the **More options (three dots)**.
3. Select **Playback Speed** and choose a desired speed.

Practical Uses of Playback Speed Control

- **Slow down (0.5x or 0.75x)** – Useful for tutorials, lectures, or learning new skills.
- **Speed up (1.5x or 2x)** – Helps save time when watching long videos or podcasts.

Managing Video Looping and Manual Skipping

Looping a Video on Desktop

1. Right-click on a YouTube video.
2. Select **Loop** to continuously repeat the video.

Skipping Forward and Backward

- **On desktop:** Use the left/right arrow keys to skip 5 seconds.
- **On mobile:** Double-tap the left/right side of the video to skip 10 seconds.

Conclusion

Managing playback preferences on YouTube allows users to have a smoother and more tailored viewing experience. Whether adjusting video quality, enabling captions, controlling autoplay, or changing playback speed, these settings provide greater flexibility and efficiency in how you consume content.

By taking a few minutes to customize these options, you can enhance your YouTube experience, save data, and improve accessibility. In the next section, we will discuss how to secure your YouTube account, ensuring safe and uninterrupted usage.

4.1.2 Controlling Notifications and Alerts

YouTube notifications and alerts help users stay updated with new videos, comments, and activities related to their interests. However, managing these notifications is essential to prevent information overload and ensure a smooth viewing experience. This section will cover everything you need to know about controlling YouTube notifications and alerts, from understanding different types of notifications to customizing and troubleshooting them effectively.

Understanding YouTube Notifications

Before diving into notification settings, it's important to understand the different types of notifications YouTube provides:

1. Channel Subscriptions Notifications

When you subscribe to a YouTube channel, you have the option to receive notifications about new uploads, live streams, and community posts from that channel. These notifications ensure you never miss content from your favorite creators.

- **All notifications:** You receive every new video upload, live stream, and community post.
- **Personalized notifications:** You receive notifications based on YouTube's algorithm, which determines what you're most likely to watch.
- **No notifications:** You remain subscribed but won't receive any alerts.

2. General YouTube Notifications

Apart from subscription-based notifications, YouTube also sends notifications about:

- **Recommended videos** based on your watch history.
- **Activity from your comments** (likes, replies, and mentions).
- **Updates from YouTube** (new features, promotions, or app updates).
- **Reminders for live streams or premieres** from subscribed channels.

3. YouTube Community Notifications

These notifications relate to YouTube's community features, including:

- Polls, announcements, or status updates from channels you follow.
- Comments on shared videos.
- Mentions in video descriptions or community posts.

Now that you know the different types of notifications, let's explore how to control them.

Managing Notification Settings on YouTube

YouTube allows users to manage notifications on both desktop and mobile devices. Here's how you can customize your notification preferences:

1. Adjusting Notifications on Desktop

Step 1: Accessing Notification Settings

1. Open YouTube and sign in to your account.
2. Click on your profile picture in the top-right corner.
3. Select **Settings** from the drop-down menu.
4. In the left panel, click **Notifications**.

Step 2: Customizing Notifications

In the **Notifications** settings, you will find different categories to adjust:

- **Desktop Notifications**: Toggle ON/OFF to receive pop-up alerts on your computer.
- **Email Notifications**: Choose whether you want updates via email.
- **Subscription Notifications**: Control alerts from channels you've subscribed to.
- **Recommended Videos**: Enable or disable video suggestions based on your activity.
- **Mentions & Comments**: Get notified when someone replies to your comments or mentions you.

2. Adjusting Notifications on Mobile (Android & iOS)

Step 1: Accessing Notification Settings

1. Open the **YouTube app** on your phone.
2. Tap on your **profile picture** in the top-right corner.
3. Select **Settings** > **Notifications**.

Step 2: Managing Notification Preferences

Once inside the **Notifications** menu, you can:

- Toggle **Mobile Notifications** ON/OFF.
- Enable **Scheduled Digest**, which compiles notifications into a single daily update.
- Mute notifications during specific hours using **Quiet Hours**.
- Control in-app notifications for **subscriptions, comments, mentions, and recommendations**.

Customizing Notifications for Subscribed Channels

If you want more control over notifications from specific channels, follow these steps:

1. On Desktop

1. Go to the channel's **YouTube page**.
2. Click the **bell icon** next to the **Subscribe** button.
3. Choose from:
    - **All notifications (🔔)** – Receive all updates.
    - **Personalized notifications** – Receive selected updates based on YouTube's recommendations.
    - **None** – Turn off notifications for that channel.

2. On Mobile

1. Open the **YouTube app**.
2. Navigate to a subscribed channel's page.

3. Tap the **bell icon** and select your notification preference.

By customizing these settings, you can control which channels send you alerts and reduce unnecessary notifications.

Managing Email and Push Notifications

Apart from in-app alerts, YouTube also sends **email notifications** and **push notifications** to your devices. You can manage them through:

1. Email Notification Settings

1. Open **YouTube Settings** > **Notifications**.
2. Scroll to the **Email Notifications** section.
3. Toggle **ON/OFF** based on your preference.
4. Select which emails you want:
    - Updates from YouTube (features, promotions, account security).
    - Community activity (replies, mentions, comment interactions).
    - Recommendations for new videos.

2. Disabling Unwanted Email Notifications

If you want to stop receiving YouTube emails:

- Open a YouTube email and scroll to the bottom.
- Click **"Unsubscribe"** to stop receiving emails from that category.

3. Adjusting Push Notifications on Mobile

1. Open **Settings** on your phone.
2. Go to **Apps & Notifications** > **YouTube**.
3. Tap **Notifications** and customize which alerts you want to receive.
4. Toggle off notifications completely if you prefer.

Using "Do Not Disturb" and "Quiet Hours"

To prevent notifications from disturbing you at night or during work hours, YouTube offers **Quiet Hours** and **Do Not Disturb** settings.

1. Enabling Quiet Hours on Mobile

1. Open **YouTube Settings > Notifications**.
2. Scroll to **Scheduled Digest & Quiet Hours**.
3. Set a time range (e.g., **10:00 PM – 7:00 AM**) when notifications won't appear.

2. Using Do Not Disturb Mode (System Settings)

- On Android/iOS, enable **Do Not Disturb Mode** to mute all notifications, including YouTube.
- Customize exceptions if you still want alerts for important apps.

Troubleshooting Notification Issues

If you're not receiving notifications or receiving too many, try these fixes:

1. Fixing Missing Notifications

- **Ensure Notifications Are Enabled** – Double-check settings on both YouTube and your device.
- **Clear Cache & Data** – On mobile, go to **Settings > Apps > YouTube > Storage > Clear Cache**.
- **Check Email Spam Folder** – Some YouTube emails may be flagged as spam.
- **Update YouTube App** – Outdated versions may cause notification delays.

2. Fixing Too Many Notifications

- **Turn Off Unnecessary Alerts** – Disable community updates or recommended videos.
- **Unsubscribe from Unwanted Emails** – Reduce email clutter.
- **Use Personalized Notifications** – Let YouTube's algorithm filter important updates.

Final Thoughts

Controlling YouTube notifications and alerts allows you to balance staying informed with minimizing distractions. By adjusting notification settings for subscriptions, emails, and mobile alerts, you can ensure a better user experience tailored to your preferences.

By following this guide, you can:
✓ Customize your **YouTube notification settings** effectively.
✓ Reduce **unnecessary notifications** while keeping important updates.
✓ Enable **Quiet Hours** and **Do Not Disturb** for a distraction-free experience.

With these settings in place, you can **navigate, watch, and enjoy YouTube** without being overwhelmed by constant alerts.

4.1.3 Customizing Dark Mode and Appearance

In today's digital age, customization is key to enhancing user experience. YouTube provides several options to adjust its appearance to suit your preferences, including Dark Mode, font settings, and layout changes. Customizing these settings can make watching videos more comfortable, especially in different lighting conditions. In this section, we'll explore how to enable Dark Mode, adjust appearance settings, and optimize YouTube's visual experience for better usability.

Understanding Dark Mode on YouTube

Dark Mode, also known as "Dark Theme," is a feature that changes the background of YouTube from white to black or dark gray. This mode is particularly useful for reducing eye strain, especially when watching videos in low-light environments. Dark Mode also helps conserve battery life on OLED and AMOLED screens by minimizing the amount of light emitted by the display.

Benefits of Dark Mode

- **Reduces Eye Strain:** Bright white screens can cause discomfort, particularly in dimly lit rooms. Dark Mode provides a more comfortable viewing experience.

- **Saves Battery Life:** On OLED and AMOLED screens, Dark Mode can extend battery life since fewer pixels need to be illuminated.
- **Enhances Visual Focus:** Dark Mode can make colors appear more vibrant and reduce distractions, allowing you to focus more on video content.
- **Aesthetic Appeal:** Many users find Dark Mode visually appealing and prefer the sleek, modern look it provides.

How to Enable Dark Mode on Different Devices

On Desktop (Web Browser)

If you primarily use YouTube on a computer, enabling Dark Mode is simple:

1. **Open YouTube** in your preferred web browser (Chrome, Firefox, Edge, etc.).
2. Click on your **profile picture** in the top-right corner.
3. Select **"Appearance"** from the dropdown menu.
4. Choose **"Dark theme"** to enable Dark Mode.

Alternatively, you can set YouTube to match your device's system theme by selecting **"Use device theme"**. This option allows YouTube to switch between light and dark modes automatically based on your operating system's settings.

On Mobile (YouTube App - Android & iOS)

Dark Mode can also be enabled in the YouTube mobile app:

1. Open the **YouTube app** on your smartphone or tablet.
2. Tap on your **profile picture** in the top-right corner.
3. Select **"Settings"** from the menu.
4. Tap **"General"** and then select **"Appearance"**.
5. Choose **"Dark theme"** to activate Dark Mode.

If you want YouTube to follow your phone's system-wide settings, select **"Use device theme"**. This is useful if you have Dark Mode scheduled to turn on at night automatically.

On Smart TVs and Gaming Consoles

If you use YouTube on a smart TV or gaming console, Dark Mode might not be available directly in the settings. However, you can reduce brightness manually or enable a dark mode option in your device's system settings (if supported).

Additional Appearance Customization Options

Beyond Dark Mode, YouTube offers other appearance settings that help personalize your viewing experience.

Changing YouTube's Layout

- **Compact Layout:** If you want to fit more videos on your screen, YouTube offers a compact view, which reduces thumbnail sizes.
- **Theater Mode:** This mode enlarges the video player while keeping the rest of the page visible, offering a more immersive experience without going full-screen.
- **Fullscreen Mode:** This removes all distractions, maximizing the video across your screen.

Customizing Video Player Appearance

YouTube allows some customization options for the video player itself:

- **Adjusting Playback Speed:** You can slow down or speed up videos using the settings icon.
- **Subtitle and Caption Settings:** Change the font style, size, and background color of captions for better readability.
- **Mini Player Mode:** Shrinks the video to a small window while allowing you to browse YouTube simultaneously.

Adjusting Font and Text Size

If you have difficulty reading small text, you can adjust font sizes by:

- Zooming in on your browser (Ctrl + "+" on Windows, Cmd + "+" on Mac).
- Changing text size in your device's accessibility settings.

Hiding or Customizing Video Thumbnails

If you find video thumbnails distracting, certain browser extensions allow you to disable them or replace them with simpler images. This can be useful if you want a clutter-free experience.

Optimizing Dark Mode for Maximum Comfort

While Dark Mode is beneficial, you can enhance its effects by making additional adjustments:

1. Adjust Screen Brightness

Dark Mode works best when combined with moderate screen brightness. If the screen is too bright, it can still cause eye strain, even with Dark Mode enabled. Consider using:

- Auto-brightness settings (available on most devices).
- Blue light filters (such as Night Mode on phones and computers).

2. Enable Blue Light Filters

Many devices include a **Night Mode** or **Blue Light Filter**, which reduces blue light emissions from screens. This can be especially helpful when watching videos late at night.

3. Use Dark Mode Extensions for Browsers

If you use YouTube on a browser, you can install extensions like:

- **Dark Reader** (Chrome, Firefox) – Enables Dark Mode across all websites, including YouTube.
- **Enhancer for YouTube** – Provides additional customization, including themes and video player adjustments.

4. Schedule Dark Mode Automatically

If you don't want to toggle Dark Mode manually, many devices allow you to schedule Dark Mode to turn on at night and off in the morning. This ensures a comfortable experience without needing constant adjustments.

Troubleshooting Dark Mode Issues

Sometimes, users experience issues when enabling Dark Mode on YouTube. Here are some common problems and solutions:

Dark Mode Not Applying on Desktop

Solution:

- Clear your browser cache and cookies.
- Disable browser extensions that may interfere with YouTube's settings.
- Ensure your browser is up to date.

Dark Mode Keeps Reverting to Light Mode

Solution:

- Make sure you're logged into your Google account.
- If you selected "Use device theme," check your system's display settings.
- Restart your browser or app to apply changes.

Dark Mode Not Available on Older Devices

Solution:

- Update the YouTube app to the latest version.
- If using an old browser, switch to a modern browser like Chrome or Edge.

Conclusion

Customizing YouTube's Dark Mode and appearance settings can greatly improve your viewing experience, making it more comfortable, efficient, and visually appealing. Whether you're using YouTube on a computer, mobile device, or TV, understanding how to tweak these settings will allow you to enjoy videos without unnecessary strain or distractions.

By enabling Dark Mode, adjusting font sizes, optimizing playback settings, and utilizing additional tools, you can create a YouTube experience tailored to your needs. Take a few minutes to explore these settings and transform the way you watch content on YouTube!

4.2 Keeping Your Account Secure

4.2.1 Enabling Two-Factor Authentication

Introduction to Two-Factor Authentication (2FA)

In today's digital landscape, cybersecurity is more critical than ever. With millions of users accessing YouTube daily, accounts are prime targets for hackers attempting to steal personal information or hijack channels. One of the best ways to safeguard your YouTube account is by enabling **Two-Factor Authentication (2FA)**, an additional security layer that helps prevent unauthorized access even if someone manages to obtain your password.

2FA works by requiring not only your password but also a second verification step—such as a code sent to your mobile device or an authentication app—to log in. This extra step significantly reduces the risk of unauthorized access, making it a crucial security feature for all YouTube users.

Why Should You Enable Two-Factor Authentication?

Many people assume that having a strong password is enough to secure their accounts. However, passwords alone are no longer sufficient due to security breaches, phishing attacks, and password leaks. Here's why enabling 2FA is essential:

- **Enhanced Security:** Even if your password is compromised, hackers won't be able to access your account without the second verification factor.
- **Protection Against Phishing Attacks:** Phishing scams trick users into providing their login credentials. With 2FA enabled, even if you accidentally enter your credentials on a fake website, the hacker still cannot log in.
- **Prevention of Unauthorized Logins:** If someone tries to access your account from an unknown device, you will receive a security alert. This allows you to take immediate action to secure your account.
- **Essential for YouTube Creators:** If you have a YouTube channel, enabling 2FA is crucial to prevent unauthorized access and potential damage to your content and audience.

How to Enable Two-Factor Authentication for Your YouTube Account

Since YouTube is owned by Google, enabling 2FA for YouTube requires setting it up on your **Google account**. Follow these steps to enable 2FA:

Step 1: Sign in to Your Google Account Security Page

1. Open your web browser and go to Google Account Security.
2. Sign in with the Google account associated with your YouTube profile.

Step 2: Locate the Two-Step Verification Option

1. Under the **"Signing in to Google"** section, find the **"2-Step Verification"** option.
2. Click **"Get Started"** to begin the setup process.

Step 3: Choose a Verification Method

Google offers several options for receiving your second verification code. You can choose one of the following:

- **Google Prompt:** A notification sent to your phone for approval.
- **SMS or Voice Call:** A code sent via text message or voice call.
- **Authenticator App (Recommended):** Use Google Authenticator or another authentication app to generate codes.
- **Backup Codes:** Pre-generated one-time-use codes that can be used when other methods are unavailable.

Step 4: Verify Your Identity

- If prompted, enter your current password to verify your identity.
- Google will send a test verification code to the method you selected. Enter the code and confirm.

Step 5: Enable and Confirm 2FA

- Once verified, **click "Turn On"** to activate Two-Factor Authentication.
- Google will now require this additional step whenever you sign in from a new device.

Choosing the Best 2FA Method for You

While SMS verification is the most common method, it is not the most secure. Hackers can intercept text messages through SIM swapping or phone number hijacking. The best 2FA method depends on your needs:

Method	Pros	Cons
Google Prompt	Fast and easy	Requires internet access
SMS or Voice Call	Works without an internet connection	Vulnerable to SIM swapping
Authenticator App	Most secure option	Requires initial setup
Backup Codes	Can be used when no other options are available	Limited number of uses

For **maximum security**, using an authenticator app such as **Google Authenticator** or **Authy** is recommended.

Managing and Updating 2FA Settings

After enabling Two-Factor Authentication, it's important to manage and update your settings periodically.

1. Changing Your 2FA Method

If you want to switch from SMS verification to an authentication app:

- Go to **Google Account Security** settings.
- Select **2-Step Verification** and click **Change Phone or Switch to Authenticator App**.
- Follow the prompts to set up a new verification method.

2. Adding Backup Methods

To prevent being locked out of your account:

- Enable multiple 2FA methods (e.g., Google Prompt + Backup Codes).
- Store backup codes in a **safe location**, such as a password manager.

3. Updating Your Phone Number

If you lose your phone or change your number, update your 2FA settings immediately:

- Sign in to **Google Account Security** and navigate to **2-Step Verification**.
- Update your phone number or verification method.

Troubleshooting Two-Factor Authentication Issues

Sometimes, you may encounter issues with 2FA. Here's how to resolve common problems:

Problem 1: Lost Phone or Authenticator App

- Use a **backup code** to log in.
- If you don't have backup codes, visit **Google's Account Recovery Page** to regain access.

Problem 2: Not Receiving SMS Codes

- Check if your phone has a strong network signal.
- Restart your device and request a new code.
- If you changed your phone number recently, update it in your Google Account settings.

Problem 3: Locked Out of Your Account

- Try logging in from a previously trusted device.
- Contact **Google Support** if you cannot recover your account.

Frequently Asked Questions About 2FA on YouTube

1. Can I disable Two-Factor Authentication after enabling it?

Yes, but it's **not recommended**. Disabling 2FA removes an essential security layer, making your account more vulnerable to hacking.

2. Do I need to enter a verification code every time I log in?

Not necessarily. If you log in from a **trusted device**, Google may not ask for a 2FA code unless it detects unusual activity.

3. What happens if I forget my password and lose my 2FA device?

You can recover your account using backup codes or Google's account recovery options.

4. Is Two-Factor Authentication mandatory for YouTube creators?

Yes, as of **November 2021**, YouTube requires **all monetized creators** to enable 2FA to protect their accounts.

5. Can hackers bypass Two-Factor Authentication?

While 2FA significantly enhances security, advanced phishing techniques (such as **man-in-the-middle attacks**) can sometimes bypass it. Using an **Authenticator App** instead of SMS further reduces this risk.

Conclusion

Enabling Two-Factor Authentication is a simple yet powerful way to secure your YouTube account against cyber threats. By taking a few minutes to set up 2FA, you significantly reduce the risk of unauthorized access, ensuring that your personal data and YouTube activity remain protected.

To further enhance your security, consider using an authenticator app instead of SMS verification, regularly updating your security settings, and keeping backup codes in a safe place. Taking these proactive steps will help you enjoy a safer and more secure YouTube experience.

4.2.2 Managing Account Recovery Options

Your YouTube account is linked to your Google account, making account recovery an essential step in maintaining security and ensuring uninterrupted access to your videos, playlists, and subscriptions. Losing access to your account can be frustrating, but Google provides multiple recovery options to help users regain control. In this section, we'll explore the different methods available for recovering your account, how to set up and manage your recovery options effectively, and best practices to keep your account secure.

1. Why Account Recovery is Important

Account recovery is a crucial security feature that helps users regain access to their YouTube accounts if they forget their passwords, lose access to their devices, or experience unauthorized access. Here are some reasons why managing account recovery is essential:

- **Protection Against Unauthorized Access** – If your account is compromised, having recovery options allows you to reset your password and regain control.
- **Accidental Lockouts** – Forgetting your password or losing access to your authentication device can lock you out of your account. Proper recovery settings prevent this from happening.
- **Device Changes** – If you change or lose your phone, you may need to verify your identity to log in to your account on a new device.
- **Security Breaches** – In the event of a security breach or hacking attempt, you can use recovery options to secure your account quickly.

To minimize risks, it's essential to set up multiple recovery methods and keep them updated.

---

2. Setting Up Recovery Options in Google

Since YouTube accounts are managed through Google, all account recovery settings are configured in your Google account settings. Here's how you can set up and manage your recovery options:

2.1 Adding a Recovery Email

A recovery email helps you regain access to your account if you forget your password or if suspicious activity is detected.

How to Add or Update a Recovery Email:

1. Go to Google Account Settings.
2. Click on **Security** from the left-hand menu.
3. Scroll down to **Ways we can verify it's you** and click on **Recovery email**.
4. Enter your preferred recovery email address.

5. Click **Next** and follow the on-screen verification process.
6. Check your recovery email for a verification code and enter it to confirm the update.

Best Practices for Recovery Emails:

- Use an email account that you regularly check.
- Avoid using the same email for both your Google and recovery account to prevent a complete lockout if one is compromised.
- Keep your recovery email updated, especially if you change email providers.

2.2 Adding a Recovery Phone Number

A recovery phone number allows Google to send you verification codes via SMS or a phone call when you need to reset your password.

How to Add or Update a Recovery Phone Number:

1. Go to Google Account Security Settings. https://myaccount.google.com/security
2. Under **Ways we can verify it's you**, click on **Recovery phone**.
3. Enter your phone number and click **Next**.
4. Google will send a verification code to your phone. Enter the code and click **Verify**.

Benefits of a Recovery Phone Number:

- Faster account recovery compared to email.
- Immediate notifications if suspicious login attempts occur.
- An extra layer of security for two-factor authentication.

Tip: If you lose access to your phone number, update it immediately in your account settings to avoid recovery issues.

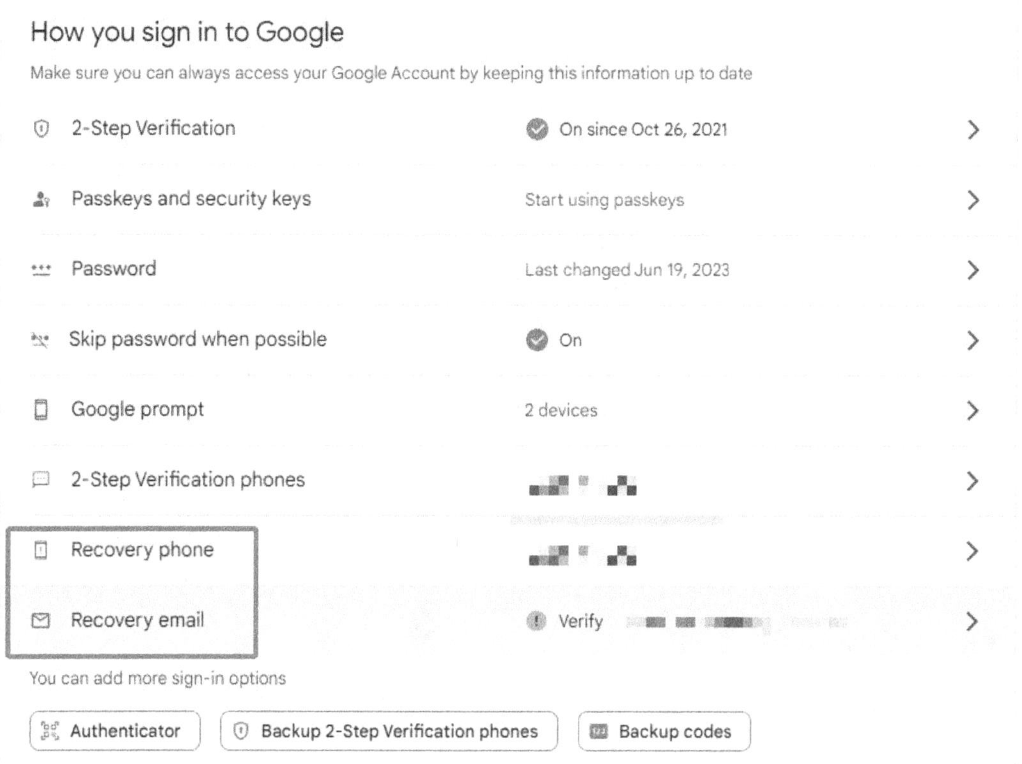

2.3 Enabling Backup Codes for Emergency Access

Backup codes are one-time passcodes that allow you to access your account if you lose access to your phone or recovery options.

How to Generate Backup Codes:

1. Visit Google's Two-Step Verification page.
   https://myaccount.google.com/security-checkup

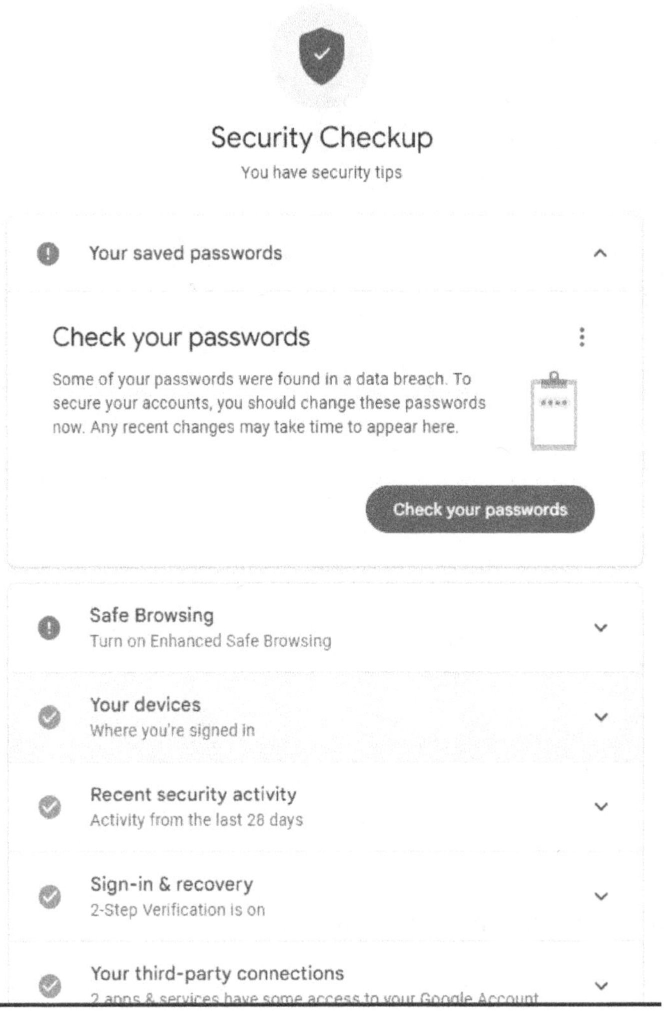

2. Click on **Backup codes** under the **2-Step Verification** section.
3. Click **Get backup codes** to generate a list of codes.
4. Save these codes in a secure location (offline storage is recommended).

When to Use Backup Codes:

- If you lose access to your phone and can't receive SMS codes.
- If you are traveling and unable to receive phone-based verification.

- If you suspect your account has been hacked and need immediate access.

Warning: Backup codes can be used only once. If you exhaust them, generate a new set immediately.

---

3. Recovering a Locked or Hacked YouTube Account

If you're unable to access your YouTube account, follow these steps to regain control:

3.1 Resetting Your Password

If you forgot your password, follow these steps to reset it:

1. Go to the Google Account Recovery page.
   https://accounts.google.com/v3/signin/recovery

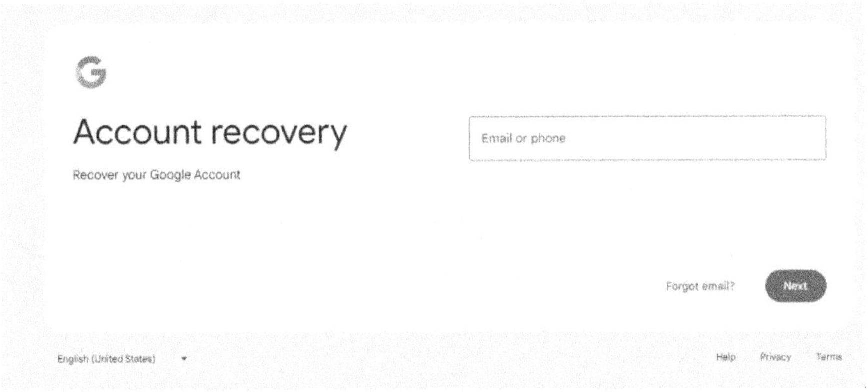

2. Enter your YouTube email address or phone number.
3. Follow the on-screen instructions to verify your identity.
4. Choose a new, strong password and confirm the reset.

Tip: Use a unique and complex password that you don't use for other accounts.

3.2 Recovering a Hacked YouTube Account

If your account has been hacked and you no longer have access, follow these steps:

1. Go to Google Account Help.
   https://support.google.com/accounts/answer/6294825

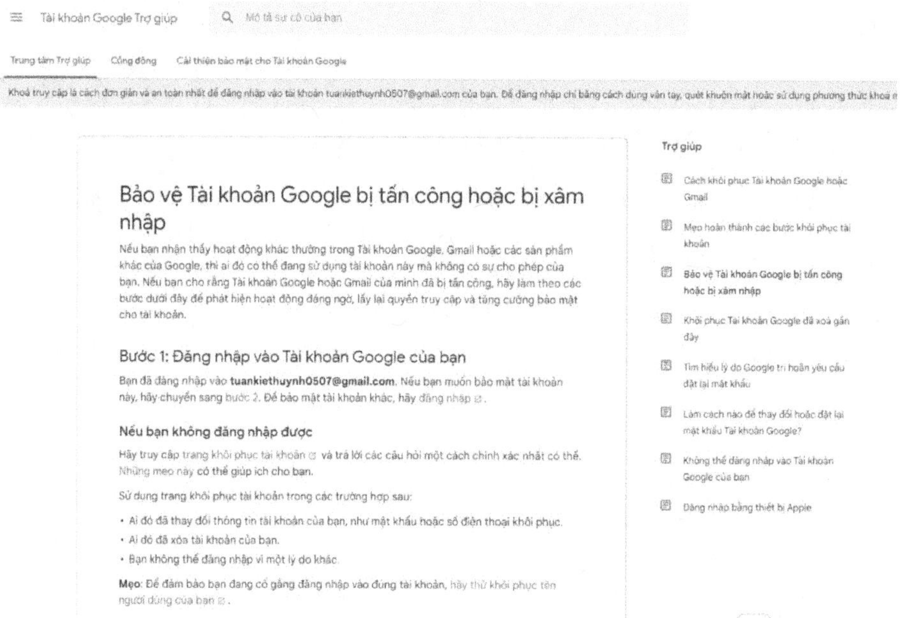

2. Click **Follow the steps to recover your account.**
3. Answer the security questions to verify your identity.
4. Check your recovery email for account recovery instructions.
5. If recovery fails, use Google's support options for additional help.

Once you regain access, follow these security steps:

- Change your password immediately.
- Review recent activity for suspicious logins.
- Remove any unknown devices from your account settings.
- Enable two-factor authentication for added security.

---

4. Additional Tips for Secure Account Recovery

- **Use a Password Manager:** Store your passwords securely and generate strong passwords.
- **Keep Recovery Information Updated:** Regularly check and update your recovery email and phone number.
- **Beware of Phishing Scams:** Never enter your Google credentials on suspicious websites.
- **Enable Security Alerts:** Turn on Google's security alerts to get notified of unauthorized login attempts.

Conclusion

Managing your YouTube account recovery options is crucial for maintaining security and ensuring uninterrupted access to your videos and subscriptions. By setting up a recovery email, phone number, and backup codes, you create multiple ways to regain control of your account if needed. Additionally, staying vigilant against phishing attacks and updating your recovery options regularly will help protect your account from unauthorized access.

By following these best practices, you can enjoy a safe and secure experience on YouTube while keeping your account protected from potential threats.

4.2.3 Recognizing and Avoiding Scams

The internet is a great place to explore, learn, and connect with others, but it also comes with risks—especially when it comes to scams. YouTube, as one of the largest online platforms, is not immune to fraudulent activities. Scammers use various tactics to trick users into providing personal information, clicking on malicious links, or engaging in schemes that can lead to financial loss. Understanding how to recognize and avoid scams is crucial for maintaining a safe and secure YouTube experience.

In this section, we'll explore common YouTube scams, how to identify warning signs, and best practices to protect yourself from falling victim to fraudulent activities.

---

1. Common Types of YouTube Scams

Scammers use different techniques to deceive users. Here are some of the most prevalent scams on YouTube:

1.1 Phishing Scams

Phishing scams involve fraudulent messages that attempt to trick users into revealing personal information such as passwords, credit card details, or other sensitive data. These scams often appear in the form of:

- Fake emails claiming to be from YouTube or Google, asking you to verify your account.
- Comments or messages containing suspicious links, claiming that you have won a prize.
- Pop-up ads directing you to login pages that resemble YouTube's official site but are actually fake.

How to recognize phishing scams:

- The email or message contains urgent requests, such as "Your account will be deleted if you don't respond immediately."
- The sender's email address looks suspicious (e.g., "youtube-security@gmail.com" instead of an official YouTube address).
- Links in the message do not lead to YouTube's official website.

1.2 Fake Giveaways and Prize Scams

Many scammers lure users by pretending to host giveaways, claiming that you have won a prize such as a new smartphone, gaming console, or cash. These scams often ask users to:

- Click on a link to claim their prize.
- Provide personal details such as name, address, and bank account information.
- Pay a "small fee" to process the prize.

How to recognize fake giveaways:

- YouTube itself does not send messages informing users that they have won prizes.
- Legitimate giveaways from content creators usually follow official rules and do not ask for money or sensitive information.

- Scammers often use phrases like "Act now before it's too late!" to create urgency.

1.3 Fake Copyright Strikes and Account Suspension Warnings

Some scammers send fake emails or messages claiming that your YouTube channel has violated copyright rules or community guidelines. They may ask you to:

- Click on a link to "resolve" the issue.
- Enter your login credentials to dispute the strike.
- Pay a fee to remove the copyright claim.

How to recognize fake copyright strikes:

- YouTube only sends copyright-related notifications through official channels.
- A real copyright strike can be checked within your YouTube Studio under "Copyright & Strikes."
- Legitimate copyright claims never ask for payment or personal details.

1.4 Impersonation Scams

Scammers create fake YouTube accounts pretending to be famous creators, brands, or YouTube employees. They leave comments or send messages asking users to:

- Visit a specific website for exclusive offers.
- Share personal information.
- Participate in fake promotions.

How to recognize impersonation scams:

- Real YouTube creators and verified accounts have a checkmark next to their names.
- If a message seems suspicious, check the creator's official YouTube page to verify if they are running any promotions.
- YouTube employees will never send direct messages offering monetization opportunities or account upgrades.

---

2. How to Protect Yourself from YouTube Scams

Now that you know the common scams, here are some ways to protect yourself and your account:

2.1 Verify the Source

Before clicking on any link or responding to a message, always verify if it is from an official source. YouTube will only contact you through its official email domain, which ends in **@youtube.com** or **@google.com**.

How to check:

- If you receive an email claiming to be from YouTube, hover over the sender's email address to see the full details.
- Avoid clicking on suspicious links in the comment section or messages.

2.2 Enable Two-Factor Authentication (2FA)

Two-factor authentication adds an extra layer of security to your account by requiring a second verification step. Even if a scammer obtains your password, they won't be able to access your account without the second verification code.

How to enable 2FA:

1. Go to your Google Account settings.
2. Click on "Security" and find "Two-Step Verification."
3. Follow the setup instructions using your phone number or an authentication app.

2.3 Use Strong and Unique Passwords

A weak password makes it easier for scammers to hack your account. Ensure that your password is:

- At least 12 characters long.
- A mix of uppercase and lowercase letters, numbers, and special symbols.
- Unique and not used for other websites.

Consider using a password manager to store your passwords securely.

2.4 Be Cautious with Links and Downloads

Never click on links in suspicious emails, comments, or messages—especially if they claim to offer free prizes or urgent account updates.

How to check a link before clicking:

- Hover over the link to preview the actual URL.
- If it doesn't match YouTube's official site (www.youtube.com or **accounts.google.com**), avoid it.
- Use Google's **Safe Browsing Site Status** to check if a website is safe.

2.5 Report and Block Suspicious Users

If you encounter a scammer, report them immediately to YouTube to prevent others from becoming victims.

How to report scams on YouTube:

1. Click on the three-dot menu next to the comment, message, or video.
2. Select "Report" and choose the appropriate reason (e.g., "Spam or misleading").
3. Block the user if necessary.

---

3. What to Do If You Fall Victim to a YouTube Scam

If you accidentally fall for a scam, take immediate action to minimize the damage:

3.1 Change Your Password

If you suspect that your YouTube or Google account has been compromised, change your password immediately.

Steps to change your password:

1. Go to **myaccount.google.com/security**.
2. Select "Password" and enter a new, strong password.
3. Log out of all devices to prevent unauthorized access.

3.2 Secure Your Financial Information

If you entered payment details into a fraudulent site, contact your bank or credit card provider to report unauthorized transactions.

3.3 Scan Your Device for Malware

Some scams involve malicious downloads that install spyware or viruses on your device. Run a full security scan using trusted antivirus software.

3.4 Report the Scam to YouTube and Google

Inform YouTube about the scam so they can investigate and take action against fraudulent accounts.

- Use YouTube's **Help Center** to submit a scam report.
- If your Google account was compromised, visit **Google Account Recovery** to regain control.

Conclusion

Scammers are constantly finding new ways to deceive users, but by staying informed and cautious, you can protect yourself from falling victim to fraud. Always verify sources, enable security features, and report suspicious activity to keep YouTube a safe platform for everyone.

By following these best practices, you can enjoy YouTube without the risk of scams and cyber threats. Stay alert, stay safe, and keep enjoying your YouTube experience!

4.3 Using YouTube Kids and Restricted Mode

4.3.1 Setting Up YouTube Kids for Child Safety

Introduction to YouTube Kids

In today's digital world, children are more exposed to online content than ever before. YouTube, being one of the largest video-sharing platforms, offers a wealth of educational and entertaining videos. However, not all content on YouTube is appropriate for young viewers. To address this concern, YouTube introduced **YouTube Kids**, a separate, child-friendly version of the platform designed to offer a safer and more controlled environment for children to explore video content.

YouTube Kids allows parents to filter content, set time limits, and customize viewing preferences to ensure a positive and secure experience for their children. This section will guide you through the process of setting up YouTube Kids, configuring parental controls, and ensuring that your child's online experience remains safe and appropriate.

Step 1: Downloading and Installing YouTube Kids

The first step to using YouTube Kids is downloading the app on your preferred device. YouTube Kids is available on:

- **Smartphones (Android and iOS)**
- **Tablets**
- **Smart TVs**
- **Web browsers (via the YouTube Kids website: www.youtubekids.com)**

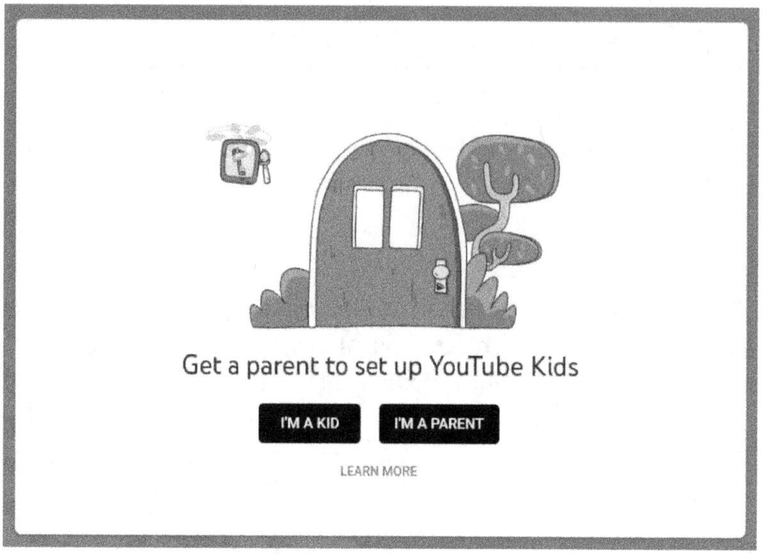

To install the app on a mobile device:

1. Open the **Google Play Store** (Android) or the **Apple App Store** (iOS).
2. Search for **YouTube Kids** and tap **Install** or **Get**.
3. Once the installation is complete, open the app to begin the setup process.

Step 2: Setting Up a Parent Account

Before your child can start using YouTube Kids, you must configure a **Parent Account** to manage the settings and restrictions.

1. **Sign in with Your Google Account**
    - When you open the app for the first time, YouTube Kids will ask you to sign in using a Google account.
    - This account will be used to manage parental controls and preferences.
2. **Agree to the Privacy Terms**
    - YouTube Kids provides a summary of how the platform handles child data.
    - Carefully read and agree to the privacy policy before proceeding.

3. **Enter Your Child's Information**
    - You will be asked to enter your child's name, age, and birth month.
    - YouTube Kids uses this information to recommend age-appropriate content.

Step 3: Selecting the Right Content Experience

YouTube Kids offers different content experiences based on your child's age group. This allows you to provide content that matches their developmental stage.

- **Preschool (Ages 4 & Under):** Designed for very young children, this mode offers educational videos, nursery rhymes, and simple entertainment.
- **Younger (Ages 5–7):** Offers a mix of educational and entertaining content with some interactive features.
- **Older (Ages 8–12):** Provides access to a broader range of videos, including music, gaming, and science-related content while still maintaining safety controls.

Parents can manually switch between these experiences or allow YouTube Kids to recommend the most suitable content for their child's age.

Step 4: Customizing Parental Controls

To ensure a safe viewing experience, YouTube Kids offers several parental control options that allow you to manage content access.

1. Approving Content Yourself (Parental Whitelist)

Parents can choose to **manually approve videos, channels, and collections** that their child can watch. This feature allows greater control over what content is accessible.

To enable this:

1. Open **YouTube Kids** and go to **Settings** (Tap the Lock icon in the bottom corner).
2. Select **Approved Content Only** mode.
3. Browse and add specific videos or channels to the approved list.

2. Blocking Inappropriate Videos or Channels

Even though YouTube Kids aims to provide a safe experience, inappropriate content may sometimes slip through. Parents can **block videos or channels** by:

- Tapping on the **three-dot menu** on a video or channel.
- Selecting **Block this video** or **Block this channel**.
- Confirming the action with a parental passcode.

3. Setting Viewing Time Limits

To prevent excessive screen time, parents can set viewing time limits:

1. Open the **Settings Menu**.
2. Select **Timer** and set the maximum amount of time your child can watch per session.
3. When time is up, the app will automatically lock.

4. Disabling Search to Limit Exposure

If you want to restrict your child's ability to search for videos, you can **turn off the search feature**:

- Open **Settings**.
- Navigate to **Search Settings** and **disable search**.

This ensures that children can only watch pre-approved videos and recommendations.

Step 5: Monitoring and Reviewing Watch History

Parents can review their child's viewing history to ensure they are watching appropriate content.

To access history:

- Open **Settings** > **Watch History**.
- Browse recently watched videos.
- Remove any video that seems inappropriate.

If you notice any concerns, you can refine content restrictions or block unwanted channels.

Step 6: Using YouTube Kids on Multiple Devices

YouTube Kids allows you to sync settings across multiple devices. This means that restrictions and parental controls will remain consistent whether your child is using a tablet, smartphone, or smart TV.

To enable multi-device access:

- Sign in with the same **Google Account** on all devices.
- Enable **syncing** in the parental control settings.

Additional Safety Tips for Parents

In addition to YouTube Kids settings, parents should consider these extra safety measures:

1. **Supervise Content Consumption**
    - Sit with your child while they watch videos.
    - Discuss what they are watching and encourage critical thinking.
2. **Use Family Link for Extra Controls**
    - Google's **Family Link** app offers additional parental controls, including screen time monitoring and app restrictions.
3. **Encourage Offline Activities**
    - Promote offline playtime and educational activities to balance screen exposure.
4. **Teach Digital Responsibility**
    - Help children understand the importance of **online safety, privacy, and respectful communication**.

Conclusion

Setting up **YouTube Kids** ensures a safer and more controlled viewing environment for children. By selecting appropriate content experiences, configuring parental controls, and monitoring viewing habits, parents can create a positive online experience. While no system is perfect, **active parental involvement** combined with YouTube Kids' built-in safety features can significantly reduce risks and promote healthy video consumption habits for children.

By following these steps, you can confidently allow your child to explore educational and entertaining content on YouTube Kids while keeping them safe from inappropriate material.

4.3.2 Enabling Restricted Mode for Safe Browsing

Introduction

YouTube is a vast platform with content catering to all audiences, from educational videos to entertainment, music, and more. However, it also contains material that may not be suitable for younger viewers or individuals who prefer a more curated experience. To help users filter out potentially inappropriate content, YouTube offers **Restricted Mode**—a feature designed to provide a safer browsing experience by hiding mature or explicit videos.

In this section, we will explore what Restricted Mode is, how it works, its limitations, and how to enable and manage it across different devices. By the end of this chapter, you will have a clear understanding of how to use Restricted Mode to create a safer YouTube environment.

Understanding Restricted Mode

What is Restricted Mode?

Restricted Mode is an optional setting on YouTube that helps filter out potentially inappropriate content. It is particularly useful for parents, educators, and workplaces where controlling exposure to explicit or sensitive content is important.

When enabled, Restricted Mode:

- **Hides videos flagged as potentially mature or inappropriate** by YouTube's automated system and user community.
- **Prevents comments from appearing on videos** (if the feature is enabled in your settings).
- **Applies content restrictions across the entire account** (if locked by an administrator or parent).

How Does Restricted Mode Work?

YouTube's Restricted Mode uses various methods to filter content, including:

- **Community Feedback**: Videos that receive multiple reports for inappropriate content may be flagged and removed from visibility in Restricted Mode.
- **Machine Learning Algorithms**: YouTube employs AI to analyze video titles, descriptions, metadata, and captions to detect and restrict mature content.
- **Manual Review**: Some videos are manually reviewed by YouTube moderators to determine their appropriateness.

Despite these efforts, **Restricted Mode is not 100% accurate** and may occasionally allow inappropriate content to slip through or mistakenly block harmless videos.

How to Enable Restricted Mode on Different Devices

1. Enabling Restricted Mode on a Web Browser

If you primarily use YouTube on a desktop or laptop, enabling Restricted Mode is simple:

1. Open **YouTube** in your web browser.
2. Click on your **profile picture** in the upper-right corner.
3. Scroll down and select **"Restricted Mode"**.
4. Toggle the switch to **"On"** to enable Restricted Mode.
5. If you want to prevent others from turning it off, click **"Lock Restricted Mode on this browser"** (requires signing in).

To disable Restricted Mode: Follow the same steps and toggle the switch to **"Off"**.

2. Enabling Restricted Mode on Mobile Devices

On Android and iOS (YouTube App)

1. Open the **YouTube app**.
2. Tap on your **profile icon** in the top-right corner.
3. Go to **"Settings"**.
4. Tap **"General"**.
5. Scroll down and locate **"Restricted Mode"**.
6. Toggle it **On** to enable or **Off** to disable.

Note: Restricted Mode settings on mobile devices are account-based, meaning they apply across all logged-in devices.

3. Enabling Restricted Mode on Smart TVs and Gaming Consoles

1. Open the **YouTube app** on your smart TV or console.
2. Navigate to **"Settings"**.
3. Look for the **Restricted Mode** option.
4. Toggle it **On** to enable or **Off** to disable.

This setting may not be available on some older smart TVs or streaming devices.

4. Enabling Restricted Mode for a Child's Account (Supervised Experience)

For greater control, parents can set up **YouTube Kids** or use **Google's Family Link** to manage their child's viewing experience.

1. Download and open the **Family Link** app.
2. Select your child's profile.
3. Navigate to **"Manage settings"** → **"YouTube"**.
4. Enable **Restricted Mode** or customize content filters.

This ensures the child's account stays in a safer environment without the risk of them disabling the setting.

Limitations and Challenges of Restricted Mode

1. Restricted Mode is Not Foolproof

Although YouTube's filtering system is robust, it is **not perfect**. Some inappropriate content might still slip through, while some safe videos may get mistakenly restricted.

2. Content Filtering Varies by Region

Restricted Mode settings may work differently depending on **regional laws and regulations**. Some countries may have stricter content filtering, while others may be more lenient.

3. Restricted Mode is Device-Specific

- If you enable Restricted Mode on one device, it **does not automatically sync** to other devices unless set under a controlled account (like **Family Link** or **Supervised Accounts**).
- You must manually **enable Restricted Mode on every device** where you want it applied.

4. Users Can Circumvent Restricted Mode

- Restricted Mode is **not a replacement for parental supervision**.
- Tech-savvy users may find ways to bypass it, such as switching accounts, using incognito mode, or accessing YouTube through third-party browsers.

Best Practices for Ensuring a Safe YouTube Experience

1. Combine Restricted Mode with Other Safety Tools

- Use **YouTube Kids** for younger children.
- Enable **SafeSearch** on Google to filter inappropriate content across search results.
- Regularly check your child's **watch history** to monitor viewing habits.

2. Educate Children and Users on Safe Browsing

- Teach kids to **identify inappropriate content** and report it.

- Encourage discussions about **online safety and digital responsibility**.
- Set screen time limits to promote a balanced media diet.

3. Monitor and Adjust Settings Regularly

- Periodically check **Restricted Mode settings** to ensure they remain enabled.
- Stay updated on **YouTube's policy changes** regarding content filtering.

Conclusion

Restricted Mode is a useful tool for filtering out inappropriate content, creating a safer viewing experience for families, schools, and workplaces. While it is not a foolproof solution, it provides an extra layer of control over what content appears on YouTube.

To maximize safety, it is essential to combine Restricted Mode with **parental controls, digital literacy education, and active monitoring**. By following the steps outlined in this chapter, you can effectively manage Restricted Mode on your devices and ensure a more secure YouTube experience for yourself and others.

4.3.3 Monitoring and Controlling Viewing Habits

YouTube offers a vast amount of content, ranging from educational videos to entertainment and everything in between. While this variety is beneficial, it also presents challenges, especially for parents, educators, or guardians who want to ensure that children are consuming appropriate and beneficial content. Monitoring and controlling viewing habits is crucial in maintaining a safe and productive YouTube experience.

This section explores different methods and tools available for monitoring and managing YouTube viewing habits effectively. It includes built-in features like **YouTube's Watch History, Restricted Mode, YouTube Kids parental controls**, and third-party monitoring solutions.

---

1. Understanding the Importance of Monitoring Viewing Habits

Before diving into the tools and strategies, it is essential to understand why monitoring YouTube activity matters. Some key reasons include:

- **Ensuring Age-Appropriate Content:** YouTube is an open platform where both family-friendly and mature content exist. Without proper monitoring, children might be exposed to inappropriate material.
- **Reducing Screen Time:** Excessive screen time can negatively impact health, productivity, and social interactions. Monitoring helps create a balanced approach to media consumption.
- **Preventing Harmful Trends:** YouTube trends and viral challenges can sometimes be dangerous. Supervision helps in avoiding harmful influences.
- **Encouraging Productive Content Consumption:** Monitoring allows parents and educators to guide users toward educational and constructive content.

---

2. Tools for Monitoring and Controlling Viewing Habits

2.1 Using YouTube's Watch History and Activity Log

One of the simplest ways to monitor YouTube usage is by reviewing **Watch History**. This feature keeps track of all videos watched while signed into a YouTube account.

How to Access and Review Watch History:

1. Open YouTube and sign in to the account you want to monitor.
2. Click on the **Library** tab in the left menu.
3. Select **History** to see the list of watched videos.
4. Click on any video to review its content.

Managing and Clearing Watch History

You can **pause**, **delete**, or **disable** Watch History if needed:

- To **pause history tracking**, go to **YouTube History Settings** and toggle off **"Include YouTube videos you watch"**.
- To **delete specific videos**, click the **three-dot menu** next to a video in Watch History and select **Remove from Watch History**.

- To **clear all history**, click **Clear all watch history** in the settings menu.

Why This Matters:

- It allows parents to check what children are watching.
- It enables users to remove videos that might influence YouTube recommendations negatively.
- It helps in maintaining a clean browsing experience.

2.2 Enabling and Configuring YouTube's Restricted Mode

Restricted Mode is a built-in feature that helps filter out potentially inappropriate content. It is useful for workplaces, schools, and homes where parents want to prevent access to mature content.

How to Enable Restricted Mode:

1. Open **YouTube** and sign in.
2. Scroll to the bottom of the **YouTube homepage**.
3. Click on **Restricted Mode**.
4. Toggle the switch to **On**.
5. If monitoring a child's account, **lock Restricted Mode** with a Google password to prevent deactivation.

How Effective is Restricted Mode?

- It **hides** videos that contain potentially mature or sensitive topics.
- It **filters out** inappropriate comments.
- It **limits search results** by blocking certain keywords.

However, **Restricted Mode is not foolproof**. Some inappropriate content may still bypass the filters. Therefore, it should be used alongside other monitoring strategies.

2.3 Setting Up and Using YouTube Kids for Safer Viewing

For younger children, **YouTube Kids** provides a safer, child-friendly alternative. This platform features content curated for kids, with strong parental controls.

How to Set Up YouTube Kids:

1. Download the **YouTube Kids** app from the App Store or Google Play.
2. Open the app and sign in with a parent's Google account.
3. Set up a **child profile**, including age and preferences.
4. Choose the **content level** (Preschool, Younger, or Older).
5. Enable **Parental Controls** to manage viewing preferences.

Parental Control Features in YouTube Kids:

- **Content Filters:** Blocks unsuitable videos based on age.
- **Timer Feature:** Limits screen time.
- **Approved Content Mode:** Parents can manually approve what their child can watch.
- **Search Restrictions:** Parents can disable the search function to prevent children from finding unwanted content.

By using YouTube Kids, parents can ensure that young children are only exposed to appropriate material while still enjoying their favorite videos.

---

3. Additional Strategies for Monitoring YouTube Usage

3.1 Setting Screen Time Limits

One of the biggest challenges of online video platforms is **overuse**. To prevent excessive screen time, parents and users can set limits using:

- **YouTube's Built-in Reminder Feature:**
    - Go to **Settings > Remind me to take a break** and set a reminder interval.
- **Google Family Link:**
    - Allows parents to limit total YouTube usage time per day.

- **iOS and Android Screen Time Controls:**
    - In device settings, limit app usage for YouTube.

By enforcing screen time limits, users can maintain a **healthy balance** between online and offline activities.

3.2 Encouraging Safe and Educational Content Consumption

Instead of just restricting content, parents and educators can also encourage **educational and productive viewing habits** by:

- **Subscribing to Educational Channels**
    - Channels like **TED-Ed, National Geographic, CrashCourse**, and **Khan Academy** offer valuable content.
- **Creating Playlists of Approved Videos**
    - Parents can create **custom playlists** with pre-approved educational content.
- **Engaging in Co-Viewing**
    - Watching YouTube together can help discuss video content and guide children towards appropriate material.

By fostering **intentional** and **educational video consumption**, YouTube can become a **valuable learning tool** rather than just an entertainment platform.

3.3 Using Third-Party Monitoring Apps

For parents who want more detailed monitoring, third-party parental control apps offer advanced features. Some popular options include:

- **Bark**: Monitors YouTube activity and alerts parents of inappropriate content.
- **Qustodio**: Blocks specific content and sets screen time limits.
- **Net Nanny**: Filters YouTube content and provides detailed activity reports.

While YouTube provides built-in tools, **third-party apps** can offer additional layers of **monitoring, filtering, and reporting**.

Conclusion

Monitoring and controlling YouTube viewing habits is essential for **safe, balanced, and meaningful** content consumption. While YouTube provides tools like **Watch History, Restricted Mode, and YouTube Kids**, users should also consider additional strategies like **screen time limits, educational playlists, and third-party monitoring tools**.

By combining **technology with active supervision**, parents, educators, and individuals can create a **positive, enriching YouTube experience** while avoiding potential risks.

CHAPTER V
YouTube Premium and Advanced Features

5.1 What is YouTube Premium?

YouTube Premium is a subscription-based service offered by YouTube that enhances the user experience by removing ads, enabling offline downloads, providing background playback, and giving access to exclusive content. Launched originally as YouTube Red in 2015 and later rebranded to YouTube Premium in 2018, the service aims to provide users with a more seamless and enriched viewing and listening experience.

For those who spend a lot of time watching videos, listening to music, or consuming content on YouTube, Premium offers several perks that can significantly improve usability. Whether you are looking to watch videos without interruptions, listen to music on the go, or enjoy YouTube Originals, YouTube Premium provides a more convenient and flexible way to engage with content.

In this section, we will explore the key features and benefits of YouTube Premium and explain how it enhances the viewing experience.

5.1.1 Features and Benefits of YouTube Premium

YouTube Premium offers a variety of features that enhance both video and music streaming. Let's take a closer look at each of the main benefits:

1. Ad-Free Viewing Experience

One of the biggest benefits of YouTube Premium is the removal of advertisements. Regular YouTube users are familiar with pre-roll ads (ads that play before a video starts), mid-roll ads (ads that interrupt a video), banner ads, and pop-ups. These can sometimes disrupt the viewing experience, especially during long videos.

With YouTube Premium, users can watch videos without any ad interruptions. This is particularly useful for those who frequently watch educational content, listen to music, or enjoy long-form videos. Eliminating ads not only enhances user experience but also saves time by avoiding interruptions.

2. Background Playback

Another major advantage of YouTube Premium is background playback. Normally, when you exit the YouTube app on your mobile device or lock your phone screen, the video stops playing. This can be frustrating, especially when listening to music, podcasts, or interviews.

With YouTube Premium, videos continue to play in the background, even if you switch to another app or lock your phone. This feature is especially beneficial for users who enjoy listening to content while multitasking, such as working, exercising, or commuting.

3. Offline Downloads for Videos and Music

YouTube Premium allows users to download videos for offline viewing. This is particularly useful when traveling, commuting, or in areas with limited internet access. Users can download their favorite content and watch it later without needing an internet connection.

The offline download feature is available on both YouTube and YouTube Music. It enables users to save playlists, individual videos, or even entire albums from YouTube Music, making it a valuable tool for people who want uninterrupted access to their favorite content.

4. YouTube Music Premium

Subscribers of YouTube Premium automatically get access to YouTube Music Premium, a dedicated music streaming service that competes with Spotify and Apple Music.

Key benefits of YouTube Music Premium include:

- **Ad-free music streaming** – No interruptions while listening to songs.
- **Background playback** – Continue listening to music while using other apps or when the screen is off.
- **Offline music downloads** – Save songs, albums, or playlists to listen to without an internet connection.

- **Smart recommendations** – Personalized music suggestions based on listening habits.

For users who already rely on YouTube for music discovery, YouTube Music Premium is a convenient alternative to traditional streaming services.

5. Exclusive YouTube Originals

Another perk of YouTube Premium is access to **YouTube Originals**, a collection of exclusive shows, movies, and series produced by YouTube.

While YouTube Originals are not as widely recognized as Netflix or Disney+ originals, they offer a unique mix of documentaries, reality shows, and scripted series featuring popular YouTube creators and celebrities. Some well-known YouTube Originals include:

- **Cobra Kai** – A continuation of the *Karate Kid* franchise.
- **Scare PewDiePie** – A reality series featuring PewDiePie.
- **Liza on Demand** – A comedy series starring Liza Koshy.

Although YouTube has scaled back its production of Originals, Premium members still enjoy exclusive content unavailable to free users.

6. Improved Live Stream Experience

For users who watch a lot of live streams, YouTube Premium offers an improved experience by removing mid-roll ads. Live streaming on YouTube often includes ads that can interrupt the flow of events, especially during sports broadcasts, concerts, or gaming streams.

With YouTube Premium, users can watch live content without disruptions, ensuring they don't miss important moments.

7. Picture-in-Picture Mode (PiP)

Another useful feature for mobile users is **Picture-in-Picture (PiP) mode**. This allows users to minimize the YouTube video into a small floating window while continuing to browse other apps on their device.

PiP mode is especially helpful for:

- Watching tutorial videos while following instructions in another app.
- Multitasking while keeping an eye on the video.

- Checking messages or emails without pausing the video.

This feature is available on both Android and iOS devices for YouTube Premium subscribers.

8. No More Forced Breaks or Pop-Ups

Some free users may have noticed **YouTube's "Take a Break" reminders** or pop-ups that encourage healthier viewing habits. While these are useful, they can be annoying for users who prefer uninterrupted viewing.

With YouTube Premium, these interruptions are minimized, allowing users to watch content without distractions.

9. Premium Membership Sharing (Family Plan)

YouTube Premium offers a **Family Plan**, which allows up to **five family members** to share a single subscription under one billing account. This makes the service more affordable when split among multiple users.

Each family member gets their own personalized YouTube experience, including individual recommendations, watch history, and offline downloads.

Conclusion: Is YouTube Premium Worth It?

The features offered by YouTube Premium significantly improve the user experience, particularly for those who spend a lot of time on the platform. Whether it's ad-free viewing, background playback, offline downloads, or access to YouTube Music, the subscription provides several advantages.

The value of YouTube Premium depends on individual usage habits. If you frequently watch videos, listen to music, and want an uninterrupted experience, YouTube Premium is a worthwhile investment. However, if you only use YouTube occasionally, the free version might be sufficient.

In the next section, we will explore how to subscribe to YouTube Premium and manage your payments effectively.

5.1.2 How to Subscribe and Manage Payments

Introduction

YouTube Premium offers an enhanced experience by removing ads, enabling offline viewing, and providing access to exclusive features like background play and YouTube Music. To take advantage of these benefits, you need to subscribe and manage your payments effectively. This section provides a step-by-step guide on how to subscribe to YouTube Premium and manage your subscription, including payment methods, billing cycles, and cancellation procedures.

---

1. How to Subscribe to YouTube Premium

Subscribing to YouTube Premium is a straightforward process, whether you are using a web browser, a mobile device, or a smart TV. Below are detailed steps for each platform.

1.1 Subscribing via a Web Browser

If you are using a laptop or desktop computer, follow these steps to subscribe:

1. **Go to the YouTube Premium Page**
    - Open a web browser and go to https://www.youtube.com/premium.

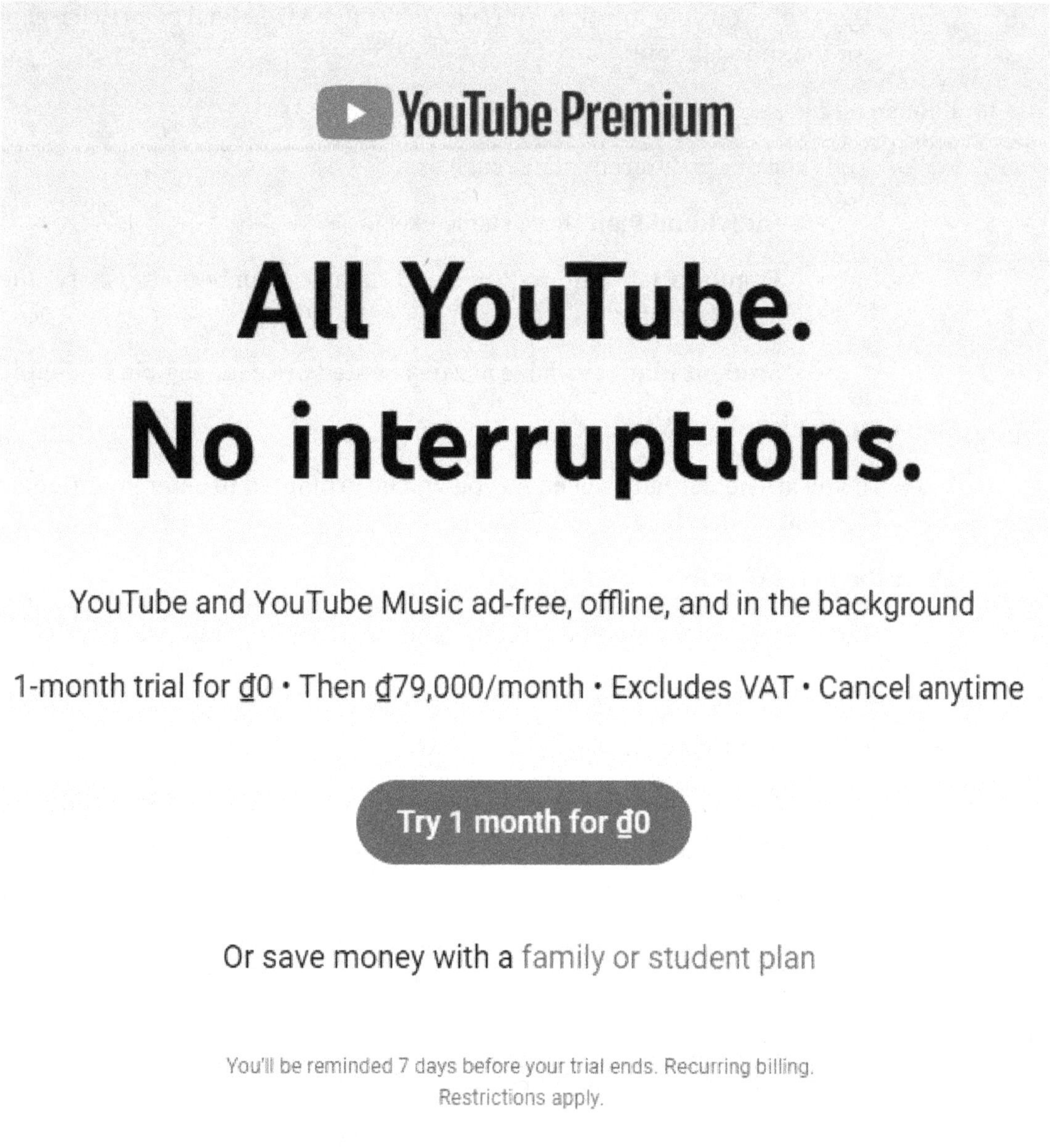
YouTube Premium
All YouTube.
No interruptions.
YouTube and YouTube Music ad-free, offline, and in the background
1-month trial for ₫0 • Then ₫79,000/month • Excludes VAT • Cancel anytime
Try 1 month for ₫0
Or save money with a family or student plan
You'll be reminded 7 days before your trial ends. Recurring billing.
Restrictions apply.

- This page provides information about the benefits and pricing of YouTube Premium in your region.

2. **Click on "Try It Free" or "Get YouTube Premium"**

- Depending on your location, YouTube may offer a **free trial** before charging for the subscription.

3. **Choose a Plan**
   - YouTube offers different plans, such as:
     - **Individual Plan** (for a single user).
     - **Family Plan** (allows up to 5 family members to share the subscription).
     - **Student Plan** (available at a discounted price for eligible students).
4. **Sign in to Your Google Account**
   - If you are not already signed in, you will be prompted to enter your Google account credentials.
5. **Enter Payment Details**
   - Choose a payment method (credit/debit card, PayPal, or Google Pay).
   - Enter the required billing details and agree to the terms.
6. **Confirm Your Subscription**
   - After entering your payment information, click **"Start Membership"** to activate your subscription.
   - You will receive a confirmation email from YouTube.

1.2 Subscribing via the YouTube Mobile App

If you prefer to subscribe using your smartphone or tablet, follow these steps:

1. **Open the YouTube App**
   - Ensure you are signed in to the Google account you wish to use for the subscription.
2. **Go to YouTube Premium**
   - Tap your profile picture in the top right corner.

- Select **"Get YouTube Premium"** from the menu.

3. **Select a Plan**
   - Choose between **Individual, Family, or Student** plans.
4. **Confirm Subscription via Google Play or App Store**
   - If you are using an **Android** device, the subscription will be processed through **Google Play**.
   - If you are using an **iPhone or iPad**, it will be processed via the **Apple App Store**.
5. **Approve Payment**
   - Follow the on-screen instructions to confirm your payment.
6. **Start Enjoying YouTube Premium**
   - Once subscribed, you can immediately enjoy ad-free videos, background play, and YouTube Music.

Note: Subscribing through the Apple App Store may be more expensive due to Apple's transaction fees. Consider subscribing through a web browser for better pricing.

1.3 Subscribing via a Smart TV or Streaming Device

If you watch YouTube on a smart TV, gaming console, or streaming device, you can also subscribe through these platforms:

1. **Open the YouTube App on Your Smart TV**
   - Navigate to the **YouTube Premium** section, usually found in the menu.
2. **Select a Subscription Plan**
   - Choose from the available plans and proceed with the sign-up process.
3. **Use a Secondary Device to Complete Payment**
   - YouTube will provide a unique code.
   - Visit **https://youtube.com/activate** on a smartphone or computer.

- Enter the code and complete the subscription.

4. **Confirm and Start Using YouTube Premium**
    - Once the payment is confirmed, YouTube Premium will be activated on your smart TV account.

---

2. Managing Your YouTube Premium Subscription

After subscribing, it's important to know how to manage your payments, update billing details, and cancel your subscription if needed.

2.1 Updating Payment Methods

If you need to change your payment method, follow these steps:

1. **Go to Google Payments Center**
    - Visit https://pay.google.com and sign in.

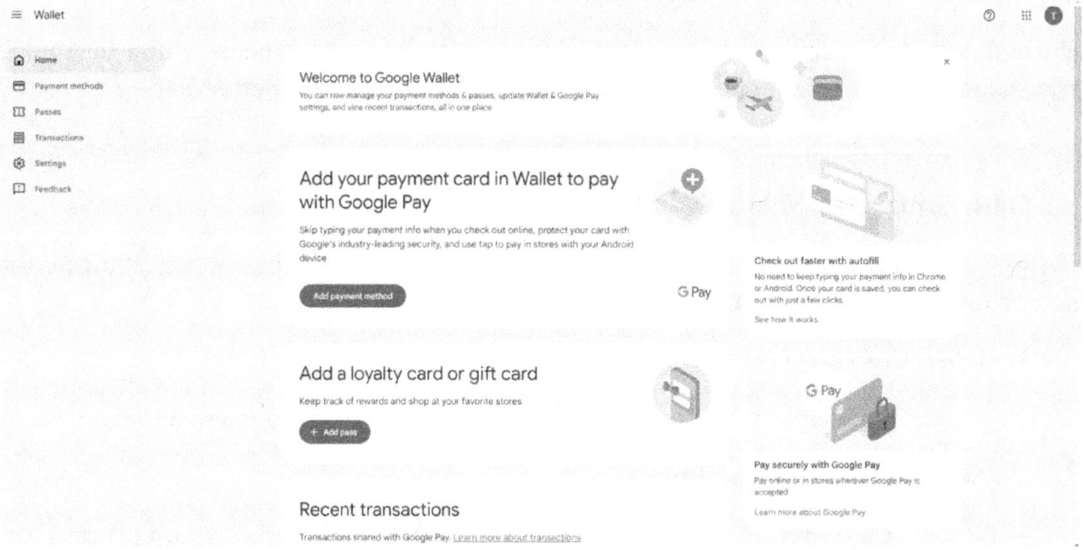

2. **Find Your YouTube Premium Subscription**
    - Under **Subscriptions & Services**, locate YouTube Premium.
3. **Click on "Manage Payment Methods"**

  - Add a new card, PayPal account, or another available payment option.
  - Remove outdated payment methods if necessary.
4. **Save Your Changes**
  - Ensure your billing details are up to date to avoid service interruptions.

2.2 Viewing and Downloading Payment Invoices

If you need invoices for your records:

1. **Visit Google Payments Center**
  - Go to https://pay.google.com.
2. **Select YouTube Premium Subscription**
  - Under **Transaction History**, find the invoice for a specific billing cycle.
3. **Download or Print the Invoice**
  - Click on the invoice and choose **Download as PDF** or **Print**.

2.3 Cancelling Your YouTube Premium Subscription

If you decide that YouTube Premium is not for you, you can cancel at any time:

Cancelling via Web Browser

1. **Go to YouTube Premium Settings**
  - Visit https://youtube.com/premium.
2. **Select "Manage Membership"**
  - Click on **"Cancel Membership"** or **"Pause Subscription"**.
3. **Choose a Reason for Cancellation**
  - YouTube may ask why you are canceling (optional).
4. **Confirm Cancellation**

- Click **"Yes, Cancel"** to finalize the process.

Cancelling via Mobile App

1. **Open YouTube App and Tap on Your Profile**
2. **Go to "Purchases & Memberships"**
3. **Select YouTube Premium and Tap "Cancel Membership"**
4. **Confirm Your Decision**

---

3. What Happens After Cancelling?

- **Immediate Access Until End of Billing Cycle**
  - You will still enjoy Premium features until your current billing period ends.
- **No Refunds for Partial Months**
  - YouTube does not offer refunds for unused days after cancellation.
- **Downgrade to Free Version**
  - You will see ads again, lose background play, and cannot download videos.
- **Easily Resubscribe**
  - You can reactivate YouTube Premium anytime without losing your watch history or subscriptions.

Conclusion

Subscribing to YouTube Premium is a simple process that can significantly enhance your viewing experience. Managing your subscription effectively—whether updating payment details, downloading invoices, or canceling—ensures you stay in control of your membership. By understanding these processes, you can make informed decisions about whether YouTube Premium is right for you.

If you frequently use YouTube, enjoy ad-free streaming, and want access to exclusive features, YouTube Premium is a valuable investment. However, if you find yourself not using its benefits often, you now know how to cancel or pause your membership without hassle.

5.1.3 Is YouTube Premium Worth It?

Whether **YouTube Premium** is worth the cost depends on how you use YouTube and what you value in a streaming service. The subscription costs around **$11.99 per month** for an individual plan, with discounted options for **family plans ($17.99/month for up to 5 members)** and **students ($6.99/month)**. Here, we will analyze the value of YouTube Premium based on various aspects.

1. Who Benefits Most from YouTube Premium?

A. Heavy YouTube Users

If you spend a significant amount of time watching YouTube videos daily, YouTube Premium might be an excellent investment. Ads can be disruptive, and frequent interruptions can make long-form content (such as educational videos, documentaries, and podcasts) frustrating to watch. By eliminating ads, you save time and improve the viewing experience.

B. Music Lovers

Subscribers of **YouTube Music Premium** gain access to a dedicated music streaming platform similar to **Spotify** and **Apple Music**. It allows background play, offline downloads, and ad-free listening. If you already use YouTube for music instead of other streaming services, upgrading to **YouTube Premium** can be a game-changer.

C. Travelers and Offline Users

If you often travel or have limited access to Wi-Fi, **offline video downloads** can be a lifesaver. You can save videos in advance and watch them anytime without worrying about data usage. This feature is especially useful for commuters, students, or those in regions with slow internet connections.

D. Multitaskers

The **background play** feature is great for users who like to listen to YouTube videos while using other apps. Whether you're listening to a podcast, tutorial, or music playlist, background play ensures uninterrupted audio without needing to keep the app open.

2. Is the Ad-Free Experience Worth It?

One of the biggest selling points of **YouTube Premium** is ad-free viewing. Ads on YouTube have become more frequent, longer, and sometimes unskippable. If you find them annoying and disruptive, the ability to watch videos without ads could be the most compelling reason to subscribe.

Here's a simple breakdown:

- The average YouTube video contains **3-5 ads** (pre-roll, mid-roll, and post-roll).
- If you watch **1 hour of YouTube per day**, you might encounter **10-20 minutes of ads** daily.
- Over a month, that's **5-10 hours of saved time** by avoiding ads.

If you value your time and prefer an uninterrupted experience, YouTube Premium is likely worth the price.

3. YouTube Music Premium vs. Other Music Streaming Services

A major advantage of YouTube Premium is its **bundled music service, YouTube Music Premium**. But how does it compare to other popular music streaming platforms?

Feature	YouTube Music Premium	Spotify Premium	Apple Music	Amazon Music Unlimited
Ad-Free Listening	✅ Yes	✅ Yes	✅ Yes	✅ Yes
Offline Downloads	✅ Yes	✅ Yes	✅ Yes	✅ Yes
Background Play	✅ Yes	✅ Yes	✅ Yes	✅ Yes
Music Videos	✅ Yes	❌ No	❌ No	❌ No
Price (Individual Plan)	$11.99	$10.99	$10.99	$10.99

What Makes YouTube Music Unique?

- It offers a **massive collection of official music videos** alongside traditional audio tracks.
- It allows users to switch **seamlessly between video and audio**.

- It provides access to **unofficial remixes, live performances, and covers** not available on other platforms.

If you enjoy discovering unique music content, **YouTube Music Premium** could be a valuable part of your subscription.

---

4. Is YouTube Originals a Game-Changer?

YouTube Originals provides exclusive movies, documentaries, and series. However, **unlike Netflix, Disney+, or HBO Max, YouTube Originals has fewer high-profile productions**. While it offers unique content from **popular creators like MrBeast, Markiplier, and Liza Koshy**, it may not be a primary reason to subscribe.

If exclusive content is a priority, platforms like **Netflix or Amazon Prime Video** offer a larger selection.

---

5. YouTube Premium vs. Free Alternatives

If you're unsure about subscribing, consider these free alternatives:

A. YouTube with Ads + Ad Blockers

Many users install **ad blockers** to remove YouTube ads for free. However, this method:

- Does not work on the **mobile app**.
- May violate YouTube's policies.
- Does not include other Premium features (offline downloads, background play, etc.).

B. YouTube Music Free Tier

The free version of YouTube Music allows streaming but comes with:

- **Ads** between songs.
- **No offline downloads**.
- **No background play** (music stops when you leave the app).

For users who listen to YouTube music frequently, **the Premium upgrade significantly improves the experience**.

Final Verdict: Is YouTube Premium Worth It?

Yes, YouTube Premium is worth it if you:

✅ Watch YouTube frequently and hate ads.
✅ Listen to YouTube Music and want an ad-free experience.
✅ Download videos for offline viewing regularly.
✅ Use YouTube as a primary source of entertainment.
✅ Enjoy listening to long-form content with background play.

It may not be worth it if you:

❌ Only watch YouTube occasionally.
❌ Don't mind watching ads.
❌ Already subscribe to another music service.
❌ Prefer other streaming platforms like Netflix for exclusive content.

Ultimately, YouTube Premium is an excellent choice for **power users**, but for casual viewers, the free version of YouTube is still a fantastic option. If you're unsure, **take advantage of the free trial** to decide whether it's right for you.

5.2 Downloading Videos for Offline Viewing

Downloading YouTube videos for offline viewing is a valuable feature that allows users to watch their favorite content without an active internet connection. This is particularly useful for travelers, students, or anyone who wants to conserve mobile data. However, not all YouTube videos can be downloaded legally, and it's essential to understand the guidelines and best practices to ensure compliance with YouTube's terms of service.

5.2.1 How to Download Videos Legally

Downloading videos from YouTube legally means using methods that comply with YouTube's policies and copyright laws. YouTube provides official ways to download videos for offline viewing, mainly through YouTube Premium and YouTube's mobile app. Below, we will explore the legal ways to download YouTube videos, the steps to do so, and the limitations you need to be aware of.

Understanding YouTube's Policies on Downloading

YouTube's terms of service clearly state that users are not allowed to download videos unless YouTube provides a download button or feature. This is to protect content creators' rights and ensure that views, ad revenue, and analytics are correctly tracked. Downloading videos using unauthorized third-party applications or websites violates YouTube's policies and can result in account suspension or legal action.

According to YouTube's **Terms of Service (Section 5B)**:
"You shall not download any content unless YouTube specifically provides a download button or similar functionality for that content."

This means that the only legal ways to download YouTube videos are:

1. **Using YouTube's official download feature on the mobile app**
2. **Subscribing to YouTube Premium for offline viewing**

Let's explore these methods in detail.

---

1. Using YouTube's Free Download Feature on Mobile

YouTube provides an **official download button** on its mobile app for certain videos. This feature is available in many regions and allows users to save videos within the app for offline viewing. However, these videos remain within the YouTube app and cannot be transferred to other devices.

Steps to Download Videos Using the Free Feature:

1. Open the **YouTube app** on your smartphone or tablet.
2. Search for the video you want to download.
3. Check if there is a **Download** button below the video (not all videos have this option).
4. Tap the **Download** button.
5. Select the **video quality** (Low, Medium, or High).
6. Wait for the download to complete.
7. Access the downloaded video from the **Library** → **Downloads** section.

Limitations of the Free Download Feature:

- Not all videos are available for download.
- Videos can only be played within the YouTube app.
- Downloaded videos expire after a certain period (usually **48 hours**), requiring an internet connection to refresh.
- Some regions may not have access to this feature due to licensing restrictions.

---

2. Using YouTube Premium for Offline Viewing

For users who want more flexibility in downloading videos, **YouTube Premium** offers a paid subscription that unlocks advanced features, including offline downloads. This option allows users to download almost any video available on YouTube for offline playback without ads.

Steps to Download Videos with YouTube Premium:

1. **Subscribe to YouTube Premium** (monthly fee applies).

2. Open the **YouTube app** on your mobile device.
3. Find the video you want to save for offline viewing.
4. Tap the **Download** button below the video.
5. Choose the **video quality** (Low, Medium, High, or Full HD).
6. The video will be saved in your **Library** → **Downloads**.
7. Watch the video anytime offline.

Benefits of Using YouTube Premium for Downloads:

- **Ad-free viewing**: No interruptions while watching videos.
- **Higher-quality downloads**: Up to **1080p resolution**.
- **Wider access**: More videos are available for download.
- **Background play**: Videos continue playing even when the app is minimized.

Limitations of YouTube Premium Downloads:

- Videos remain inside the YouTube app and cannot be shared externally.
- You need to **connect to the internet at least once every 30 days** to keep downloaded content accessible.
- Some videos may still be unavailable due to copyright restrictions.

---

3. Downloading YouTube Shorts for Offline Viewing

YouTube Shorts, the platform's short-form video feature, can also be downloaded using YouTube Premium. The process is the same as regular videos, but Shorts downloads are often restricted due to music licensing issues.

To download Shorts:

1. Open the **YouTube Shorts** section in the app.
2. Tap on a **Shorts video** you want to save.
3. If the **Download button** is available, tap to save it.

4. Access the downloaded Shorts in the **Library** tab.

Note: Many Shorts videos contain copyrighted music, which may prevent downloads.

---

4. Using YouTube Go (For Limited Internet Access)

In some regions, Google offers an alternative app called **YouTube Go**, designed for users with limited internet access. This app allows users to download and watch videos offline using minimal data.

Key Features of YouTube Go:

- Allows **low-data video downloads**.
- Videos can be shared with friends **without using mobile data**.
- Available only in selected regions (mainly developing countries).

How to Download Videos Using YouTube Go:

1. Install **YouTube Go** from the Play Store (if available in your region).
2. Open the app and sign in with your Google account.
3. Find the video you want to download.
4. Choose the **quality** (Basic, Standard, or High).
5. Tap **Download** and wait for the process to finish.

Unlike the regular YouTube app, YouTube Go is designed to **work offline**, making it ideal for users with slow internet connections.

Why Legal Downloading Matters

Downloading YouTube videos legally is crucial for several reasons:

- **Supports content creators**: Unauthorized downloads prevent creators from earning revenue through ads and views.
- **Prevents account suspension**: YouTube can ban accounts that violate its policies.

- **Ensures video quality and security**: Third-party apps may contain malware or low-quality video files.
- **Protects intellectual property**: Many videos are copyrighted, and unauthorized downloads are considered piracy.

By using YouTube's official download features, users can enjoy offline viewing while respecting copyright laws and supporting content creators.

Final Thoughts

Downloading YouTube videos legally is easy and convenient with YouTube's built-in features. Whether you use the **free download option**, **YouTube Premium**, or **YouTube Go**, there are plenty of ways to save videos for offline playback without breaking any rules.

For those who frequently watch YouTube offline, **subscribing to YouTube Premium** is the best option, as it provides **ad-free viewing, higher-quality downloads, and background play**. However, even without Premium, the **standard download feature** allows users to save selected videos for later viewing.

By following these methods, you can enjoy your favorite YouTube content anytime, anywhere—legally and hassle-free.

5.2.2 Managing Downloaded Content

Downloading videos for offline viewing is a valuable feature of YouTube, especially for users who want to watch content without relying on an internet connection. However, effectively managing downloaded content is crucial to ensure a smooth viewing experience, optimal storage use, and easy access to your favorite videos. This section will cover where to find your downloaded videos, how to organize them, troubleshooting common issues, and optimizing your device's storage.

Understanding Where Your Downloaded Videos Are Stored

When you download a video from YouTube using the official mobile app, the file is stored within the app itself and cannot be accessed directly through your device's file manager.

YouTube encrypts downloaded videos to prevent unauthorized distribution and playback outside the app.

To access your downloaded content:

1. Open the **YouTube app** on your mobile device.
2. Tap on the **Library** tab at the bottom of the screen.
3. Select **Downloads** from the menu.
4. Here, you will see a list of all videos available for offline viewing.

Downloaded videos remain within the YouTube app and can only be played from there, ensuring that YouTube maintains control over copyrighted content.

Organizing Your Downloaded Videos for Easy Access

If you frequently download videos, your downloads list can quickly become cluttered. Organizing your downloaded content can help you find videos more efficiently and manage storage space effectively.

Using Playlists for Organization

Although YouTube does not provide a direct way to create folders for downloaded content, you can use playlists as a workaround:

1. **Create a playlist** with a meaningful name (e.g., "Offline Tutorials," "Workout Videos," or "Travel Vlogs").
2. Add the downloaded videos to the corresponding playlist.
3. When you need to watch something specific, go to your playlist rather than scrolling through a long list of downloads.

This method makes it easier to locate videos, especially if you frequently download educational content, entertainment, or series episodes.

Sorting and Filtering Downloaded Videos

In the Downloads section, YouTube provides options to **sort videos** by:

- **Most recent** (default setting)

- **Oldest first**
- **File size**

Using these filters, you can quickly find older videos that may no longer be needed and delete them to free up space.

Managing Storage Space for Downloaded Content

Downloaded YouTube videos take up storage space on your device. If your phone or tablet has limited storage, it's essential to monitor and optimize the space used by offline videos.

Checking Storage Usage

To see how much space your downloaded content is taking up:

1. Open the **YouTube app** and go to **Settings**.
2. Tap **Downloads** or **Storage** (depending on your device).
3. You will see a breakdown of how much storage is used by downloaded videos.

Adjusting Video Quality to Save Space

By default, YouTube allows users to select the quality of downloaded videos. Higher quality videos consume more storage, so adjusting this setting can help manage space.

To change the default download quality:

1. Go to **YouTube Settings → Downloads**.
2. Select **Download quality**.
3. Choose from:
    - **Low (144p–360p)** – Uses the least storage but may have poor clarity.
    - **Medium (480p–720p)** – A balance between quality and storage.
    - **High (1080p and above)** – Best quality but consumes a lot of space.

For most users, **480p or 720p** provides a good balance between video clarity and storage efficiency.

Deleting Old or Unused Videos

To remove videos that you no longer need:

1. Go to **Library → Downloads**.
2. Tap the **three-dot menu** next to a video.
3. Select **Remove from downloads**.

If you want to clear all downloaded videos at once:

1. Open **YouTube Settings → Downloads**.
2. Tap **Delete all downloads**.

This is useful if you need to quickly free up space before downloading new content.

Troubleshooting Downloaded Videos

Sometimes, users may encounter issues with their downloaded videos. Here are some common problems and solutions:

1. Downloaded Video is Missing or Unavailable

If a video you previously downloaded is no longer available, possible reasons include:

- The creator has **deleted** or **made the video private**.
- The video has been **removed due to copyright issues**.
- Your YouTube Premium subscription has expired (for premium downloads).

In these cases, you will need to find an alternative version or re-download it if it becomes available again.

2. Downloaded Video Won't Play Offline

If your downloaded video is not playing offline, try the following:

- Ensure your device is not in **Airplane Mode** if verification is required.
- Update the **YouTube app** to the latest version.
- Restart your **device**.
- Check if your **YouTube Premium subscription is active** (if applicable).

3. Unable to Download New Videos Due to Storage Issues

If your device does not have enough space to download new videos:

- Delete **unused apps** or **old photos and videos**.
- Transfer files to an **external storage device or cloud storage**.
- Reduce the **download quality setting** to lower file sizes.

Downloading Videos on Different Devices

Managing downloaded videos may differ slightly depending on the device you are using.

On Smartphones and Tablets (iOS & Android)

- You can only download videos via the **YouTube app**.
- Videos are accessible in the **Downloads section**.
- **No direct file access** to downloaded videos.

On Laptops and Desktops

- YouTube Premium subscribers can **download videos on the web version** for offline playback.
- Downloads are stored within the browser cache and cannot be moved or shared.
- Downloaded videos expire after **30 days** unless re-verified online.

On Smart TVs and Streaming Devices

- YouTube **does not support** offline downloads on most Smart TVs.
- However, **YouTube Music** allows offline listening on some devices.

Best Practices for Managing YouTube Downloads

To get the best experience from YouTube's offline viewing feature, consider these **best practices**:
✅ **Download only what you need** – Avoid unnecessary downloads to save space.
✅ **Keep an eye on expiration dates** – Some videos expire after 30 days, so re-verify if

needed.
✅ **Use playlists for organization** – Helps in finding and managing downloaded content easily.
✅ **Adjust video quality** – Optimize between clarity and storage use.
✅ **Regularly clean up your downloads** – Free up space for new videos.

By following these guidelines, you can ensure a smooth and efficient experience when managing your YouTube downloaded content.

Conclusion

Managing downloaded content effectively is key to enjoying YouTube's offline features. By organizing your downloads, optimizing storage, and troubleshooting issues, you can make the most of this feature without cluttering your device. Whether you're traveling, saving data, or simply prefer to watch without interruptions, these strategies will help you maintain a well-managed offline library.

In the next section (**5.2.3 Offline Viewing Limitations**), we will discuss the restrictions of YouTube's offline feature, including content expiration, playback limitations, and how downloads work across different devices.

5.2.3 Offline Viewing Limitations

Downloading videos for offline viewing is one of the most attractive features of YouTube, especially for users who frequently travel or have limited internet access. However, while this feature is highly convenient, it comes with several limitations that users should be aware of. These limitations include restrictions on availability, time constraints, quality settings, device limitations, and content eligibility. Understanding these constraints will help you make the most of YouTube's offline viewing feature without unexpected disruptions.

---

1. Content Availability Restrictions

Not all videos on YouTube can be downloaded for offline viewing. The availability of the download feature depends on several factors:

1.1. YouTube Premium Requirement

- **Paid Subscription Needed:** Free YouTube users have limited access to offline downloads. The feature is primarily available for **YouTube Premium subscribers**, who pay a monthly fee to access benefits like ad-free viewing, background play, and offline downloads.
- **Limited Free Downloads:** In some regions, YouTube allows free users to download certain videos through the YouTube mobile app, but this is often restricted to **educational content, specific partnerships, or government initiatives** promoting internet accessibility.

1.2. Creator's Restrictions

- **Not All Videos are Downloadable:** Content creators have the option to disable downloading for their videos. If a creator decides that their content should not be available for offline viewing, YouTube will **block the download button** for that video.
- **Copyright Restrictions:** Videos that contain copyrighted music, movies, or TV shows are often **restricted from downloading** due to licensing agreements. Even YouTube Premium users may not be able to download these types of videos.

1.3. Regional Limitations

- **Different Rules in Different Countries:** The ability to download videos varies by country. Some nations have stricter **copyright and licensing laws**, preventing offline downloads in their region.
- **Geo-Blocked Content:** Even if a user downloads a video in one country, they may not be able to access it when traveling to another country where that content is restricted.

---

2. Time Restrictions and Expiry Rules

2.1. Download Expiration

- **Videos Expire After 30 Days:** YouTube does not allow indefinite offline storage of videos. Most downloaded content will **automatically expire after 30 days** unless the user reconnects to the internet.

- **Online Refresh Required:** To maintain access to downloaded videos, users must **connect to the internet at least once every 30 days**. This ensures that the video is still available and that the uploader has not removed or restricted it.

2.2. Content Removal and Changes

- **Deleted Videos Become Unavailable:** If a YouTube creator **deletes a video or makes it private**, it will also be **removed from your offline library**, even if you downloaded it before the change.
- **Regional Licensing Changes:** If a video becomes unavailable in your country due to licensing updates, it will also disappear from your offline downloads.

---

3. Quality and Format Limitations

3.1. Limited Download Quality Options

- **Resolution Restrictions:** While YouTube allows users to choose from multiple resolutions when streaming, **offline downloads are often limited** to **standard definition (SD) or lower high definition (HD) options**.
- **No 4K or Full HD in Some Cases:** Many videos are not available in **1080p (Full HD) or 4K resolution** for offline viewing, especially on mobile devices.

3.2. Storage Space Considerations

- **High-Quality Downloads Require More Space:** HD videos take up **significantly more storage**, which can **quickly fill up** a smartphone or tablet.
- **Storage Limits on Devices:** Some devices may **restrict the number of offline videos** based on available storage or app limitations.

3.3. No External File Access

- **Files Are Encrypted:** YouTube's offline videos are **encrypted and stored within the app**, meaning users cannot **move them to other folders or share them with other devices**.
- **No Third-Party Player Support:** Unlike downloaded MP4 files, offline videos can **only be played through the YouTube app** and cannot be opened with other media players.

4. Device and Platform Limitations

4.1. Limited to Mobile Apps

- **No Downloads on Desktop:** YouTube's official download feature is **only available on the mobile app** (Android and iOS). Desktop users **cannot download videos for offline use**, unless they use third-party software, which often violates YouTube's Terms of Service.
- **No Downloads on Smart TVs or Consoles:** The download feature does not work on **Smart TVs, gaming consoles, or other streaming devices**.

4.2. Account and Device Limitations

- **Limited Number of Devices:** YouTube restricts the number of devices that can store offline downloads under the same account. Users cannot **download videos on multiple devices simultaneously** beyond the allowed limit.
- **Downloads Are Linked to the Account:** If a user **logs out of their YouTube account**, all downloaded videos will **be deleted from the device** and must be re-downloaded upon logging back in.

---

5. Restrictions on Sharing and Editing

5.1. No Sharing Between Users

- **No Direct File Transfers:** Offline videos **cannot be transferred** between different devices or users. They are stored within the YouTube app and **cannot be shared via Bluetooth, USB, or cloud storage**.
- **Family Accounts Have Separate Downloads:** Even if users are part of the same **YouTube Premium family plan**, each account must **download videos separately**—they cannot share offline content.

5.2. No Editing or External Use

- **Cannot Use in Video Editing Software:** Downloaded videos cannot be **imported into video editing programs** like Adobe Premiere Pro or iMovie. This prevents users from **reusing or modifying** the content.

- **No Background Usage:** Even though YouTube Premium allows background play for online videos, **offline videos must still be played within the YouTube app**, preventing multitasking in some cases.

---

6. YouTube's Enforcement of Offline Viewing Rules

6.1. Terms of Service Compliance

- **YouTube's Strict Policies:** Downloading videos outside of YouTube's official offline feature **violates the platform's Terms of Service**.
- **Third-Party Downloaders Are Prohibited:** Many third-party apps or websites allow users to download YouTube videos illegally, but these tools can **result in account suspension or legal consequences**.

6.2. Consequences of Violating Download Rules

- **YouTube Can Disable Offline Downloads:** If a user attempts to manipulate or bypass YouTube's download restrictions, their account may **lose access** to offline viewing.
- **Account Bans for Repeated Violations:** Using unauthorized methods to download videos **can result in permanent account suspension**.

Conclusion

Offline viewing on YouTube is a convenient feature, but it comes with several important limitations. Users must consider **content availability, expiration rules, resolution constraints, device limitations, and sharing restrictions** when using this feature. While YouTube Premium provides more flexibility, it still enforces strict policies to prevent unauthorized distribution of content. Understanding these rules will help users **maximize their offline viewing experience while staying compliant with YouTube's guidelines**.

By being aware of these limitations, users can **enjoy a seamless offline viewing experience** without unexpected issues or lost content.

5.3 Using YouTube Music and YouTube TV

5.3.1 Exploring YouTube Music for Audio Streaming

Introduction to YouTube Music

YouTube Music is a dedicated music streaming service offered by YouTube, designed to provide users with a seamless and personalized audio experience. Unlike traditional music streaming platforms like Spotify or Apple Music, YouTube Music integrates YouTube's vast video library, allowing users to listen to official songs, albums, remixes, live performances, and even user-generated content.

With features like smart recommendations, offline playback, and background listening, YouTube Music has grown into a popular alternative for music enthusiasts who want more than just standard audio tracks.

This section explores how YouTube Music works, its key features, and how you can optimize your listening experience.

Getting Started with YouTube Music

Creating an Account and Accessing YouTube Music

To use YouTube Music, you need a Google account. If you already have a YouTube or Gmail account, you can use the same credentials to sign in. YouTube Music is available in several ways:

- **Website:** Visit music.youtube.com on your browser.

- **Mobile App:** Download the YouTube Music app on iOS or Android from the App Store or Google Play.
- **Smart Devices:** Use YouTube Music on smart speakers, Chromecast, or Android Auto.

Once signed in, YouTube Music will automatically start recommending content based on your listening history and preferences.

Navigating the YouTube Music Interface

The YouTube Music interface consists of several key sections:

1. **Home Tab** – Displays recommended playlists, albums, and trending songs based on your listening habits.
2. **Explore Tab** – Helps you discover new releases, top charts, and music by genre.
3. **Library Tab** – Stores your liked songs, created playlists, and downloaded content for offline listening.
4. **Search Bar** – Allows you to find specific songs, artists, or albums. You can also use voice search for quick access.

The user-friendly design makes it easy to browse, discover, and play your favorite tracks.

Key Features of YouTube Music

1. Personalized Playlists and Recommendations

One of the standout features of YouTube Music is its ability to curate playlists based on your listening habits. The more you use the platform, the better its recommendations become.

- **Your Mix** – A constantly updated playlist featuring songs you like and new tracks you might enjoy.
- **Discover Mix** – Weekly suggestions for new music based on your listening history.
- **New Release Mix** – Features the latest songs from artists you follow or have listened to before.
- **Mood & Genre Playlists** – Offers playlists for different moods (e.g., "Chill Vibes," "Workout Hits") and genres (e.g., "Rock Classics," "Hip-Hop Essentials").

These recommendations help users discover new music effortlessly.

2. Background Play and Offline Listening

With YouTube Music Premium (the paid version), users can enjoy:

- **Background Play:** Listen to music while using other apps or when the screen is off. This is a major advantage over free YouTube, which stops playing when you leave the app.
- **Offline Listening:** Download songs, albums, or playlists to listen without an internet connection. This is especially useful for traveling or commuting.
- **Smart Downloads:** YouTube Music automatically downloads songs based on your listening history so you always have music available offline.

3. High-Quality Audio Streaming

YouTube Music allows users to adjust audio quality based on their internet connection.

- **Low Quality (48kbps AAC)** – Suitable for slow networks.
- **Normal Quality (128kbps AAC)** – Standard quality with balanced performance.
- **High Quality (256kbps AAC)** – Premium sound for a better listening experience.

Users can set streaming quality preferences in the settings menu to optimize data usage.

4. Lyrics and Music Videos

A unique feature of YouTube Music is its ability to switch between audio and video modes. If a song has an official music video, you can seamlessly toggle between the music video and the audio-only version.

Additionally, YouTube Music provides **real-time lyrics**, allowing you to sing along or understand the lyrics better.

5. Integration with YouTube and Google Services

YouTube Music is deeply integrated with other Google services, offering a seamless experience:

- **Google Assistant Support:** Voice commands allow you to play songs hands-free.
- **YouTube Integration:** Since YouTube Music pulls from YouTube's massive library, you can listen to rare tracks, live performances, and remixes that aren't available on other streaming platforms.
- **Cross-Device Sync:** Your playlists, liked songs, and preferences sync across all devices where you use YouTube Music.

How to Find and Organize Your Favorite Music

1. Searching for Songs and Artists

You can search for music in several ways:

- By **song title**, **artist name**, or **album name**.
- Using **lyrics** – If you remember a few words from a song, YouTube Music can identify the track.
- Through **voice search** – Simply say, "Play [song name]" using Google Assistant.

2. Creating and Managing Playlists

To organize your music collection, you can create custom playlists.

- Tap **"Create a Playlist"** in the Library tab.
- Add songs manually or let YouTube Music suggest tracks.
- Share your playlists with friends or make them private.

Playlists allow users to build a personalized music experience tailored to their tastes.

3. Following Artists and Subscribing to Channels

If you enjoy a specific artist, you can **subscribe** to their YouTube Music profile. This ensures you get notified of new releases and automatically adds new songs to your New Release Mix.

YouTube Music Free vs. YouTube Music Premium

YouTube Music is available in two versions:

Feature	YouTube Music Free	YouTube Music Premium
Background Play	✗ No	✓ Yes
Offline Listening	✗ No	✓ Yes
Ad-Free Experience	✗ No	✓ Yes
High-Quality Audio	✗ No	✓ Yes
Smart Downloads	✗ No	✓ Yes

For users who want an uninterrupted, high-quality listening experience, **YouTube Music Premium** is worth considering.

Pros and Cons of YouTube Music

Pros:

✓ Huge music library, including exclusive content from YouTube.
✓ Smart recommendations based on listening habits.
✓ Background play and offline mode (for premium users).
✓ Real-time lyrics and seamless audio-video switching.

Cons:

✗ Free version has ads and no background play.
✗ Not as many high-quality curated playlists as competitors like Spotify.
✗ Some songs are unavailable due to licensing restrictions.

Final Thoughts

YouTube Music is an excellent choice for users who want a versatile streaming service with access to both traditional music tracks and unique YouTube content. With features like smart recommendations, offline listening, and seamless integration with YouTube, it offers a powerful alternative to other music platforms.

Whether you're looking for your favorite songs, discovering new music, or enjoying rare live performances, YouTube Music provides a dynamic and personalized experience.

In the next section, we'll explore **YouTube TV**, another powerful feature that enhances your YouTube experience by providing live television streaming.

5.3.2 Watching Live TV with YouTube TV

In recent years, traditional cable TV has faced growing competition from streaming services, and one of the leading contenders in this space is **YouTube TV**. This service, launched by YouTube in 2017, provides live TV streaming over the internet, eliminating the need for cable boxes or satellite dishes. With a subscription-based model, YouTube TV offers access to live broadcasts from major networks, sports channels, and entertainment options.

This section will cover everything you need to know about YouTube TV, including how it works, its features, pricing, channel offerings, DVR functionality, and tips to enhance your viewing experience.

What is YouTube TV?

YouTube TV is a **live TV streaming service** that provides access to more than 100 live channels, including **news, sports, entertainment, and local networks**. It operates entirely over the internet, allowing users to watch live television without needing a cable subscription.

Some of the most popular channels available on YouTube TV include:

- **News**: CNN, FOX News, MSNBC, ABC News
- **Sports**: ESPN, FOX Sports, NBC Sports, CBS Sports Network
- **Entertainment**: TNT, TBS, FX, AMC, Comedy Central

- **Kids & Family**: Disney Channel, Nickelodeon, Cartoon Network
- **Local Channels**: CBS, ABC, FOX, NBC (availability varies by location)

YouTube TV is available on **smart TVs, streaming devices, computers, and mobile devices**, making it a flexible option for users who want to watch live television anytime, anywhere.

Features of YouTube TV

1. Live Streaming of Popular Channels

YouTube TV offers a **comprehensive selection of live channels**, covering news, sports, and entertainment. Unlike traditional cable, there are no hidden fees for HD quality or additional hardware.

2. Unlimited Cloud DVR Storage

One of YouTube TV's standout features is its **cloud-based DVR**, which allows users to record live TV shows without storage limits.

- **Record multiple shows at once** without worrying about running out of space.
- **Saved recordings are stored for up to nine months.**
- **Skip commercials on recorded content** when watching later.

3. Multiple Streams and Family Sharing

A **single YouTube TV subscription can support up to six user profiles**, making it a great option for families.

- Each user gets their own personal DVR, recommendations, and settings.
- Up to **three devices can stream simultaneously** from the same account.

4. On-Demand Content

In addition to live TV, YouTube TV also provides **on-demand content**, allowing users to watch previously aired episodes of certain shows without needing to record them.

5. No Long-Term Contracts

Unlike cable providers that require long-term commitments, YouTube TV operates on a **month-to-month subscription basis**, allowing users to cancel anytime without penalties.

How to Subscribe to YouTube TV

Step 1: Check Availability in Your Area

Since YouTube TV offers **local network channels**, availability may vary depending on your location. You can check channel availability on the YouTube TV website. https://tv.youtube.com/

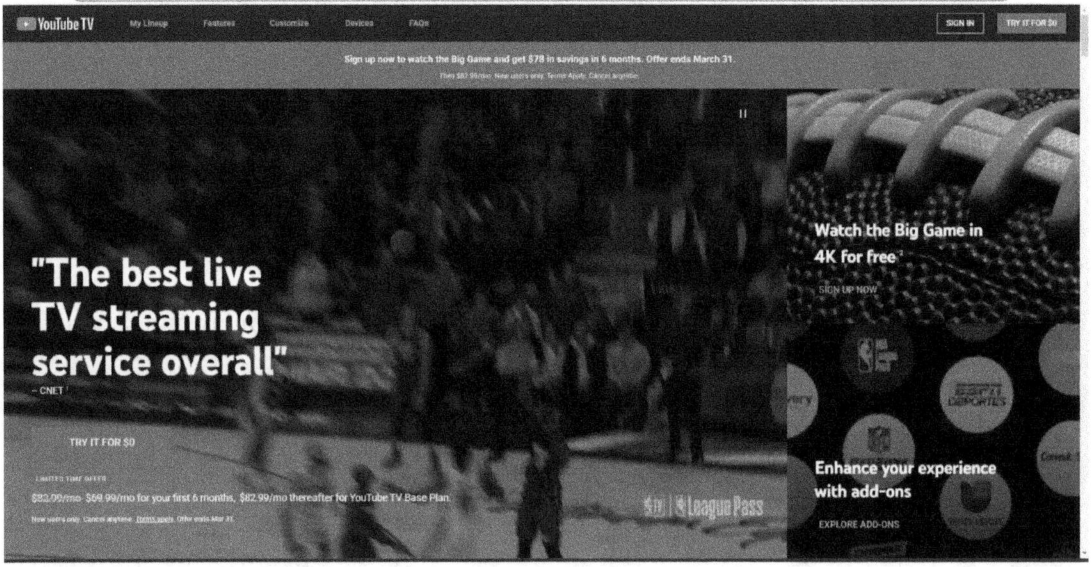

Step 2: Sign Up for a Subscription

To subscribe to YouTube TV:

1. Visit **tv.youtube.com**.
2. Click **"Try It Free"** (if a free trial is available).
3. Sign in with your Google account.
4. Choose your desired **base package** (add-ons like premium networks are optional).
5. Enter **payment details** and start your subscription.

Step 3: Download the YouTube TV App

You can watch YouTube TV on:

- **Smart TVs** (Samsung, LG, Sony, etc.)
- **Streaming devices** (Roku, Apple TV, Chromecast, Fire TV)
- **Mobile apps** (iOS & Android)
- **Web browsers** (Chrome, Edge, Safari, Firefox)

Watching Live TV with YouTube TV

Once you have subscribed and set up YouTube TV, watching live television is simple.

Navigating the YouTube TV Interface

The YouTube TV homepage is divided into three main sections:

1. **Home Tab** – Displays recommended live TV, recorded content, and trending shows.
2. **Library Tab** – Houses your **recorded shows** and saved content.
3. **Live Tab** – Shows a **live TV guide**, similar to cable TV listings.

To watch a live TV channel:

- Open the **Live Tab** to browse available channels.
- Click on the **channel name** to start streaming.
- Use the **DVR option** to record a show if you want to watch it later.

Customizing Your Live TV Experience

YouTube TV allows you to **customize the channel lineup**, hide unwanted channels, and rearrange your favorites for easier access.

Steps to customize your channel guide:

1. Open **Settings > Live Guide**.
2. Drag and reorder channels as per your preference.

3. Hide channels that you don't watch.

YouTube TV vs. Traditional Cable

Feature	YouTube TV	Traditional Cable
Monthly Cost	$72.99/month (as of 2024)	Varies ($80–$150)
Contract	No contract, cancel anytime	Usually requires a long-term contract
Cloud DVR	Unlimited storage	Limited storage, requires additional fees
Device Compatibility	Mobile, PC, Smart TVs, streaming devices	Limited to set-top boxes
Hidden Fees	No additional fees	Extra fees for HD, DVR, and equipment

YouTube TV provides a more flexible and cost-effective solution compared to traditional cable, with additional features like **unlimited DVR storage and multi-device support**.

Tips for the Best YouTube TV Experience

1. Optimize Streaming Quality

To prevent buffering and ensure the best viewing experience:

- Use a stable **internet connection with at least 10 Mbps** for HD streaming.
- Close unused applications if watching on mobile devices.
- Adjust video quality settings to **Auto** for optimal playback.

2. Utilize Keyboard Shortcuts (For Desktop Users)

- **M** – Mute/unmute audio
- **F** – Full-screen mode
- **J** – Rewind 10 seconds
- **L** – Fast forward 10 seconds

3. Manage DVR Recordings

Since YouTube TV offers **unlimited DVR**, take advantage of it by:

- Setting up series recordings for your favorite shows.
- Watching content offline if downloaded on mobile.
- Deleting unwanted recordings to keep your library organized.

4. Watch Live Sports More Effectively

- Use **"Key Plays" feature** to catch up on highlights.
- Enable **Live Sports Stats** for real-time updates.
- Pause and rewind live matches if needed.

Conclusion

YouTube TV is a powerful alternative to traditional cable, providing **live TV, unlimited DVR storage, and flexible viewing options** across multiple devices. Whether you are watching the latest news, live sports, or your favorite TV shows, YouTube TV ensures a smooth and user-friendly experience.

By understanding how to subscribe, navigate the interface, and customize settings, you can **fully enjoy live TV streaming** without the restrictions of a cable subscription.

If you are looking for an **affordable and convenient** way to watch live television, **YouTube TV is an excellent choice**!

5.3.3 Integrating YouTube Services for a Seamless Experience

YouTube is more than just a video-sharing platform—it's an ecosystem of services that work together to enhance your entertainment experience. With **YouTube Premium**, **YouTube Music**, and **YouTube TV**, Google has created an interconnected suite of services that allow users to seamlessly transition between watching videos, streaming music, and enjoying live television. This section explores how these services integrate, how you can maximize their benefits, and tips for optimizing your experience across multiple devices.

---

1. Understanding the YouTube Ecosystem

YouTube has expanded beyond its traditional role as a platform for user-generated content. Today, it offers specialized services designed to cater to different entertainment needs:

- **YouTube Premium**: An ad-free experience with background play, offline downloads, and exclusive content.
- **YouTube Music**: A dedicated music streaming service with curated playlists, personalized recommendations, and offline listening.
- **YouTube TV**: A live TV service offering access to major networks, sports channels, and cloud DVR functionality.

Each of these services can function independently, but when integrated, they provide a more seamless and immersive experience across different types of media.

---

2. Linking YouTube Premium, Music, and TV for a Unified Experience

2.1 Syncing Your Google Account Across Services

All YouTube services are linked to your **Google Account**, which means you can access them with the same login credentials. This integration ensures that your preferences, subscriptions, and recommendations remain consistent across platforms.

How to ensure proper synchronization:

1. Sign in to your **Google Account** on all your devices (smartphone, tablet, computer, smart TV).
2. Open **YouTube**, **YouTube Music**, or **YouTube TV** and verify that you're logged in with the same account.
3. Adjust personalized settings in **YouTube Settings > Connected Apps & Accounts** to ensure seamless integration.

2.2 Shared Subscriptions and Benefits

If you subscribe to **YouTube Premium**, you automatically get **YouTube Music Premium** included in your plan. This means:

- **No ads** across both YouTube and YouTube Music.

- **Offline downloads** available for both videos and music.
- **Background play**, allowing uninterrupted listening and watching.

For **YouTube TV subscribers**, certain features also integrate:

- Access to **YouTube Originals** (if included in your region).
- Ability to use **YouTube's cloud DVR** for recording live shows and watching them later.
- Seamless transition between **YouTube videos and TV content**, allowing users to watch clips related to TV shows and sports events directly on YouTube.

---

3. Enhancing Your Experience with Cross-Platform Features

3.1 Seamless Playback Across Devices

One of the biggest advantages of the YouTube ecosystem is the ability to start watching on one device and continue on another.

- **Smart TV Integration**: If you're watching a YouTube video or listening to music on your phone, you can **cast** it to a smart TV or **Chromecast** device for a bigger-screen experience.
- **Cross-Device Syncing**: If you pause a video on your laptop, you can resume it from the same spot on your phone or tablet.
- **Google Assistant Compatibility**: Use voice commands to control YouTube playback across devices, such as "Hey Google, play my YouTube Music playlist on my smart speaker."

3.2 Integrated Search and Recommendations

Google's powerful AI ensures that your preferences and search history are used to curate content across different services.

For example:

- If you frequently watch **music videos** on YouTube, those artists and genres will be **recommended in YouTube Music**.

- If you watch **sports highlights** on YouTube, related live games or sports channels may appear in **YouTube TV recommendations**.

How to optimize your recommendations:

- Use the **"Like" and "Dislike"** buttons to fine-tune suggestions.
- Regularly clear your watch history to reset personalized recommendations if needed.
- Explore the **"Trending" and "For You"** sections in each service to discover new content.

---

4. Multi-Tasking and Cross-Content Consumption

4.1 Using Background Play for a Continuous Experience

One of the best features of **YouTube Premium** is the ability to play videos or music in the background while using other apps.

- **Example 1**: You can start a **YouTube podcast**, switch to your email app, and continue listening without interruption.
- **Example 2**: You can stream **music videos on YouTube Music**, lock your phone, and still listen like a traditional music streaming service.

4.2 Watching YouTube While Browsing YouTube TV

- YouTube TV allows you to **minimize live TV playback** in a floating window while browsing other channels.
- On mobile, **Picture-in-Picture (PiP) mode** lets you watch a YouTube video while checking social media or sending messages.

---

5. Advanced Tips for a Seamless YouTube Experience

5.1 Automating Playlists Across Services

- Use **YouTube Music's Auto-Generated Playlists** to automatically save recently played songs.
- Create custom playlists that mix **YouTube Music** tracks with YouTube videos.

- On **YouTube TV**, use the **DVR feature** to automatically record favorite shows for later viewing.

5.2 Using Family Sharing for Multiple Users

If you have a **YouTube Premium Family Plan**, you can share the benefits with up to **five family members**. This ensures:

- Each user gets **personalized recommendations** and **separate watch histories**.
- Shared access to **ad-free YouTube, background play, and downloads**.

To set up Family Sharing:

1. Go to **Google Account Settings** and select **Family Sharing**.
2. Add family members by sending invites.
3. Each member gets their own customized experience while using the same subscription.

5.3 Integrating with Smart Home Devices

YouTube services work seamlessly with Google's **smart home ecosystem**:

- Play YouTube Music on **Google Nest speakers**.
- Cast YouTube videos to your **smart TV** using voice commands.
- Watch **YouTube TV** live channels on Google Chromecast or Android TV.

Example voice commands:

- "Hey Google, play my workout playlist on YouTube Music."
- "Hey Google, cast the latest news on YouTube TV to my living room TV."

Conclusion

By integrating **YouTube Premium, YouTube Music, and YouTube TV**, you can create a truly seamless entertainment experience. Whether you're watching videos, streaming music, or enjoying live TV, these services work together to provide **uninterrupted, ad-free, and personalized content** across multiple devices.

To fully optimize your experience:
✅ Ensure all services are linked to the same **Google Account**.
✅ Use **cross-device playback** to switch between mobile, TV, and desktop easily.
✅ Customize **settings, recommendations, and playlists** to suit your preferences.
✅ Explore **background play, offline downloads, and Family Sharing** for more flexibility.

With the right setup, YouTube's ecosystem becomes a **powerful all-in-one media hub** that adapts to your lifestyle—whether you're watching, listening, or live streaming!

CHAPTER VI
Interacting with the YouTube Community

6.1 Following and Supporting Your Favorite Creators

YouTube is more than just a video-sharing platform; it is a thriving community where creators and viewers connect over shared interests. If you have favorite YouTubers whose content you love, there are multiple ways to support them. Watching their videos, liking and commenting, and sharing their content with others are great starting points. However, YouTube also offers direct support methods, such as **channel memberships and Patreon**, which allow fans to contribute financially while receiving exclusive perks in return.

In this section, we'll explore **YouTube Memberships and Patreon**, how they work, and how you can use them to support your favorite content creators.

6.1.1 Joining Memberships and Patreon

What Are YouTube Memberships?

YouTube Memberships is a feature that allows viewers to become paying members of a YouTube channel in exchange for exclusive perks. It is similar to a subscription service, where fans can contribute a **monthly fee** to support a creator while gaining access to benefits such as:

- **Exclusive badges** that appear next to your name in comments and live chats.
- **Custom emojis** that can be used in chats.

- **Members-only videos, posts, and live streams.**
- **Early access to content** before it is available to the public.
- **Shoutouts and recognition from the creator.**

Memberships provide a way for fans to show appreciation for their favorite creators while getting unique rewards in return.

How to Join a YouTube Membership

If a creator has enabled **YouTube Memberships**, you will see a **"Join" button** next to the **"Subscribe" button** on their channel. Here's how you can become a member:

1. **Click the "Join" Button** – This will open a pop-up showing the different membership tiers available.
2. **Select a Membership Tier** – Some channels offer multiple tiers with different benefits. Choose the one that best suits your budget and interest.
3. **Enter Your Payment Information** – YouTube supports various payment methods, including credit/debit cards and Google Pay.
4. **Confirm Your Membership** – Once your payment is processed, you will receive access to the exclusive perks immediately.

You can manage or cancel your membership anytime through **YouTube settings** under **"Purchases and Memberships."**

What is Patreon?

Patreon is an external **crowdfunding** platform that allows creators to receive direct financial support from their fans. Unlike YouTube Memberships, Patreon operates outside of YouTube and provides a flexible way for creators to **offer exclusive content, personalized interactions, and other rewards** to their supporters.

Many YouTubers use Patreon to:

- Provide **behind-the-scenes content** about their creative process.
- Offer **one-on-one interactions**, such as Q&A sessions or private messages.

- Share **exclusive videos, early access to content, and downloadable resources.**
- Sell **personalized merchandise** or offer custom services.

Patreon allows creators to build a **dedicated fanbase** while offering rewards that go beyond what YouTube provides.

How to Support a YouTuber on Patreon

If a YouTuber has a Patreon page, they will usually include a **link in their video descriptions, channel banner, or pinned comments.** Here's how you can become a patron:

1. **Visit the Creator's Patreon Page** – This link is typically provided by the YouTuber in their videos or social media.
2. **Choose a Membership Tier** – Patreon offers multiple tiers with different levels of benefits. Select the one that fits your budget and interests.
3. **Set Up Your Payment** – Patreon accepts credit/debit cards and PayPal. You will be charged either **per month** or **per creation**, depending on the creator's setup.
4. **Access Your Exclusive Perks** – Once subscribed, you can log in to Patreon and access all the exclusive content you have unlocked.

You can modify or cancel your Patreon membership anytime through your Patreon account settings.

YouTube Memberships vs. Patreon: Which One is Better?

Both YouTube Memberships and Patreon provide ways to support content creators, but they have key differences:

Feature	YouTube Memberships	Patreon
Platform	Integrated into YouTube	External platform
Perks	Badges, emojis, members-only videos, live streams	Exclusive content, behind-the-scenes access, one-on-one interactions
Payment Model	Monthly subscription	Monthly subscription or per-creation payment

Flexibility	Limited customization for creators	Fully customizable rewards
Interaction	Chat-based recognition	Direct creator-to-fan engagement

- If you **watch YouTube regularly** and enjoy live chats, **YouTube Memberships** may be a better option.
- If you want **more personalized content** and deeper engagement, **Patreon** offers more flexibility.

Some creators use **both platforms**, allowing fans to **choose** how they prefer to support them.

Why Supporting Your Favorite Creators Matters

Content creation requires **time, effort, and resources**. Many YouTubers rely on **ads, sponsorships, and direct fan support** to sustain their channels. By joining **YouTube Memberships or Patreon**, you help your favorite creators:

✅ **Continue producing quality content** without depending solely on advertisements.
✅ **Improve their content** with better equipment and production value.
✅ **Dedicate more time** to their channel instead of balancing other jobs.
✅ **Foster a strong community** with deeper engagement between fans and creators.

Even if you can't contribute financially, simple actions like **liking, commenting, and sharing videos** help creators grow.

Final Thoughts

Joining a **YouTube Membership or Patreon** is a great way to **support the creators you love** while gaining **exclusive content and perks**. Whether you prefer **custom emojis in live chats, early access to videos, or behind-the-scenes content**, both platforms offer unique benefits.

If you regularly watch and appreciate a creator's work, consider **becoming a member or patron** to help them **continue making amazing content** for their audience.

6.1.2 Understanding Super Chats and Donations

Introduction

YouTube has evolved into more than just a video-sharing platform; it has become a thriving community where viewers and creators connect, engage, and support one another. For those who want to actively contribute to their favorite creators beyond simply watching their videos, YouTube offers several monetization features, including **Super Chats and Donations**. These tools allow viewers to financially support creators during live streams and premieres, giving them the opportunity to stand out in the chat and interact directly with the streamer.

This section will provide a comprehensive guide to understanding Super Chats and donations, including how they work, why they are beneficial, how to use them, and key considerations before making a contribution.

---

1. What Are Super Chats?

Super Chats are a feature available during **YouTube live streams and Premieres** that allows viewers to pay to have their messages highlighted in the chat. This feature enables fans to get noticed by their favorite creators and sometimes even receive a direct response during the stream.

1.1 How Super Chats Work

- When a creator hosts a **live stream** or a **Premiere**, a live chat appears next to the video where viewers can interact in real time.
- Viewers can purchase a Super Chat, which highlights their message in a different color and pins it to the top of the chat for a specific duration.
- The more a viewer pays, the **longer their Super Chat remains pinned** and the **more prominent** it appears.
- Super Chats help fans support their favorite creators financially while also making their messages more noticeable.

1.2 Super Chat Pricing and Display Duration

The amount paid for a Super Chat determines:

- **Color Coding** – Different price ranges result in different colors that stand out in the chat.
- **Message Length** – Higher payments allow longer messages.
- **Pinned Duration** – More expensive Super Chats stay pinned longer at the top of the chat.

Here's an approximate breakdown of how Super Chats work based on payment:

Price (USD)	Message Color	Maximum Message Length	Pinned Duration
$1 - $4.99	Light Blue	50 characters	No pinning
$5 - $9.99	Green	150 characters	30 seconds
$10 - $24.99	Yellow	200 characters	1 minute
$25 - $49.99	Orange	225 characters	5 minutes
$50 - $99.99	Magenta	250 characters	10 minutes
$100 - $500	Red	270 characters	5 hours max

Super Chats provide a **tiered system**, where higher contributions gain more visibility and longer exposure.

---

2. What Are Super Stickers?

In addition to Super Chats, YouTube also offers **Super Stickers**, which allow viewers to purchase animated stickers to display in the chat. These stickers add a **fun and expressive** way to interact with the creator.

2.1 Differences Between Super Chats and Super Stickers

- **Super Chats** allow users to send a **custom message** along with their contribution.
- **Super Stickers** are **pre-designed animated stickers** without a custom message but still highlight the viewer's support.

Super Stickers come in different categories and price levels, making them a great way for fans to show enthusiasm without needing to type a message.

---

3. How to Send a Super Chat or Super Sticker

3.1 Steps to Purchase a Super Chat or Super Sticker

1. **Join a Live Stream or Premiere**

- Ensure the creator has **Super Chats enabled.**
- Open the **live chat window** during the stream.

2. **Click on the Dollar Sign ($) Icon**
    - Located in the chatbox, this icon allows access to YouTube's monetization options.
3. **Choose "Super Chat" or "Super Sticker"**
    - Selecting **Super Chat** allows you to enter a custom message.
    - Selecting **Super Sticker** lets you pick an animated sticker.
4. **Select the Payment Amount**
    - Drag the slider or enter a specific amount to determine your contribution.
5. **Complete the Payment**
    - Use a linked **credit card, debit card, or Google Pay** to finalize the transaction.
6. **Enjoy Your Highlighted Message or Sticker!**
    - Your message will be **pinned in the chat** based on the payment tier.

---

4. Benefits of Using Super Chats and Donations

4.1 For Viewers

- **Direct Interaction** – Super Chats make it easier for your favorite creator to see and respond to your messages.
- **Support the Creator** – Contributions help fund content creation and encourage creators to continue producing high-quality videos.
- **Exclusive Recognition** – High-value Super Chats often receive **shoutouts from the creator** during the stream.

4.2 For Creators

- **Monetization Boost** – Super Chats serve as an additional revenue stream.

- **Increased Engagement** – Encouraging Super Chats fosters a more interactive and supportive community.
- **Live Content Sustainability** – Many creators rely on Super Chats to fund better equipment, research, and time investment.

---

5. Important Considerations Before Donating

5.1 Age and Payment Restrictions

- Users must be **18+ or have parental permission** to purchase Super Chats.
- Some regions have **restrictions** on YouTube monetization features.

5.2 Refund Policy

- Super Chats are **non-refundable**, so double-check your message before submitting.
- If a creator **deletes a live stream**, Super Chats sent during that session will not be refunded.

5.3 Avoiding Scams and Misuse

- Only donate to **verified creators** with **monetization enabled**.
- Avoid sending **personal information** in Super Chats.

---

6. Alternative Ways to Support Creators

If Super Chats are not available in your country or if you prefer other methods, consider:

- **YouTube Channel Memberships** – Subscribe for exclusive perks.
- **External Platforms like Patreon** – Many creators offer **additional content** on other platforms.
- **Merchandise Purchases** – Buy official merchandise to support the creator.

Conclusion

Super Chats and donations provide an engaging way to support creators financially while gaining **special recognition** in live chat. Whether you're looking to **interact more closely with your favorite YouTuber** or simply **show appreciation**, these features enhance the viewing experience for both fans and content creators.

Before making a contribution, always **review payment policies, set a budget, and ensure responsible spending**. Supporting creators should be a fun and positive experience for everyone involved!

6.1.3 Engaging in Live Streams and Premieres

YouTube Live Streams and Premieres provide exciting opportunities for viewers to interact with content creators in real-time. Whether you are watching a live Q&A session, a gaming stream, or the premiere of a new video, these features allow for direct engagement with both creators and fellow viewers. In this section, we will explore how to participate in live streams and premieres, the benefits of engaging in these events, and tips for maximizing your experience.

Understanding Live Streams and Premieres

What Are YouTube Live Streams?

Live streaming on YouTube enables creators to broadcast video content in real-time, allowing them to connect instantly with their audience. These streams can be planned events or spontaneous sessions, and they may include various formats such as:

- **Q&A Sessions** – Creators answer audience questions live.
- **Gaming Streams** – Gamers showcase their gameplay and interact with viewers.
- **Music Performances** – Artists perform live music or host virtual concerts.
- **Tutorials and Workshops** – Creators share educational or how-to content.
- **Behind-the-Scenes Content** – Exclusive insights into a creator's life or work process.

What Are YouTube Premieres?

YouTube Premieres allow creators to debut pre-recorded videos as live events. Unlike regular uploads, Premieres provide a shared viewing experience where viewers can watch and chat with others while the video plays for the first time. Creators can also participate in the chat, making it feel like a live event even though the content is pre-recorded.

Key benefits of Premieres include:

- **Real-time engagement** – Viewers can chat with the creator and other fans.
- **Hype-building** – Creators can promote their content before release.
- **Scheduled viewing** – Viewers know exactly when the video will be available.

How to Participate in Live Streams and Premieres

Finding Live Streams and Premieres

You can discover live streams and upcoming Premieres in several ways:

- **YouTube Homepage** – The "Live" section highlights trending live streams.
- **Subscriptions Tab** – If a creator you follow is live, their stream appears here.
- **YouTube Notifications** – If you enable notifications, YouTube alerts you when a creator goes live.
- **Search and Filters** – Searching for a topic and using the "Live" filter helps find relevant streams.

Joining a Live Stream or Premiere

To join a live stream or Premiere:

1. Click on the video thumbnail when it appears on your feed.
2. If it is an upcoming event, you can set a reminder.
3. Once the stream starts, engage through the chat and reactions.

Interacting During a Live Stream

Using Live Chat

Live chat is a real-time messaging feature that allows viewers to communicate during a live stream or Premiere. Here's how to use it:

- **Typing Messages** – Simply enter your message in the chatbox and press send.
- **Tagging Users** – Use "@username" to address a specific person.
- **Using Emojis and Stickers** – Express yourself with fun visuals.
- **Engaging with the Creator** – Creators often read and respond to chat messages.

Sending Super Chats and Super Stickers

Super Chats and Super Stickers allow viewers to support creators financially while getting their messages highlighted in the chat.

- **Super Chat** – Paid messages that stand out and are pinned for a period.
- **Super Stickers** – Animated images that users can purchase to grab attention.

To send a Super Chat or Super Sticker:

1. Click on the dollar sign ($) in the chatbox.
2. Choose the amount you want to send.
3. Enter a message (for Super Chats).
4. Complete the payment process.

Participating in Polls and Q&A Sessions

Many creators use polls and Q&A sessions to engage with their audience during a stream.

- **Polls** – Creators post questions with multiple-choice answers.
- **Q&A Sessions** – Viewers submit questions, and the creator answers live.

To participate:

1. Click on the poll options to vote.
2. Submit your question through the chat when prompted.

Engaging in YouTube Premieres

Before the Premiere Starts

Creators can schedule Premieres in advance, giving fans time to prepare for the event.

- **Set a Reminder** – Click the "Set Reminder" button to receive a notification.
- **Join the Countdown** – Before the video plays, a countdown timer builds anticipation.

During the Premiere

Once the Premiere starts, you can interact in several ways:

- **Live Chat** – Chat with other viewers and the creator.
- **Super Chats and Super Stickers** – Support the creator while standing out in the chat.
- **Reactions and Comments** – Express your thoughts as the video plays.

After the Premiere Ends

Once the Premiere concludes, it turns into a regular video on the creator's channel.

- **Leave a Comment** – Share your thoughts after watching.
- **Like and Share** – Support the video by giving it a thumbs up and sharing it.
- **Watch Again** – You can rewatch the video anytime.

Best Practices for Engaging in Live Streams and Premieres

1. Be Respectful and Follow Community Guidelines

- Avoid spamming the chat.
- Use appropriate language and be kind to others.
- Do not engage in harassment or offensive behavior.

2. Support Creators Responsibly

- If you send Super Chats, make sure they fit within your budget.
- Engage positively and encourage meaningful discussions.

3. Maximize Your Viewing Experience

- Use a stable internet connection to prevent buffering.
- Adjust video quality settings for a smoother stream.
- Participate actively to make the most of the live experience.

Conclusion

Engaging in YouTube Live Streams and Premieres enhances your viewing experience by allowing real-time interaction with creators and the community. By participating in live chats, supporting your favorite channels through Super Chats, and making the most of Premieres, you can enjoy a more immersive and social experience on YouTube.

6.2 Reporting and Blocking Content

The YouTube community is vast, with millions of creators and users interacting daily. While most content on the platform adheres to community standards, inappropriate videos and comments can occasionally appear. To ensure a safe and enjoyable experience, YouTube provides tools for reporting harmful content and blocking disruptive users.

6.2.1 Reporting Inappropriate Videos and Comments

YouTube has clear guidelines on acceptable content, and the platform encourages users to report violations. Reporting helps keep YouTube a safe space by flagging harmful, offensive, or misleading material. In this section, we'll explore what constitutes inappropriate content, how to report videos and comments, and what happens after a report is submitted.

What Is Considered Inappropriate Content on YouTube?

YouTube has established **Community Guidelines** that define the types of content that are not allowed. Some common violations include:

- **Hate Speech and Harassment** – Content that promotes violence, discrimination, or hate against individuals or groups based on attributes such as race, gender, religion, or nationality.
- **Misinformation and Fake News** – False information that could cause harm, such as misleading medical advice or fabricated news stories.
- **Violence and Graphic Content** – Videos that depict excessive violence, self-harm, or other distressing content.
- **Spam and Scams** – Repetitive, misleading, or deceptive content designed to manipulate viewers for financial gain.
- **Child Exploitation and Harmful Activities** – Any content that endangers minors, including child abuse, exploitation, or inappropriate behavior towards children.

- **Nudity and Sexual Content** – Explicit adult content or inappropriate sexual material.

By reporting content that falls into these categories, users help YouTube enforce its policies and maintain a respectful environment.

How to Report a Video on YouTube

If you come across a video that violates YouTube's guidelines, you can report it in just a few steps:

1. **Sign in to Your YouTube Account** – You need to be logged in to submit a report.
2. **Locate the Video** – Find the video that contains inappropriate content.
3. **Click the "More" Button (Three Dots)** – Below the video player, click on the three vertical dots next to the share button.
4. **Select "Report"** – From the dropdown menu, choose the "Report" option.
5. **Choose a Reason for Reporting** – A list of reporting categories will appear, including "Hateful or abusive content," "Violent or repulsive content," "Misinformation," and more. Select the most appropriate option.
6. **Provide Additional Details (If Needed)** – Some reports allow you to provide extra information to explain why the video is problematic.
7. **Submit the Report** – Click "Submit," and YouTube's moderation team will review the report.

Once a report is submitted, YouTube evaluates it based on its policies. If the video violates guidelines, it may be removed, restricted, or demonetized.

How to Report a Comment on YouTube

Comments are an essential part of YouTube's interactive experience, but they can sometimes be offensive, harmful, or spammy. YouTube provides a simple way to report such comments:

1. **Go to the Comment Section** – Scroll down to the comments under a video.
2. **Find the Inappropriate Comment** – Identify the comment that violates YouTube's guidelines.

3. **Click the "More" Button (Three Dots) Next to the Comment** – A small menu will appear.
4. **Select "Report"** – Choose "Report" from the dropdown list.
5. **Choose the Reason for Reporting** – Select an option such as "Harassment or bullying," "Hate speech," or "Spam."
6. **Submit the Report** – Click "Submit," and YouTube will review the comment.

YouTube uses automated systems and human moderators to assess reported comments. If a comment is found to be in violation, it may be removed, and the commenter may face penalties, including temporary or permanent bans.

How to Report a Channel on YouTube

In some cases, an entire YouTube channel may consistently violate community guidelines. You can report a channel as follows:

1. **Go to the Channel's Homepage** – Click on the channel's name to open its profile.
2. **Click the "About" Tab** – Scroll to the "About" section.
3. **Click the Flag Icon** – You will see a small flag icon; click on it.
4. **Select "Report User"** – Choose the appropriate reporting reason, such as "Impersonation" or "Hate speech."
5. **Provide Additional Information (If Required)** – In some cases, YouTube will ask for more details.
6. **Submit the Report** – YouTube will review the channel and take action if necessary.

Channels that repeatedly violate guidelines may face demonetization, suspension, or permanent removal.

What Happens After You Report Content?

Once a report is submitted, YouTube reviews it through a combination of **AI detection and human moderation**. Depending on the severity of the violation, YouTube may:

- **Take No Action** – If the content does not violate guidelines, it will remain on the platform.

- **Age-Restrict the Video** – If the content is inappropriate for younger audiences but not harmful, YouTube may apply an age restriction.
- **Remove the Content** – If the video or comment is clearly against YouTube's policies, it will be taken down.
- **Strike the Creator's Account** – If a channel repeatedly violates guidelines, YouTube may issue a warning or a **Community Guidelines Strike**. After three strikes, the channel can be permanently removed.

Using the YouTube Feedback System

If you disagree with YouTube's decision on a report, you can **appeal** in certain cases. The appeal process is available for creators whose content was removed or restricted. To appeal, follow these steps:

1. **Check Your YouTube Studio Dashboard** – You'll receive a notification if your content was removed.
2. **Find the Appeal Option** – Click on the notification and select "Appeal."
3. **Submit a Justification** – Provide a clear explanation of why you believe the content does not violate guidelines.
4. **Wait for YouTube's Response** – Appeals are usually reviewed within a few days.

Best Practices for Reporting Content

- **Only Report Legitimate Violations** – False reporting can lead to **your account being penalized** if YouTube detects misuse.
- **Do Not Engage with Harmful Users** – Instead of arguing with someone posting inappropriate content, report and move on.
- **Use YouTube's Block Feature** – If someone continuously harasses you, consider blocking them (discussed in the next section).

Final Thoughts

Reporting inappropriate videos and comments is a vital part of maintaining a positive and safe YouTube experience. By understanding YouTube's policies and using reporting tools responsibly, you contribute to a respectful and enjoyable community. In the next section, we'll explore how to **block users and manage your personal YouTube space** to further enhance your experience.

6.2.2 Blocking Users and Managing Your Community

YouTube is a vast platform where millions of users interact daily. While most interactions are positive and constructive, there may be times when you encounter negative or disruptive behavior. Whether you are a casual viewer or an active content creator, managing your YouTube experience by blocking users and moderating interactions is essential for maintaining a positive and safe environment.

In this section, we will explore the different ways to block users, manage your comment section, and build a healthy YouTube community.

Understanding Why You Might Need to Block Users

Blocking users on YouTube is not just about avoiding negativity—it's about creating a more enjoyable and constructive experience. Here are some common reasons why you might need to block someone:

- **Harassment and Bullying** – Some users engage in personal attacks, hate speech, or persistent harassment in the comments section.
- **Spam and Unwanted Promotions** – Many bots or individuals flood comment sections with links, ads, or irrelevant content.
- **Trolls and Disruptive Behavior** – Some people post offensive or provocative comments just to cause trouble.
- **Personal Safety Concerns** – If someone is threatening you or sharing personal information without your consent, blocking is a necessary step.
- **Maintaining a Professional Community** – If you are a content creator, blocking disruptive users can help keep your audience engaged in meaningful discussions.

By blocking problematic users, you can ensure a safer and more enjoyable browsing or content creation experience.

How to Block a User on YouTube

Blocking a user on YouTube prevents them from commenting on your videos and sending you messages. However, they will still be able to view your public content. Here's how you can block someone:

Blocking a User from a Comment Section

If someone is posting inappropriate or spammy comments on your videos, you can block them directly from the comment section.

1. Locate the comment from the user you want to block.
2. Click on the **three-dot menu** (□) next to the comment.
3. Select **Hide user from channel** (this prevents them from commenting on any of your videos).
4. Confirm your action.

The user will no longer be able to comment on your videos, but they won't be notified that they have been blocked.

Blocking a User from Their Channel Page

If you want to block a user before they even comment on your videos, you can do so from their channel page.

1. Visit the **YouTube channel** of the person you want to block.
2. Click on the **About** tab.
3. Click on the **flag icon** (⚑) and select **Block user**.
4. Confirm your action.

After this, the user will be unable to comment on your videos or send you direct messages.

Blocking a User on YouTube Mobile App

The process is similar on mobile devices.

1. Open the **YouTube app** and go to the user's channel.
2. Tap the **three-dot menu** (□) in the top right corner.
3. Select **Block user** and confirm.

This method ensures that the blocked user can no longer interact with you through comments or messages.

Managing Your YouTube Community

Blocking users is just one part of managing your YouTube community. To create a positive and engaging environment, you also need to moderate comments, set interaction guidelines, and use YouTube's built-in tools for community management.

1. Setting Up Comment Moderation

YouTube allows creators to moderate their comment sections using various tools. Here's how you can manage comments effectively:

A. Enabling Comment Review Before Posting

If you want to review comments before they appear on your videos, follow these steps:

1. Go to **YouTube Studio** and select **Settings**.
2. Click on **Community** and navigate to **Defaults**.
3. Under **Comments on your channel**, choose:
    - **Hold all comments for review** (if you want to approve each comment manually).
    - **Hold potentially inappropriate comments for review** (if you want YouTube to automatically filter certain comments).
4. Save changes.

This setting helps prevent spam and offensive comments from appearing on your videos.

B. Adding Words to the Blocked List

If there are certain words or phrases you do not want in your comment section, you can add them to a blocked list:

1. Go to **YouTube Studio** > **Settings** > **Community**.
2. Scroll down to the **Blocked words** section.
3. Enter the words or phrases you want to block.
4. Save changes.

Comments containing these words will be automatically held for review or deleted.

C. Turning Off Comments on Specific Videos

If you don't want to deal with comments at all, you can disable them for specific videos:

1. Go to **YouTube Studio** and select the video you want to edit.
2. Click on **More Options** under the **Comments and Ratings** section.
3. Select **Disable comments** and save changes.

This can be useful for preventing spam on old videos or when discussing sensitive topics.

---

2. Using YouTube's Community Management Features

YouTube provides additional tools to help manage your community and maintain a positive environment.

A. Using "Hidden Users" to Silence Persistent Troublemakers

Instead of just blocking a user, you can hide them from your entire channel:

1. Go to **YouTube Studio** > **Settings** > **Community**.
2. Scroll down to the **Hidden Users** section.
3. Add the user's channel URL to prevent them from commenting on your videos.
4. Save changes.

This ensures that their comments won't appear, even if they try to comment multiple times.

B. Assigning Moderators to Your Channel

If you have a large audience, assigning moderators can help keep your community safe.

1. Go to **YouTube Studio** > **Settings** > **Community**.
2. Under **Moderators**, add the channel URL of the person you want to assign as a moderator.
3. Save changes.

Moderators can help remove unwanted comments and maintain a friendly environment.

---

3. Encouraging Positive Engagement in Your Community

Blocking users and moderating comments are reactive measures, but it's also important to take proactive steps in creating a welcoming space. Here are some tips:

- **Set clear community guidelines** – Let your audience know what behavior is acceptable in your comment section.
- **Engage with your audience** – Respond to constructive comments and encourage discussions.
- **Reward positive interactions** – Highlight meaningful comments and pin them to the top of your videos.
- **Use the YouTube Community Tab** – If you have 500+ subscribers, use the Community Tab to interact with viewers and keep discussions focused.

Conclusion

Blocking users and managing your YouTube community is essential for maintaining a positive and safe environment. By using YouTube's blocking features, moderating your comment section, and fostering healthy discussions, you can create a space that is enjoyable for both you and your audience.

Remember, YouTube is a platform for creativity and learning—by setting the right boundaries, you ensure that your experience remains enjoyable and free from unnecessary negativity.

6.2.3 Understanding YouTube's Community Guidelines

YouTube, as one of the largest video-sharing platforms in the world, has a responsibility to ensure a safe, fair, and respectful environment for all users. To maintain this, YouTube has developed **Community Guidelines**—a set of rules and policies that govern what is and isn't allowed on the platform. These guidelines help protect users from harmful content while promoting creativity and open discussion in a responsible manner.

In this section, we will explore YouTube's Community Guidelines in detail, including their purpose, major categories, enforcement measures, and what you can do to ensure compliance as a viewer or content creator.

---

1. What Are YouTube's Community Guidelines?

YouTube's Community Guidelines are rules that set the standard for what type of content is permitted on the platform. They apply to everyone, from casual viewers to professional content creators. Violations of these guidelines can lead to warnings, video removals, account strikes, demonetization, or even permanent bans.

These guidelines are different from **YouTube's Terms of Service**, which primarily cover legal agreements between YouTube and its users. Community Guidelines specifically focus on content policies and interactions on the platform.

The guidelines evolve over time as YouTube adapts to new trends, challenges, and potential risks. It is essential to stay updated to avoid unintentional violations.

---

2. Key Categories of YouTube's Community Guidelines

YouTube's Community Guidelines cover various types of content violations. Below are the major categories that all users should be aware of:

2.1 Spam, Scams, and Deceptive Practices

YouTube prohibits misleading and fraudulent content designed to deceive users. This includes:

- **Scams**: Videos or comments that trick users into providing personal information, money, or sensitive data (e.g., fake giveaways, phishing attempts).
- **Clickbait and Misleading Content**: Videos with deceptive thumbnails, exaggerated titles, or misleading descriptions that trick viewers.
- **Artificial Engagement**: Buying views, likes, or comments to manipulate engagement metrics.

2.2 Misinformation and Harmful Content

YouTube actively fights against the spread of false information that can harm users. Examples include:

- **Medical Misinformation**: Videos that promote false cures or discourage medical treatments.
- **Election and Political Misinformation**: Spreading false claims about elections, voting, or political events.
- **Conspiracy Theories**: Content that promotes baseless conspiracy theories that could incite harm.

2.3 Hate Speech and Harassment

YouTube does not allow content that promotes hate or targets individuals based on identity, including:

- **Hate Speech**: Content that attacks people based on race, gender, religion, nationality, sexual orientation, or other protected characteristics.
- **Harassment and Cyberbullying**: Threatening, doxxing, or encouraging harassment of individuals or groups.

2.4 Violence, Dangerous Acts, and Self-Harm

Videos that promote or glorify violence and dangerous behavior are strictly prohibited, including:

- **Graphic Violence and Gore**: Videos showing extreme violence, injury, or death.
- **Self-Harm and Suicide Promotion**: Content that encourages or provides instructions for self-harm or suicide.
- **Dangerous Challenges and Stunts**: Videos encouraging harmful challenges, such as the "Tide Pod Challenge" or other dangerous internet trends.

2.5 Child Safety and Exploitation

Protecting minors is a top priority for YouTube, and the platform enforces strict policies, including:

- **Child Exploitation and Abuse**: Any content that exploits or endangers children is banned and may be reported to law enforcement.
- **Inappropriate Content Involving Minors**: Videos featuring minors in suggestive, exploitative, or unsafe situations are removed.
- **Predatory Behavior**: Comments or messages targeting children inappropriately result in bans and account removals.

2.6 Copyright and Intellectual Property Violations

YouTube follows strict **copyright laws** to protect content creators. Violations include:

- **Uploading Copyrighted Content**: Using videos, music, or images without permission.
- **Reusing Other People's Content**: Posting content that belongs to others without adding significant original value.
- **Circumventing Copyright Enforcement**: Attempting to bypass YouTube's Content ID system to monetize copyrighted material.

2.7 Nudity, Sexual Content, and Explicit Material

YouTube restricts or removes content that includes:

- **Sexually Explicit Material**: Pornographic or explicit content is banned.
- **Sexualized Minors**: Any suggestive content involving minors results in immediate removal.

- **Educational Nudity**: Certain nudity is allowed for educational or artistic purposes, but it must be properly labeled.

---

3. How YouTube Enforces Community Guidelines

YouTube enforces these rules through a combination of **automated detection, human moderation, and user reports**. Here's how violations are handled:

3.1 Automated Detection and AI Moderation

YouTube uses artificial intelligence (AI) to detect inappropriate content **before** it is even published. This includes scanning for:

- Hate speech and offensive language.
- Copyrighted material using **Content ID**.
- Nudity and explicit content using image recognition AI.

3.2 User Reporting System

If you come across content that violates the guidelines, you can **report** it:

1. Click the **three-dot menu** below the video.
2. Select **Report**.
3. Choose the reason for reporting.
4. Provide additional details if necessary.

Reports are reviewed by human moderators, and if the content is found to violate guidelines, it may be removed.

3.3 YouTube's Strike System

YouTube uses a **three-strike policy** to manage violations:

- **First Strike**: A warning, with no penalties.
- **Second Strike**: A **temporary restriction** on uploads and live streaming.
- **Third Strike**: **Permanent channel termination**.

Serious violations (e.g., extreme hate speech, child exploitation) can lead to **immediate bans** without warnings.

---

4. How to Stay Compliant with YouTube's Community Guidelines

To avoid violating YouTube's rules, here are some best practices:

4.1 For Viewers

- **Be Mindful of What You Comment**: Avoid hate speech, harassment, or spammy behavior.
- **Report Violations Responsibly**: Only report content that genuinely violates policies, not just because you dislike it.
- **Understand Age Restrictions**: Some content is age-restricted, meaning you must be signed in and of legal age to view it.

4.2 For Content Creators

- **Review YouTube's Policies Regularly**: Guidelines change over time, so staying updated is essential.
- **Use Copyright-Free Music and Clips**: Avoid copyright claims by using royalty-free music or obtaining proper licenses.
- **Avoid Clickbait and Misleading Titles**: Be honest in video descriptions and thumbnails.
- **Moderate Your Community**: If you run a channel, manage your comments section to prevent toxic discussions.

Conclusion

YouTube's Community Guidelines exist to create a **safe, fair, and respectful** environment for all users. Whether you are watching, commenting, or creating content, it's important to understand and follow these rules to avoid penalties and ensure a positive experience.

By staying informed and acting responsibly, you can enjoy everything YouTube has to offer while helping maintain a healthy community for everyone.

6.3 Understanding YouTube Trends and Challenges

6.3.1 How Trends Emerge on YouTube

YouTube is one of the most dynamic platforms on the internet, where trends emerge, evolve, and sometimes fade away in a matter of days. Understanding how these trends develop can help viewers stay engaged with popular content and assist creators in capitalizing on viral opportunities. This section explores the mechanisms behind YouTube trends, the factors that influence their growth, and how they impact both viewers and creators.

---

1. What is a YouTube Trend?

A YouTube trend refers to a topic, format, or style of content that gains rapid popularity and engagement across the platform. These trends can take various forms, such as:

- **Viral Challenges** – Examples include the Ice Bucket Challenge, the Mannequin Challenge, and the Bottle Cap Challenge.
- **Meme-Based Videos** – These often involve popular internet jokes, edits, or remixes.
- **Reaction Videos** – Viewers reacting to trending topics, viral videos, or cultural phenomena.
- **Hashtag Trends** – Some trends are tied to hashtags, making them easier to find and participate in.
- **Trending Music and Dance Routines** – Many songs go viral because of dance challenges or remixes.
- **Emerging Topics and News** – Breaking news and cultural discussions can dominate trending pages.

Each trend follows a lifecycle where it gains momentum, peaks in popularity, and eventually declines as viewers move on to the next big thing.

---

2. Factors That Contribute to YouTube Trends

Several factors influence how trends emerge and gain traction on YouTube:

2.1 Algorithm and Recommendations

YouTube's recommendation system plays a significant role in amplifying trends. When a video gains high engagement (likes, comments, shares, and watch time), the algorithm pushes it to more users through the **"Recommended"** and **"Trending"** sections.

- The more people watch and interact with a video, the higher its chances of being featured on the homepage.
- If a specific format or topic gains momentum, YouTube may suggest similar videos to more users, accelerating the trend's growth.

2.2 Social Media and Cross-Platform Influence

Trends on YouTube often originate from or spread to other platforms like TikTok, Instagram, Twitter, and Reddit.

- A short viral video on TikTok may inspire long-form reaction videos, remixes, or commentary on YouTube.
- Twitter discussions and memes can spark YouTube creators to make analysis or response videos.
- Livestreamers on Twitch may introduce new gaming challenges that later trend on YouTube.

2.3 Celebrity and Influencer Participation

When high-profile YouTubers, celebrities, or influencers participate in a trend, it quickly gains mainstream attention.

- If a famous YouTuber engages in a challenge, their followers are likely to replicate and share their own versions.

- Celebrities appearing in a viral trend bring media coverage, further amplifying its reach.

2.4 Viewer Engagement and Community Participation

Trends thrive on engagement. A video format that allows viewers to participate—whether through challenges, reaction videos, or collaborations—has a higher chance of going viral.

- Community-driven trends, such as fan edits, remixes, and parody videos, encourage massive participation.
- Content that encourages user submissions, such as "Try Not to Laugh" challenges, keeps trends alive for longer.

2.5 Relatability and Entertainment Value

The most successful trends usually resonate with a wide audience.

- Humor, nostalgia, and emotion-driven content often become widely shared.
- Simple yet engaging trends, such as "10-Year Challenge" or "What's in My Bag?", gain traction because they are easy for anyone to participate in.

---

3. The Lifecycle of a YouTube Trend

Trends on YouTube follow a general pattern from inception to peak popularity and eventual decline.

3.1 The Birth of a Trend

A trend often starts with a single video or a small group of creators experimenting with a new concept.

- It may originate organically or be inspired by another social media platform.
- Early adopters share it, sparking curiosity among viewers.
- The YouTube algorithm starts recognizing the pattern and suggesting similar content.

3.2 Peak Popularity and Mass Adoption

Once a trend gains momentum:

- More creators jump on the bandwagon, producing variations of the original content.
- Mainstream media might cover the trend, increasing its visibility.
- Brands and advertisers may incorporate the trend into marketing campaigns.
- The YouTube "Trending" tab highlights top videos, exposing them to millions of users.

3.3 Saturation and Decline

Eventually, a trend reaches saturation when:

- Too many videos are produced, leading to audience fatigue.
- Creators move on to fresh ideas.
- A new trend emerges, shifting viewer interest.

While some trends disappear completely, others evolve into long-term content genres. For example, **"Let's Play"** gaming videos and **reaction videos** started as trends but have become mainstay content formats.

---

4. How to Identify and Participate in Trends

For viewers and creators alike, recognizing and engaging with trends can enhance their YouTube experience.

4.1 Where to Find Trending Content

To stay updated on trends, users can explore:

- **YouTube's Trending Tab** – Shows real-time popular videos.
- **Social Media Discussions** – Twitter hashtags and TikTok challenges often indicate upcoming trends.
- **Popular Creator Channels** – Following major influencers helps spot emerging topics.

- **YouTube Analytics (for Creators)** – Examining rising search queries and engagement patterns.

4.2 Best Practices for Engaging with Trends

If you're a creator looking to participate in trends:

- **Act Quickly** – Trends move fast, so timely participation is crucial.
- **Be Creative** – Put a unique spin on trending content instead of copying others.
- **Engage with the Community** – Commenting, collaborating, and encouraging participation boost visibility.
- **Balance Trends with Original Content** – Relying solely on trends may limit long-term growth.

For viewers:

- **Support Creators** – Liking, commenting, and sharing helps spread positive trends.
- **Stay Informed** – Following multiple content genres can diversify your recommendations.
- **Avoid Overconsumption** – Watching too much trending content can lead to burnout.

---

5. The Impact of Trends on YouTube Culture

Trends shape the YouTube ecosystem, influencing content styles, audience behavior, and even platform policies.

5.1 The Positive Impact of Trends

- They **encourage creativity** by inspiring new content formats.
- They **build communities** around shared interests.
- They **raise awareness** for important social issues (e.g., viral charity challenges).

5.2 The Negative Side of Trends

- Some trends promote **dangerous or harmful behavior** (e.g., reckless viral challenges).
- Clickbait trends can lead to **misinformation and misleading content**.
- Over-reliance on trends may pressure creators to **sacrifice originality** for views.

YouTube frequently updates its policies to curb harmful trends, ensuring a safer environment for viewers.

Conclusion

YouTube trends are an ever-evolving aspect of the platform, shaping content creation and viewer engagement. By understanding how trends emerge, grow, and fade, users can make informed decisions about which trends to follow and engage with. Whether you're a casual viewer or an aspiring creator, staying aware of YouTube trends can enhance your experience, connect you with a wider community, and even provide new opportunities for creativity and growth.

6.3.2 Participating in Viral Challenges

YouTube has become a hub for viral trends and challenges, attracting millions of users who want to join the latest craze. Participating in viral challenges can be a fun way to engage with the YouTube community, gain exposure, and connect with like-minded creators. However, to successfully take part in these challenges, it's important to understand their dynamics, choose the right ones, and approach them with creativity and responsibility.

This section will guide you through the process of participating in viral challenges on YouTube, from identifying popular trends to ensuring your content remains safe, entertaining, and aligned with your personal or brand identity.

Understanding Viral Challenges on YouTube

Viral challenges are video-based activities that encourage creators to attempt specific tasks, often following a set theme, rule, or format. These challenges spread rapidly across the platform, with thousands (or even millions) of users participating and adding their unique spin.

Some challenges originate from major influencers, while others emerge from social media platforms like TikTok, Instagram, or Twitter before making their way to YouTube. The virality of a challenge depends on factors such as simplicity, entertainment value, and audience participation.

Types of Viral Challenges

There are several categories of viral challenges on YouTube, each with its own appeal and level of engagement:

- **Comedy and Reaction Challenges** – These involve humorous reactions to specific situations, such as the **Try Not to Laugh Challenge**, where participants watch funny videos while attempting to keep a straight face.
- **Food and Eating Challenges** – These include eating unusual foods, consuming extremely spicy items, or completing timed food challenges (e.g., the **Spicy Noodle Challenge** or the **100-Layer Burger Challenge**).
- **Fitness and Endurance Challenges** – Many challenges push participants to test their physical limits, such as **30-Day Workout Challenges** or the **Push-Up Challenge**.
- **Dance and Lip-Sync Challenges** – Originating from TikTok, dance and lip-sync trends, such as the **Renegade Challenge**, quickly gain popularity on YouTube.
- **DIY and Creative Challenges** – These encourage users to showcase their creativity by making something unique, such as the **Blindfold Makeup Challenge** or the **Duct Tape Fashion Challenge**.
- **Social and Charity Challenges** – Some viral challenges focus on raising awareness or funds for a cause, such as the famous **Ice Bucket Challenge** that supported ALS research.

Understanding the nature of these challenges will help you decide which ones align with your interests and audience preferences.

How to Identify Popular Challenges

To participate in viral challenges effectively, you need to recognize which trends are currently gaining traction. Here's how you can stay updated:

1. Follow Trending Pages on YouTube

YouTube's **Trending** section highlights the most popular videos on the platform. By checking this regularly, you can spot emerging challenges early and jump in before they reach peak popularity.

2. Monitor Social Media Platforms

Many YouTube challenges originate from platforms like TikTok, Instagram, and Twitter. Keeping an eye on trending hashtags and viral videos on these platforms can help you predict which challenges will soon take off on YouTube.

3. Follow Popular Influencers

Top YouTubers and content creators often start or amplify viral challenges. Subscribing to influential creators in your niche can give you insight into which trends are gaining momentum.

4. Engage with the YouTube Community

Joining forums, Facebook groups, or Reddit communities related to YouTube content creation can help you stay informed about new challenges and their potential for virality.

Best Practices for Participating in a Viral Challenge

1. Put Your Unique Spin on It

Since many creators participate in the same challenges, adding a unique twist can help your video stand out. For example, if you're doing a food challenge, you could introduce a creative punishment for losing or incorporate an unexpected ingredient.

2. Stay Authentic to Your Brand

Not every viral challenge will be suitable for your channel's theme. Choose challenges that align with your niche and personality to maintain consistency with your audience. If you run an educational channel, you might adapt a challenge to include interesting facts or a learning component.

3. Optimize Your Video for Discovery

To maximize visibility, use effective **titles, descriptions, and hashtags** related to the challenge. For example, including phrases like "Extreme Spicy Noodle Challenge - Can I Survive?" can attract viewers searching for similar content.

4. Engage with Other Participants

Commenting on and collaborating with other creators participating in the challenge can help build connections and increase exposure. You can even challenge specific YouTubers to participate, encouraging cross-promotion.

5. Prioritize Safety and Responsibility

Some challenges have been controversial or even dangerous (e.g., the **Tide Pod Challenge** or extreme endurance stunts). Before participating, ensure the challenge is safe and does not promote harmful behavior. If necessary, add disclaimers or safety precautions to your video.

Recording and Editing Your Challenge Video

Once you've chosen a challenge, it's time to record and edit your video for maximum impact.

1. Plan Your Video Structure

Most successful challenge videos follow a clear format:

- **Introduction:** Explain the challenge and why you're participating.
- **The Attempt:** Perform the challenge while capturing genuine reactions.
- **Conclusion:** Wrap up the video with final thoughts, a challenge to viewers, or a call to action (e.g., asking viewers to subscribe).

2. Use High-Quality Production Techniques

Even if you're filming with a phone, proper lighting, clear audio, and engaging visuals will enhance the viewing experience. Adding multiple camera angles or close-ups of reactions can make the video more dynamic.

3. Edit for Engagement

Cut unnecessary parts to keep the video fast-paced and entertaining. Adding **text overlays, sound effects, and music** can make the content more appealing. For example, adding dramatic music during a suspenseful moment can increase viewer retention.

4. Encourage Viewer Interaction

At the end of your video, invite viewers to try the challenge themselves and tag you. This can create a community-driven effect and further boost engagement.

Leveraging Viral Challenges for Channel Growth

Participating in viral challenges can help grow your audience if done strategically. Here's how:

1. Leverage Trending Keywords

Using trending keywords in your video title, description, and tags can increase the chances of your video appearing in YouTube search results.

2. Cross-Promote on Social Media

Sharing your challenge video on Instagram, Twitter, or TikTok can bring additional traffic to your YouTube channel. You can also create short teaser clips to drive engagement.

3. Engage with Challenge Creators

Tagging the original challenge creator or engaging with their community can increase your visibility and help attract new subscribers.

4. Encourage Repeat Viewership

If a challenge gains traction, consider doing a **"Part 2"** video, where you attempt the challenge again under different conditions (e.g., trying the **Spicy Noodle Challenge** with an even hotter version).

Conclusion

Participating in viral challenges can be an exciting and effective way to engage with the YouTube community, gain exposure, and create entertaining content. By choosing the right challenges, putting a unique spin on them, optimizing your video for discovery, and ensuring safety, you can maximize the benefits while having fun.

As you explore YouTube challenges, remember that authenticity and creativity are key. Whether you're doing a hilarious reaction challenge or a meaningful charity-based challenge, staying true to your personality will help build a loyal audience and enhance your presence on the platform.

6.3.3 Recognizing Clickbait and Misinformation

YouTube is a vast platform where millions of videos are uploaded daily, covering nearly every topic imaginable. While this diversity is a strength, it also presents a challenge: not all content is reliable, and some videos are designed to manipulate viewers through misleading tactics. This section will help you recognize **clickbait** and **misinformation**, understand why they exist, and develop critical thinking skills to navigate YouTube more effectively.

---

1. What is Clickbait?

Clickbait refers to **sensationalized or misleading titles, thumbnails, and descriptions** designed to grab attention and increase video views. While clickbait is commonly used as a marketing tactic, it can sometimes be deceptive, leading to disappointment or misinformation.

1.1 Common Forms of Clickbait

Clickbait comes in various forms, including:

- **Exaggerated Titles** – Phrases like *"You Won't Believe This!"* or *"Shocking Truth Exposed!"* are often designed to spark curiosity but may not reflect the actual content.
- **Misleading Thumbnails** – Some creators use **photoshopped images** or unrelated visuals to lure viewers. For example, a video might show a celebrity in the thumbnail but not feature them at all.
- **Fake Urgency or Hype** – Words like *"Breaking News"*, *"Limited Time Only"*, or *"Must Watch Now"* create a sense of urgency to encourage immediate clicks.
- **Overpromising and Underdelivering** – Videos that claim to reveal *"secret tricks"* or *"unbelievable hacks"* may not contain any valuable information.

1.2 Why Do Creators Use Clickbait?

Clickbait is commonly used for several reasons:

- **Maximizing Views** – More clicks mean more **ad revenue** and better ranking in YouTube's algorithm.
- **Competing for Attention** – With **millions of videos** uploaded daily, creators use clickbait to **stand out** from the crowd.
- **Increasing Watch Time** – Some misleading thumbnails and titles trick users into watching longer than they intended.

While **some level of exaggeration** is common in online content, unethical clickbait can damage a creator's credibility and frustrate viewers.

1.3 How to Identify Clickbait?

Here are **practical ways** to spot and avoid clickbait:

- **Compare the Title and Thumbnail to the Video Content** – If a video claims to reveal *"an amazing secret"* but delivers basic information, it's likely clickbait.
- **Look at the Creator's History** – If a channel frequently uses **shocking headlines** but never delivers valuable content, it's best to avoid them.
- **Check the Comments** – Many viewers express their frustration in the comment section if a video is misleading.

- **Use Critical Thinking** – If something sounds **too good to be true**, it probably is.

Not all clickbait is harmful—some creators use **engaging titles** to attract views while still delivering **valuable content**. However, consistently misleading videos can lead to **mistrust** and **a poor viewing experience**.

---

2. Understanding Misinformation on YouTube

Misinformation refers to **false or misleading content** presented as fact. It can spread quickly, especially when it taps into emotions, **controversy**, or **current events**. Unlike clickbait, which is mainly about attracting views, misinformation can have **real-world consequences**, influencing opinions and decisions.

2.1 Types of Misinformation on YouTube

Misinformation can take several forms, including:

- **Fake News** – Videos that spread **false or distorted news stories**, often for political or financial gain.
- **Health Misinformation** – Some creators promote **unproven medical treatments**, fake cures, or conspiracy theories about health topics.
- **Deepfake Videos** – AI-generated videos that **alter faces or voices** to create realistic but fake footage.
- **Misleading Edits** – Some videos **splice clips** together out of context to distort reality.
- **Sensationalized Conspiracies** – Certain channels create **elaborate conspiracy theories** that lack evidence but are designed to go viral.

2.2 Why Does Misinformation Spread?

Misinformation spreads for several reasons:

- **Virality Over Accuracy** – The YouTube algorithm prioritizes **engagement (likes, shares, watch time)**, meaning **sensational** but false content often gets **recommended**.

- **Monetary Incentives** – Some channels spread false information to **generate ad revenue** or **sell products**.
- **Psychological Appeal** – People are naturally drawn to **shocking or controversial** information, making misinformation more shareable.
- **Echo Chambers** – YouTube's **recommendation system** can create **filter bubbles**, reinforcing false beliefs by only showing similar content.

2.3 How to Spot Misinformation?

To avoid falling for false content, follow these guidelines:

- **Check the Source** – Reliable sources are **well-known news outlets, experts, and fact-checking organizations**. If the creator has no credibility, be skeptical.
- **Look for Evidence** – Trust videos that provide **sources, data, or expert interviews** rather than **opinions without proof**.
- **Verify with Multiple Sources** – Compare information across **different channels or websites** to see if it's widely reported.
- **Watch for Emotional Manipulation** – If a video **plays on extreme emotions** (fear, anger, outrage) without providing **facts**, it may be misleading.
- **Check Fact-Checking Websites** – Use platforms like **Snopes, FactCheck.org, or Google Fact Check Explorer** to verify claims.

YouTube has taken steps to **combat misinformation** by **labeling authoritative sources** in search results and **removing harmful false content**, but it's still **up to viewers to think critically**.

---

3. How YouTube is Addressing Clickbait and Misinformation

YouTube has **implemented policies** to reduce misleading content and improve **content quality**. Some of these efforts include:

3.1 Algorithm Adjustments

YouTube has adjusted its algorithm to:

- Prioritize **authoritative sources** for topics like news and health.
- Reduce recommendations for **borderline content** that spreads misinformation.
- Penalize channels that **frequently use misleading tactics**.

3.2 Fact-Checking and Warning Labels

For certain searches (like health topics or elections), YouTube:

- **Displays fact-checking panels** from reliable sources.
- **Adds warning labels** on content flagged as misleading.
- **Removes harmful misinformation**, especially related to health crises or violent extremism.

3.3 Community Guidelines and Reporting Tools

YouTube allows users to:

- **Report videos for misinformation**.
- **Flag misleading thumbnails and titles**.
- **Give feedback** on whether a video is **helpful or misleading**.

While these measures help, **no system is perfect**, and misinformation can still slip through.

---

4. Developing Smart Viewing Habits

To **protect yourself from misleading content**, develop **smart viewing habits**:

- **Be Skeptical of Extreme Claims** – If a video **claims something outrageous**, verify it before believing.
- **Check the Comments and Community Feedback** – Many users **call out misleading content** in the comments section.
- **Diversify Your Sources** – Follow multiple channels with **different viewpoints** to avoid **bias and misinformation**.

- **Use External Fact-Checking Resources** – Don't rely solely on YouTube—cross-check information with **news websites, academic sources, and fact-checkers**.

By being aware of **clickbait and misinformation**, you can **enjoy YouTube responsibly** while avoiding manipulation.

Conclusion

Clickbait and misinformation are **common challenges** on YouTube, but with **critical thinking** and **smart habits**, you can navigate the platform effectively. Always question extreme claims, verify sources, and engage with **trustworthy content**. As YouTube evolves, the ability to **identify misleading videos** will become an essential skill for all users.

CHAPTER VII
Tips and Tricks for a Better YouTube Experience

7.1 Keyboard Shortcuts and Hidden Features

YouTube is designed to provide an engaging and user-friendly experience, but navigating the platform efficiently can sometimes be a challenge. Luckily, YouTube offers a range of keyboard shortcuts that can significantly enhance your viewing experience, allowing you to control videos, navigate between sections, and adjust settings with just a few keystrokes.

In this section, we will explore essential keyboard shortcuts that will help you become a more efficient YouTube user.

7.1.1 Essential Keyboard Shortcuts

YouTube provides a variety of keyboard shortcuts that allow you to control video playback, adjust volume, switch between different modes, and much more—all without using your mouse. Learning these shortcuts can help you save time and improve your overall experience.

Here's a detailed breakdown of the most useful keyboard shortcuts for YouTube:

1. Playback Controls

These shortcuts allow you to easily control video playback, including pausing, playing, skipping forward or backward, and adjusting playback speed.

- **Spacebar or 'K'** – Play/Pause the video
- **Left Arrow (←)** – Rewind the video by 5 seconds

- **Right Arrow (→)** – Fast forward the video by 5 seconds
- **'J'** – Rewind the video by 10 seconds
- **'L'** – Fast forward the video by 10 seconds
- **'<' (Shift + ,)** – Decrease playback speed
- **'>' (Shift + .)** – Increase playback speed
- **'0' (Zero key)** – Restart the video from the beginning
- **Numbers 1-9** – Jump to different points in the video (e.g., pressing '5' skips to 50% of the video)

These shortcuts make it easy to control video playback without constantly clicking on the progress bar.

---

2. Volume and Mute Controls

Adjusting the volume while watching videos is crucial, especially if you're in a shared space or need to quickly mute a video.

- **Up Arrow (↑)** – Increase volume by 5%
- **Down Arrow (↓)** – Decrease volume by 5%
- **'M'** – Mute/unmute the video

These shortcuts are particularly useful when watching videos on full-screen mode, as they allow you to adjust the volume without needing to move the mouse.

---

3. Screen and Viewing Mode Shortcuts

YouTube offers different viewing modes, such as full-screen, theater mode, and mini-player mode. The following shortcuts help you switch between them easily:

- **'F'** – Toggle full-screen mode on/off
- **'T'** – Toggle theater mode on/off
- **'I'** – Open mini-player mode

- **'Esc'** – Exit full-screen or close a pop-up

These shortcuts provide flexibility, especially when you want to switch between different viewing experiences quickly.

---

4. Subtitles and Captions Controls

For those who watch videos in different languages or need subtitles, YouTube provides several shortcuts to control captions.

- **'C'** – Toggle captions on/off
- **'+' (Shift + =)** – Increase subtitle size
- **'-' (Shift + -)** – Decrease subtitle size

These shortcuts can be especially helpful if you're watching educational content, foreign language videos, or content with unclear audio.

---

5. Playlist and Navigation Shortcuts

If you're watching a playlist or browsing YouTube, these shortcuts will help you navigate efficiently:

- **'Shift + N'** – Play the next video in a playlist
- **'Shift + P'** – Play the previous video in a playlist
- **'/'** – Activate the search bar instantly
- **'G + H'** – Go to the YouTube homepage
- **'G + L'** – Open your liked videos
- **'G + S'** – Open your subscriptions page

These shortcuts are particularly useful if you frequently watch playlists or want to navigate YouTube without using the mouse.

---

6. Comment and Engagement Shortcuts

- If you want YouTube to pause automatically when you switch tabs, use browser extensions like "Enhancer for YouTube" (not an official feature but useful for multitasking).

Conclusion

Mastering YouTube's keyboard shortcuts can dramatically improve your viewing experience, making it easier to control playback, adjust settings, and navigate the platform efficiently. Whether you're a casual viewer or a power user, these shortcuts will help you enjoy YouTube without unnecessary interruptions.

In the next section, we'll explore **Picture-in-Picture Mode**, a fantastic feature that allows you to keep watching videos while multitasking on your device.

7.1.2 Using Picture-in-Picture Mode

YouTube's **Picture-in-Picture (PiP) mode** is a powerful feature that enhances your viewing experience by allowing you to watch videos in a small, resizable window while using other apps or browsing the web. This feature is particularly useful for multitasking, as it enables you to keep watching a video while checking emails, browsing social media, or even taking notes.

In this section, we'll explore how **Picture-in-Picture mode** works, how to enable it on different devices, and the benefits of using it effectively.

---

1. What is Picture-in-Picture Mode?

Picture-in-Picture (PiP) is a **miniature video player** that appears in a floating window when you navigate away from the YouTube app or website. This allows you to continue watching your video while performing other tasks.

The **PiP window** is moveable and can be resized to fit your screen preference, providing a flexible way to keep videos playing in the background without interrupting your workflow.

How Picture-in-Picture Mode Works

When you activate PiP mode:

- The main YouTube player **minimizes into a small floating window**.
- You can **move the window around** your screen.
- The video **continues playing** even if you switch to another app or website.
- Basic playback controls, such as **play, pause, and skip**, remain accessible.

This feature is **especially useful for tutorials, podcasts, news, and educational videos**, where you might want to listen while doing something else.

---

2. How to Enable Picture-in-Picture Mode on Different Devices

PiP mode is available on various platforms, including **Android, iOS, Windows, and macOS**. Below, we'll go over how to enable and use PiP on each device.

2.1 Using Picture-in-Picture Mode on Android

On **Android devices**, YouTube's PiP mode is supported **natively**, meaning it is built into the operating system. However, the availability of PiP depends on whether you are a **YouTube Premium subscriber** or if the video is eligible for PiP playback.

Steps to Enable PiP Mode on Android

1. **Check if PiP is enabled in your settings:**
    - Go to **Settings → Apps & notifications → Advanced → Special app access → Picture-in-Picture**.
    - Find **YouTube** and ensure that PiP is **allowed**.
2. **Open YouTube and play a video.**
3. **Activate PiP mode:**
    - Simply **press the Home button** or **swipe up** (for gesture-based navigation).
    - The video should **shrink into a small floating window**.
4. **Move and resize the PiP window:**
    - Drag the window **to any corner** of the screen.

- **Pinch** to resize the window.

5. **Close PiP mode:**
   - Drag the PiP window **to the bottom of the screen** to dismiss it.

YouTube Premium Requirement on Android

- In many regions, **PiP mode requires a YouTube Premium subscription** for non-music videos.
- **For free users**, some educational and public videos may still support PiP.

2.2 Using Picture-in-Picture Mode on iOS (iPhone & iPad)

Apple's iOS supports PiP mode, but its **availability depends on your YouTube subscription.**

Steps to Enable PiP Mode on iOS

1. **Check if PiP is enabled:**
   - Go to **Settings → General → Picture-in-Picture** and turn it **ON**.
2. **Open the YouTube app and start playing a video.**
3. **Activate PiP mode:**
   - Swipe up from the bottom of the screen (on Face ID devices) or press the Home button (on Touch ID devices).
   - The video will shrink into a **floating window**.
4. **Move and resize the PiP window:**
   - Drag it around the screen.
   - Pinch to resize.
5. **Close PiP mode:**
   - Tap the "X" in the corner of the PiP window.

YouTube Premium Requirement on iOS

- Like Android, **YouTube Premium is required** for PiP on iPhones.
- Free users can only use PiP for certain **non-music** content.

2.3 Using Picture-in-Picture Mode on Windows & macOS

For **desktop users**, PiP mode is available via **web browsers** like Chrome, Edge, and Firefox.

Steps to Enable PiP Mode on a Web Browser

1. **Right-click (or double right-click) the video** while it's playing.
    - A menu will appear.
2. **Select "Picture-in-Picture" mode.**
    - The video will pop out into a small floating window.
3. **Move and resize the PiP window.**
    - Drag the window to a convenient spot on your screen.
4. **To exit PiP mode:**
    - Click the "X" in the PiP window or return to the main browser tab.

Using Browser Extensions for PiP

- Chrome users can install the **"Picture-in-Picture Extension"** from the Chrome Web Store for **one-click PiP mode activation**.

---

3. Benefits of Using Picture-in-Picture Mode

Multitasking Efficiency

- Watch YouTube **while using other apps** or websites.
- Great for **following tutorials** while working.

Enhanced Productivity

- Listen to **educational videos or podcasts** while doing other tasks.

- Keep up with **news or stock updates** in the background.

More Control Over Video Playback

- Move the video window **anywhere** on your screen.
- Resize it to match your **screen space preferences**.

---

4. Troubleshooting Picture-in-Picture Issues

PiP Mode Not Working? Here's How to Fix It

Check YouTube Premium Subscription

- If PiP doesn't work on **mobile**, check if you have an **active YouTube Premium subscription**.

Update Your Device and App

- Ensure your **OS and YouTube app are up to date**.
- Some **older versions** may not support PiP mode.

Restart the App or Device

- A simple **restart** can resolve PiP-related issues.

Try a Different Browser

- If PiP mode fails on **desktop**, try **Chrome, Edge, or Firefox**.

---

5. Final Thoughts on Picture-in-Picture Mode

Picture-in-Picture mode is a game-changer for multitasking, making it easy to keep watching YouTube videos while doing other things. Whether you're using a **smartphone, tablet, or computer**, PiP mode helps you stay productive and entertained at the same time.

By following the steps in this guide, you can make the most of **YouTube's PiP feature** and enhance your video-watching experience.

7.1.3 Customizing Playback Speed

YouTube offers users the ability to adjust video playback speed, making it a valuable tool for various purposes. Whether you want to slow down a tutorial to grasp every detail or speed up a lecture to save time, customizing playback speed can significantly enhance your viewing experience. In this section, we will explore how playback speed customization works, its practical applications, different methods to adjust it, and tips for optimizing your experience.

Understanding YouTube's Playback Speed Feature

YouTube's playback speed feature allows users to change how fast or slow a video plays without distorting the audio significantly. This function is built into YouTube's video player and is available on both desktop and mobile devices.

Available Speed Options

YouTube provides preset speed options that range from 0.25x (one-quarter speed) to 2x (double speed), including:

- **0.25x** – Very slow playback (useful for analyzing fast-moving visuals).
- **0.5x** – Half-speed playback (helpful for language learners or detailed tutorials).
- **0.75x** – Slightly slower than normal speed (ideal for understanding complex content).
- **Normal (1x)** – Standard playback speed.
- **1.25x** – Slightly faster playback (saves time while maintaining comprehension).
- **1.5x** – Moderately fast playback (good for quick content consumption).
- **1.75x** – Faster playback while still retaining most speech clarity.
- **2x** – Double speed playback (best for content that is slow-paced or repetitive).

These speed settings allow users to fine-tune their viewing experience based on their needs.

How to Adjust Playback Speed on Different Devices

On Desktop (Web Browser Version)

1. Open a YouTube video.
2. Click on the **gear icon (Settings)** in the lower right corner of the video player.
3. Select **"Playback speed"** from the menu.
4. Choose your desired speed from the available options.

Alternatively, you can use keyboard shortcuts:

- Press **Shift + . (period)** to increase speed.
- Press **Shift + , (comma)** to decrease speed.

On Mobile (YouTube App on iOS and Android)

1. Open the YouTube app and start a video.
2. Tap on the **three-dot menu** in the upper-right corner of the screen.
3. Select **"Playback speed"** from the list of options.
4. Choose a speed from the available settings.

Using Keyboard Shortcuts for Quick Adjustments

For those who frequently adjust playback speed, keyboard shortcuts provide a fast way to make changes without using menus.

- **Increase speed:** Shift + . (period)
- **Decrease speed:** Shift + , (comma)
- **Reset speed to normal:** Shift + N (not an official shortcut, but some browser extensions allow this customization).

Practical Applications of Playback Speed Customization

1. Learning and Education

Many students and professionals use playback speed adjustments to enhance their learning experience.

- **Speeding up online lectures:** Watching educational videos at 1.5x or 2x speed helps absorb information faster while saving time.
- **Slowing down tutorials:** When watching coding demonstrations, musical lessons, or language tutorials, slowing the speed to 0.75x or 0.5x can improve comprehension.

2. Content Consumption Efficiency

Busy individuals can maximize their time by adjusting playback speed.

- **Podcasts and interviews:** Many YouTube podcasts have slow dialogue. Increasing speed to 1.25x or 1.5x makes them more engaging.
- **Long-form content:** Documentaries or long discussions can be watched at higher speeds without losing key insights.

3. Entertainment and Media Analysis

Playback speed control also benefits entertainment content viewers.

- **Analyzing fast-moving scenes:** Sports enthusiasts can slow down highlight reels to study techniques.
- **Catching hidden details:** Movie fans analyzing special effects or Easter eggs may slow down playback for a better look.

4. Accessibility and Language Learning

Playback speed customization is a helpful tool for non-native speakers and individuals with different learning needs.

- **Slow playback for clear pronunciation:** Language learners can slow down dialogue-heavy videos for better understanding.
- **Hearing-impaired users:** Slowing down content helps in reading captions more comfortably.

Advanced Methods for Customizing Playback Speed

While YouTube provides preset speed options, some users may want even more control. Here are a few advanced techniques:

Using Custom Speed Controls with Browser Extensions

Some Chrome and Firefox extensions allow users to adjust playback speed more precisely, such as:

- **Video Speed Controller** (Chrome) – Enables custom speeds (e.g., 1.3x or 1.8x) and shortcuts.
- **Enhancer for YouTube** – Adds a speed control slider directly to the player.

Manually Adjusting Speed via Developer Console (Advanced Users)

For tech-savvy users, JavaScript commands in a browser's developer console can set a custom playback speed.

1. Open a YouTube video.
2. Press **F12** (or right-click > Inspect) to open the Developer Console.
3. Navigate to the **Console** tab.
4. Enter the following command:
5. document.querySelector('video').playbackRate = 1.3;

(Change 1.3 to any desired speed).

This method allows for more precise speed control, but it resets when the page is refreshed.

Using Third-Party Apps for Custom Speed Control

Some video player apps like **VLC Media Player** allow downloading YouTube videos and adjusting playback speed beyond YouTube's standard limits.

Tips for Optimizing Playback Speed Usage

- **Use small speed increases for better comprehension** – Watching at 1.25x instead of 1.5x might keep information retention high.
- **Enable captions when using high-speed playback** – Subtitles can help maintain understanding at faster speeds.

- **Combine with timestamps for better navigation** – If watching an educational video at 2x, use timestamps to jump to key points.
- **Test different speeds for different content types** – Some content is better suited for fast playback, while others require slower speeds.

Potential Downsides and Limitations

While playback speed control is highly useful, it does have some drawbacks:

- **Fast speech may become hard to follow** – Some speakers naturally talk quickly, making 2x speed difficult to understand.
- **Distorted audio quality** – At extreme speeds, voices can become robotic or unclear.
- **Loss of intended pacing** – Comedic timing, dramatic pauses, and music pacing may be lost when increasing speed.

To mitigate these issues, experiment with different speeds based on content type.

Conclusion

Customizing playback speed is a powerful feature that enhances the YouTube experience in various ways, from learning more efficiently to improving entertainment consumption. Whether you're a student, a professional, or an avid content consumer, adjusting speed allows you to tailor your viewing experience to your needs.

By mastering YouTube's speed controls, experimenting with different speeds, and using advanced tools like browser extensions or developer commands, you can take full advantage of this often-overlooked feature.

For those new to playback speed customization, start with small adjustments and find what works best for different types of content. With the right approach, you'll soon be watching smarter, learning faster, and making the most out of YouTube.

7.2 Reducing Distractions While Watching

7.2.1 Using Focus Mode Extensions

YouTube is an incredible platform for learning, entertainment, and staying updated with the latest trends. However, it can also be a major source of distraction. The constant recommendations, autoplay feature, and comment section can pull you away from your original intent, making it difficult to focus on the content you want to watch.

Focus mode extensions are browser tools designed to minimize these distractions, helping you stay engaged with the videos that matter most. In this section, we'll explore what focus mode extensions are, their benefits, and how to install and use them effectively.

Understanding Focus Mode Extensions

Focus mode extensions are browser add-ons that modify your YouTube experience by removing unnecessary elements that contribute to distractions. These tools can:

- Hide recommended videos from the sidebar
- Disable autoplay to prevent endless video consumption
- Remove the comment section to avoid unnecessary discussions
- Block homepage suggestions to keep your attention on specific content
- Enable distraction-free viewing by focusing only on the video player

By using these extensions, you can create a cleaner YouTube interface that encourages mindful watching rather than endless scrolling.

Why Use Focus Mode Extensions?

There are several reasons why using focus mode extensions can be beneficial:

1. Improve Productivity

Many people use YouTube for educational purposes, such as watching tutorials, lectures, or industry-related content. However, the platform's recommendation algorithm often suggests unrelated videos, making it easy to lose focus. Focus mode extensions help eliminate these distractions so you can stay on track.

2. Minimize Time Wasted on Unnecessary Content

YouTube's autoplay feature and sidebar recommendations can lead to hours of unintended viewing. If you've ever started watching a five-minute tutorial and ended up watching an hour of unrelated content, focus mode extensions can help by preventing autoplay and hiding suggested videos.

3. Reduce Mental Clutter

A cluttered YouTube interface with excessive thumbnails, comments, and advertisements can be visually overwhelming. Focus mode extensions create a cleaner, more streamlined experience, allowing you to concentrate on the content that truly matters.

4. Enhance Learning and Retention

For those using YouTube as a learning tool, a distraction-free interface helps with concentration and information retention. By eliminating unnecessary elements, you can fully absorb the information being presented in the video.

Popular Focus Mode Extensions for YouTube

Several browser extensions are designed to enhance focus while using YouTube. Here are some of the most popular ones:

1. Unhook – Remove YouTube Distractions

Unhook is a powerful Chrome extension that allows you to customize your YouTube experience by:

- Hiding recommended videos
- Removing the sidebar and homepage suggestions
- Disabling autoplay
- Hiding the comment section

This extension is ideal for users who want a minimalist YouTube interface focused solely on video content.

2. DF Tube (Distraction-Free for YouTube)

DF Tube is another excellent extension for blocking distractions. It provides options to:

- Hide the video recommendations sidebar
- Remove autoplay controls
- Disable comments and trending sections
- Create a cleaner, distraction-free interface

DF Tube is highly customizable, allowing users to enable or disable specific elements based on their needs.

3. Minimal YouTube

Minimal YouTube focuses on simplifying the user experience by removing clutter from the interface. It:

- Hides suggested videos
- Removes comments
- Blocks homepage distractions
- Allows users to create a cleaner, more focused YouTube environment

This extension is perfect for those who want a streamlined, distraction-free viewing experience.

4. YouTube Rabbit Hole

This extension is designed to help users avoid endless scrolling by:

- Hiding related videos
- Removing autoplay suggestions
- Disabling comments
- Focusing only on the video content

YouTube Rabbit Hole is great for users who want to stay on track with their intended viewing goals.

How to Install and Use a Focus Mode Extension

If you're new to browser extensions, installing and setting up a focus mode tool is a simple process. Here's how you can do it:

Step 1: Choose a Browser

Focus mode extensions are usually available for Chrome, Firefox, Edge, and other Chromium-based browsers. Ensure that your browser supports extensions.

Step 2: Visit the Extension Store

Go to the official extension store for your browser:

- **Google Chrome**: Chrome Web Store https://chrome.google.com/webstore/
- **Firefox**: Mozilla Add-ons https://addons.mozilla.org/en-US/firefox/
- **Microsoft Edge**: Edge Add-ons https://microsoftedge.microsoft.com/addons/Microsoft-Edge-Extensions-Home

Step 3: Search for the Extension

Type the name of the focus mode extension (e.g., "Unhook" or "DF Tube") in the search bar.

Step 4: Install the Extension

Click on the extension, then press the "Add to Browser" or "Install" button. Follow the prompts to complete the installation.

Step 5: Configure the Settings

Once installed, click on the extension icon in your browser toolbar. Customize the settings to enable or disable features according to your preferences.

Step 6: Enjoy a Distraction-Free YouTube Experience

Visit YouTube and notice the cleaner, more focused interface. Adjust settings as needed for a better experience.

Customizing Your Focus Mode Experience

Most focus mode extensions offer customization options, allowing you to:

- Enable or disable specific features (e.g., keep the comment section but hide recommendations)
- Adjust settings per session (e.g., block distractions during study hours but allow them during leisure time)
- Whitelist certain channels where you want full YouTube functionality

By personalizing these settings, you can create an experience that balances focus and enjoyment.

Alternative Ways to Reduce Distractions on YouTube

If you don't want to install extensions, there are other ways to minimize distractions on YouTube:

1. Use YouTube's Built-in Features

- **Turn off autoplay**: Click the autoplay toggle switch to stop YouTube from automatically playing the next video.
- **Use "Watch Later" playlists**: Save videos to watch at a scheduled time instead of getting lost in recommendations.

2. Watch in Full-Screen Mode

By switching to full-screen mode, you eliminate sidebar distractions and focus solely on the video content.

3. Set Time Limits

Use browser time management tools like StayFocusd or Freedom to limit the amount of time you spend on YouTube.

4. Use Productivity Apps

Apps like Cold Turkey and RescueTime can block YouTube during work hours, ensuring you stay productive.

Conclusion

Focus mode extensions are valuable tools for anyone looking to reduce distractions while watching YouTube. By removing recommended videos, autoplay, and comments, these extensions help users stay engaged with the content that truly matters.

Whether you're using YouTube for learning, work, or relaxation, a distraction-free experience can enhance focus, productivity, and enjoyment. By installing and customizing the right extension, you can transform YouTube into a more intentional and valuable resource.

If you're someone who often finds themselves watching unrelated videos for hours, give a focus mode extension a try—you might be surprised at how much more efficient your YouTube experience becomes!

7.2.2 Hiding Comments and Suggested Videos

YouTube is an excellent platform for consuming educational content, entertainment, and news, but it can also be a source of distractions. The comment section and suggested videos are two elements that can divert your focus from the main content you want to watch. This section explores the reasons for hiding comments and suggested videos, various methods to do so, and how this practice can improve your overall YouTube experience.

Why Hide Comments and Suggested Videos?

1. Reducing Negative Influence

The comment section on YouTube can be informative, entertaining, or, unfortunately, a source of toxicity. While some discussions are constructive, many contain:

- Spam and self-promotion

- Misinformation and fake news
- Negative or offensive language
- Unwanted arguments and trolling

By hiding comments, you can avoid exposure to unnecessary negativity and keep your focus on the video content itself.

2. Preventing Endless Scrolling

Many users find themselves scrolling through comments long after a video has ended, leading to wasted time. Since YouTube does not have an in-built focus mode, manually avoiding the comment section can be difficult. Hiding comments can prevent you from getting caught in this loop.

3. Avoiding Unwanted Distractions

YouTube's suggested videos algorithm recommends related or trending content based on your watch history and user behavior. While this feature is helpful, it can also:

- Lead to binge-watching unrelated videos
- Show clickbait content that does not add value
- Distract you from your primary intent

Hiding suggested videos helps you maintain focus on your learning or entertainment goals without being tempted by irrelevant content.

How to Hide Comments on YouTube

1. Using YouTube's Built-in Features

YouTube does not have a direct "hide all comments" button, but you can disable comments for your own uploaded videos if you are a creator. However, as a viewer, you have the following options:

1.1 Expanding the Video Player

One simple way to avoid seeing comments is by expanding the video player to full screen or theater mode. This removes distractions by focusing on the video content only.

- Click on the full-screen button (□□) or press F on your keyboard.
- To enter theater mode, click the rectangular theater mode button or press T.

1.2 Scrolling Past the Comment Section

While this is not a perfect solution, a simple trick is to scroll down just enough so that the comment section disappears from view while watching.

2. Using Browser Extensions to Block Comments

If you want a more permanent way to hide comments on YouTube, browser extensions are an excellent solution. Here are some popular ones:

2.1 "Hide YouTube Comments" Extension

This is a lightweight Chrome extension that automatically removes the comment section from all YouTube videos. It works instantly and does not require configuration.

2.2 "Shut Up" Extension

This extension works across multiple websites, including YouTube, by blocking all comment sections. You can toggle it on and off when needed.

2.3 Custom CSS for Advanced Users

If you use a browser that supports user styles (such as Stylus for Chrome or Firefox), you can apply custom CSS to hide comments. Use the following CSS code:

```
#comments { display: none !important; }
```

This method ensures that YouTube will never load the comment section when you visit a video page.

How to Hide Suggested Videos on YouTube

1. Turning Off Autoplay

One way to limit distractions from suggested videos is by disabling autoplay. Autoplay automatically plays the next recommended video, often leading to an endless viewing session.

- Click the autoplay switch (□) next to the video player.
- Ensure that it is toggled **off** to prevent YouTube from playing suggested videos automatically.

2. Using Browser Extensions to Hide Recommendations

Several browser extensions can completely remove suggested videos from YouTube.

2.1 "Unhook" Extension

- This extension removes the entire right-side recommendations bar.
- It also removes the homepage video suggestions.
- Users can enable or disable specific features like the trending tab.

2.2 "Distraction Free YouTube"

- This extension hides related videos, comments, and homepage recommendations.
- It allows users to customize what they want to block.

3. Modifying YouTube's URL to Prevent Suggested Videos

A little-known trick is modifying YouTube's URL to avoid distractions. If you remove the watch?v= portion and replace it with /embed/, you will get a distraction-free video.

For example:

- Normal YouTube URL:

  https://www.youtube.com/watch?v=EXAMPLEID

- Modified distraction-free URL:

  https://www.youtube.com/embed/EXAMPLEID

This method eliminates the right-side suggested videos and the comment section.

4. Using YouTube's Restricted Mode

YouTube's restricted mode is designed to filter inappropriate content, but it also modifies the recommendation algorithm, reducing clickbait and irrelevant suggestions.

- Click on your profile picture in the top right corner.
- Scroll down and toggle on **Restricted Mode**.

How Hiding Comments and Suggested Videos Improves Your Experience

1. Increases Productivity

By reducing distractions, you can focus on watching educational content, tutorials, or business-related videos without wasting time.

2. Creates a More Positive Environment

Without toxic comments and clickbait recommendations, your YouTube experience becomes more peaceful and engaging.

3. Encourages Mindful Viewing

When you are not tempted by autoplay or endless recommendations, you are more likely to watch videos that genuinely interest you.

4. Reduces Screen Time

Many users find themselves trapped in an endless cycle of watching suggested videos. By removing distractions, you regain control over your screen time.

Final Thoughts

Hiding comments and suggested videos on YouTube is a powerful way to stay focused and avoid unnecessary distractions. Whether you use built-in features like full-screen mode and autoplay controls or browser extensions to block comments and recommendations, these strategies help create a better, more intentional YouTube experience.

By implementing these methods, you can enjoy YouTube for learning, entertainment, or work without falling into the trap of endless scrolling and unnecessary content consumption.

7.2.3 Managing Autoplay for a Better Experience

YouTube's **Autoplay** feature is a convenient tool designed to keep you engaged by automatically playing the next suggested video. While this can be useful for continuous viewing, it can also be distracting or lead to excessive screen time. In this section, we will explore how Autoplay works, how to disable or customize it, and how to optimize your YouTube experience by managing Autoplay effectively.

Understanding YouTube's Autoplay Feature

Autoplay is an algorithm-driven feature that queues up and plays a recommended video immediately after your current video finishes. This feature is available on both desktop and mobile versions of YouTube, as well as on smart TVs and streaming devices.

How Autoplay Works

- **Algorithmic Recommendations**: YouTube's algorithm suggests the next video based on your watch history, video engagement (likes, shares, and comments), and trending content.
- **Continuous Play**: If Autoplay is enabled, the next video starts automatically after a short countdown (usually 5–10 seconds).
- **Cross-Device Synchronization**: If you are logged into your Google account, your Autoplay settings will be consistent across all devices.
- **Watch History Influence**: YouTube tailors Autoplay recommendations based on videos you have watched and engaged with.

While this feature can be great for discovering new content, it can also become overwhelming or lead to mindless binge-watching.

Why You Might Want to Manage Autoplay

Although Autoplay can enhance the viewing experience, there are several reasons why you might want to take control of it:

1. **Avoiding Distractions**: Autoplay can lead to endless video consumption, which can distract from important tasks.
2. **Preventing Unwanted Content**: Sometimes, Autoplay suggests videos that are not relevant or interesting to you.
3. **Saving Data and Battery Life**: On mobile devices, Autoplay can quickly consume data and drain battery power.
4. **Reducing Screen Time**: If you are trying to manage your time effectively, disabling Autoplay can help prevent prolonged sessions.

Managing Autoplay effectively allows you to **stay in control of your viewing experience** rather than letting the algorithm dictate what you watch next.

How to Turn Off or Adjust Autoplay on Different Devices

Depending on the device you are using, you can disable or customize Autoplay in different ways.

On Desktop (YouTube Website)

1. Open **YouTube** in your web browser.
2. Play any video.
3. Look for the **Autoplay toggle** (a switch) on the top-right corner of the video player.
4. Click the toggle to **turn it off** (it should no longer be blue).

Alternatively, you can disable Autoplay permanently:

1. Click on your **profile picture** in the top-right corner.
2. Go to **Settings > Playback & Performance**.
3. Locate the **Autoplay** section and turn it off.

On Mobile Devices (YouTube App - Android & iOS)

1. Open the **YouTube app**.

2. Tap on your **profile picture** in the top-right corner.
3. Select **Settings > Autoplay**.
4. Toggle **Autoplay next video** to **off**.

Additionally, you can disable Autoplay directly from the video player:

- While watching a video, look for the **Autoplay switch** at the top of the screen and toggle it off.

On Smart TVs and Streaming Devices

1. Open the **YouTube app** on your Smart TV or streaming device (e.g., Roku, Fire Stick, Apple TV).
2. Navigate to **Settings**.
3. Scroll to **Autoplay** and turn it off.

Disabling Autoplay on one device typically syncs across all devices if you are logged into the same account.

Alternative Ways to Control Autoplay

Besides turning off Autoplay completely, you can manage it in other ways to maintain a better YouTube experience.

1. Using the "Up Next" Feature

Instead of letting YouTube decide the next video, you can manually choose from the **"Up Next"** list, which appears on the right side of the screen (desktop) or below the video (mobile).

2. Using YouTube's Queue Feature

- On desktop, you can **queue videos** by clicking the **"Add to Queue"** button (represented by three dots next to a video title).
- This allows you to create a temporary playlist of videos **without relying on Autoplay**.

3. Using YouTube Playlists Instead of Autoplay

If you enjoy continuous playback but want more control, consider creating and watching **playlists** instead:

- Add videos manually to a playlist.
- Play the playlist for uninterrupted viewing without unpredictable Autoplay recommendations.

4. Adjusting Data-Saving and Battery Settings

If you're concerned about mobile data or battery life:

- **Enable "Data Saver" mode** in YouTube settings to reduce video quality and prevent excessive streaming.
- **Turn on battery-saving mode** to limit background activity, which may also reduce automatic video playback.

The Psychology Behind Autoplay and How to Resist It

YouTube's Autoplay feature is designed to **maximize user engagement** by keeping you on the platform for longer periods. Studies show that **automated content consumption increases watch time** because users are less likely to stop watching when the next video starts automatically.

Here are some strategies to resist the temptation of endless Autoplay:

1. Set Time Limits for Watching

Use a **timer** or set **screen time limits** on your device to remind yourself to take breaks.

2. Use Browser Extensions to Disable Autoplay Permanently

If you use YouTube on a desktop browser, consider installing extensions like:

- **"Unhook – Remove YouTube Distractions"** (Chrome & Firefox)
- **"Disable Autoplay for YouTube"**

These tools **permanently disable Autoplay** and hide distracting elements like recommended videos.

3. Watch Videos with a Purpose

Before opening YouTube, set an **intention** for what you want to watch. Avoid random browsing that leads to unnecessary binge-watching.

Final Thoughts on Managing Autoplay for a Better Experience

Autoplay can be a **double-edged sword**—it helps you discover great content but can also lead to **unintentional binge-watching**. Managing this feature gives you **more control over your viewing habits**, **reduces distractions**, and **helps maintain a balanced digital lifestyle**.

Key Takeaways:

✅ **Autoplay is designed to keep you engaged**, but you can disable or customize it.
✅ **Turning off Autoplay can reduce distractions and prevent excessive screen time.**
✅ **Using manual queues and playlists provides better content control.**
✅ **Browser extensions and mobile settings can permanently disable Autoplay.**
✅ **Setting viewing goals and screen time limits helps maintain balance.**

By taking control of **Autoplay settings**, you can **enjoy YouTube more intentionally** while still benefiting from its vast collection of content.

7.3 Exploring YouTube on Different Devices

7.3.1 Watching YouTube on Smart TVs

Introduction

YouTube is no longer limited to computers and mobile devices; it has become a central part of home entertainment through Smart TVs. Watching YouTube on a Smart TV allows users to enjoy high-definition videos on a large screen, making it ideal for family gatherings, educational purposes, and entertainment. This section will guide you through the different ways to access YouTube on Smart TVs, how to navigate the interface, optimize video quality, and troubleshoot common issues.

---

1. How to Access YouTube on a Smart TV

There are multiple ways to watch YouTube on a Smart TV, depending on the brand and model of your television. Here are the most common methods:

Using the Built-in YouTube App

Most modern Smart TVs come with a pre-installed YouTube app. To access it:

1. **Turn on your Smart TV** and connect it to the internet.
2. **Navigate to the app store** (on Samsung, LG, Sony, or other Smart TVs, the app store might be called the "LG Content Store" or "Google Play Store" for Android TVs).
3. **Open the YouTube app** if it's already installed. If not, download and install it.
4. **Sign in to your YouTube account** to access subscriptions, playlists, and recommendations.

Casting YouTube from a Smartphone or Tablet

Casting is an easy way to watch YouTube on your Smart TV without needing to type using a TV remote. Here's how:

1. **Ensure your Smart TV and smartphone are connected to the same Wi-Fi network.**
2. **Open the YouTube app** on your mobile device.
3. **Tap the Cast icon** (usually found at the top of the app).
4. **Select your Smart TV** from the list of available devices.
5. **Choose a video on your phone, and it will play on the TV.**

Using a Streaming Device (Chromecast, Fire Stick, Apple TV, Roku)

If your Smart TV does not have a built-in YouTube app, you can use an external streaming device:

- **Google Chromecast:** Plug the device into your TV's HDMI port and cast YouTube videos from your phone or computer.
- **Amazon Fire Stick:** Download the YouTube app and sign in to access all features.
- **Apple TV:** Open the YouTube app from the Apple TV interface and log in.
- **Roku:** Search for the YouTube channel in the Roku store, install it, and log in.

---

2. Navigating the YouTube Interface on a Smart TV

Once you have YouTube running on your Smart TV, understanding the interface is essential for a smooth experience.

The Home Screen

The YouTube home screen on Smart TVs displays a layout similar to desktop and mobile versions:

- **Recommended videos** based on your watch history.
- **Trending content** including popular videos worldwide.
- **Subscribed channels** featuring new uploads from your favorite creators.

Using the Remote to Control YouTube

Most Smart TV remotes support basic YouTube navigation:

- **Arrow buttons** move the selection cursor.
- **OK/Enter button** selects a video or menu option.
- **Back button** returns to the previous screen.
- **Fast-forward and rewind buttons** help navigate through videos.

Using Voice Search for Faster Navigation

Many modern Smart TVs and streaming devices support voice commands. You can say:

- *"Play the latest video from National Geographic."*
- *"Search for cooking tutorials on YouTube."*
- *"Show me trending gaming videos."*

To use voice search, press the microphone button on the remote and speak clearly.

---

3. Optimizing Video Quality and Playback Settings

Watching YouTube on a Smart TV provides an immersive experience, but optimizing video settings enhances it further.

Adjusting Video Resolution

By default, YouTube adjusts video quality based on internet speed, but you can manually change it:

1. **While watching a video, press the Settings (gear) icon.**
2. **Select "Quality" and choose a resolution.** Options include:
    - 144p to 480p (low quality, faster loading)
    - 720p to 1080p (high-definition)
    - 4K or 8K (ultra-high definition, requires strong internet)

Enabling Captions and Subtitles

For accessibility or language learning, captions can be turned on:

1. **Press the Settings (gear) icon during video playback.**
2. **Select "Subtitles/CC" and choose a language.**
3. **For auto-generated captions, enable "Auto-translate."**

Controlling Playback Speed

To slow down or speed up videos:

1. **Open the Settings (gear) menu.**
2. **Select "Playback Speed."**
3. **Choose from 0.25x (slower) to 2x (faster).**

---

4. Managing YouTube Features on a Smart TV

Creating and Accessing Playlists

Smart TVs allow users to create and watch playlists:

1. **Add videos to a playlist on a mobile device or computer.**
2. **Access the playlist on Smart TV via the Library tab.**

Using YouTube Kids for Family-Friendly Content

For parents, YouTube Kids provides a safer viewing experience:

1. **Download the YouTube Kids app** (if supported by your TV).
2. **Set up parental controls** and content filters.
3. **Enable Restricted Mode on regular YouTube** for additional safety.

Enabling Dark Mode for Comfortable Viewing

Dark Mode reduces eye strain during nighttime viewing:

1. **Go to Settings on your Smart TV YouTube app.**

2. **Enable Dark Mode under "Appearance."**

---

5. Troubleshooting Common Issues

YouTube App Not Opening or Crashing

- Restart your Smart TV and router.
- Update the YouTube app via the TV's app store.
- Clear app cache (if available in settings).

Buffering or Slow Video Playback

- Check your internet speed (YouTube recommends at least 5 Mbps for HD and 20 Mbps for 4K).
- Reduce the resolution if the internet is slow.
- Move the router closer to the TV or use a wired Ethernet connection.

No Sound or Audio Sync Issues

- Ensure TV volume is not muted.
- Restart the TV and YouTube app.
- Check HDMI connections if using external devices.

Conclusion

Watching YouTube on a Smart TV is an excellent way to enjoy content on a larger screen with high-quality visuals and better audio. Whether you access YouTube via the built-in app, cast from a smartphone, or use a streaming device, there are multiple ways to enhance your viewing experience. By optimizing video settings, using voice search, managing playlists, and troubleshooting common issues, you can make the most of YouTube on your Smart TV.

Next time you want to watch your favorite YouTube content, grab your remote, sit back, and enjoy a cinema-like experience from the comfort of your home!

7.3.2 Using YouTube on Mobile Apps

With the increasing use of smartphones and tablets, YouTube's mobile app has become the primary way many users access and enjoy content. The YouTube mobile app offers a user-friendly experience, allowing you to watch, search, interact, and even upload videos on the go. In this section, we'll explore how to navigate the YouTube mobile app, its key features, customization options, and some advanced tips for optimizing your viewing experience.

---

1. Downloading and Setting Up the YouTube Mobile App

Before you can start using YouTube on your mobile device, you need to download and install the app.

Downloading the App

The YouTube app is available on both **Android** (via Google Play Store) and **iOS** (via Apple App Store). To download:

- Open the **Google Play Store** or **App Store** on your device.
- Search for **"YouTube"** in the search bar.
- Select the official **YouTube** app (developed by Google LLC).
- Tap **"Install"** (on Android) or **"Get"** (on iOS).

Signing In and Setting Up Your Account

Once installed, follow these steps to sign in and customize your experience:

- Open the **YouTube** app.
- Tap the **profile icon** in the top right corner.
- Select **"Sign In"** and enter your Google credentials.
- If you have multiple accounts, choose the one you want to use.
- Adjust your **privacy and notification settings** based on your preferences.

By signing in, you unlock features such as **watch history, subscriptions, and personalized recommendations**.

---

2. Navigating the YouTube Mobile Interface

The YouTube mobile app interface is designed to be intuitive, with different sections to help users easily discover and manage content.

Home Screen

When you open the app, the **Home** tab displays personalized recommendations based on your watch history and subscriptions.

- The top section often features **shorts, trending videos, and live streams**.
- Scrolling down reveals more suggested videos tailored to your interests.

Search and Discover

The **Search bar** (magnifying glass icon) at the top allows you to find specific videos, channels, or playlists.

- You can filter results by **upload date, view count, or duration**.
- **Voice search** is also available, letting you find content hands-free.

Library and History

The **Library** tab stores your **watch history, playlists, liked videos, and downloads**.

- Use the **History** section to revisit previously watched videos.
- Create and manage **playlists** for easy access to your favorite content.

Subscriptions

The **Subscriptions** tab provides updates from the channels you follow.

- You'll see new uploads, live streams, and community posts from your favorite creators.
- Tap the **bell icon** next to a subscribed channel to customize notifications.

Shorts and Live Tab

- **Shorts**: A dedicated tab for quick, vertical-format videos similar to TikTok and Instagram Reels.
- **Live**: A section showcasing live streaming videos, including gaming, events, and real-time broadcasts.

---

3. Watching Videos on the Mobile App

Video Player Controls

When you tap on a video, the video player interface provides several controls:

- **Play/Pause**: Tap anywhere on the screen to pause or resume playback.
- **Seek Bar**: Drag the red progress bar to skip forward or rewind.
- **Captions (CC)**: Enable subtitles for better understanding.
- **Quality Settings**: Tap the three-dot menu to adjust resolution (e.g., 720p, 1080p, 4K).
- **Theater Mode**: Rotate your phone to watch in full-screen mode.
- **Playback Speed**: Speed up or slow down video playback (0.5x to 2x speed).

Picture-in-Picture (PiP) Mode

On supported devices, you can enable **Picture-in-Picture mode**, which allows the video to continue playing in a small window while using other apps. To enable PiP:

- On **Android**, go to **Settings > Apps > YouTube > Enable PiP Mode**.
- On **iOS**, swipe up or press the home button while a video is playing.

Engaging with Videos

- **Like/Dislike**: Tap the thumbs-up or thumbs-down button.
- **Comment**: Scroll down to leave or read comments.

- **Share**: Use the share button to send videos via social media, email, or messaging apps.
- **Save to Playlist**: Tap "Save" to add videos to your Watch Later or custom playlists.

---

4. Customizing the YouTube Mobile Experience

Managing Notifications

To control notifications for new videos, live streams, and recommendations:

- Go to **Profile > Settings > Notifications**.
- Enable or disable alerts for **subscriptions, comments, and trending videos**.

Dark Mode and Appearance Settings

If you prefer a darker theme for night-time viewing:

- Go to **Settings > General > Appearance > Dark Mode**.

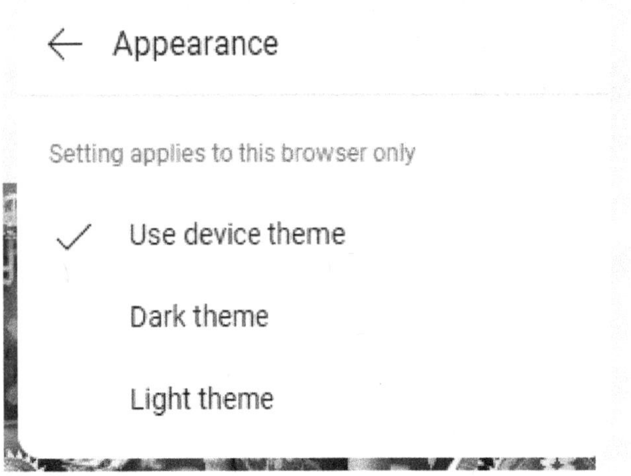

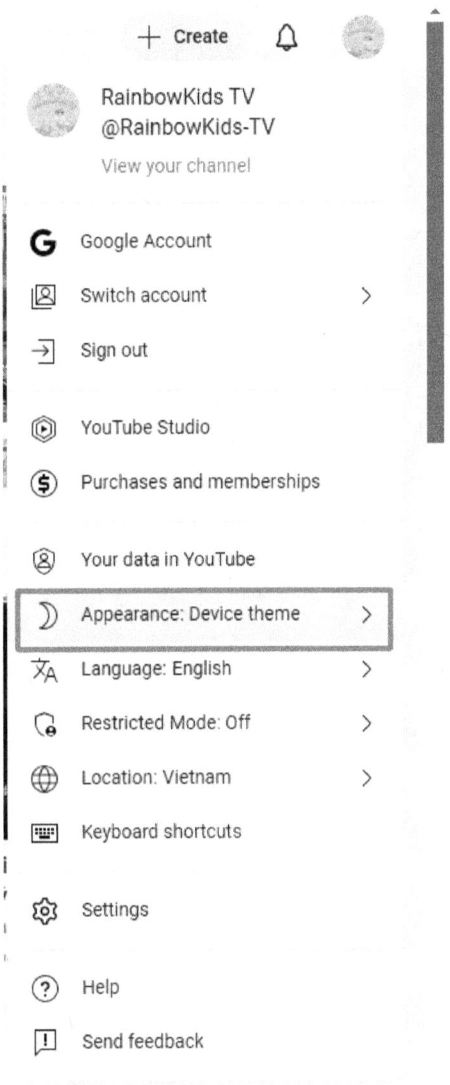

Downloading Videos for Offline Viewing

YouTube Premium subscribers can download videos to watch without an internet connection.

- Tap the **Download button** below a video.
- Choose **video quality (Low, Medium, High, or HD)**.

- Access downloaded videos in the **Library > Downloads** section.

---

5. Advanced YouTube Features on Mobile

Using YouTube Premium Features

YouTube Premium unlocks additional mobile features such as:

- **Background Play**: Videos continue playing even when you exit the app.
- **Ad-Free Experience**: No interruptions from advertisements.
- **YouTube Music Premium**: Exclusive access to an ad-free music streaming service.

YouTube Mobile for Creators

If you want to upload and manage your own content, the YouTube mobile app supports:

- **Uploading videos** directly from your phone.
- **Editing titles, descriptions, and thumbnails**.
- **Checking analytics** using the **YouTube Studio App**.

---

6. Common Issues and Troubleshooting

Video Not Loading or Buffering Issues

If videos are slow or not loading:

- Check your **internet connection** (Wi-Fi or mobile data).
- Lower the **video quality** in settings.
- Clear the **YouTube app cache** via your device settings.

App Crashes or Freezes

If the app crashes frequently:

- Ensure your **YouTube app is updated**.

- Restart your **phone**.
- Reinstall the **app** if problems persist.

Playback Errors

If you receive an error message:

- Restart the app and try again.
- Check if **YouTube is down** by visiting Downdetector. https://downdetector.com/

Conclusion

Using YouTube on a mobile device offers a convenient and immersive way to enjoy videos anytime, anywhere. With features like offline downloads, background play, and picture-in-picture mode, the app provides flexibility and efficiency. By mastering navigation, customization, and troubleshooting, you can enhance your YouTube experience and get the most out of the platform.

7.3.3 Integrating YouTube with Other Platforms

YouTube is more than just a standalone video-sharing website—it seamlessly integrates with various platforms, allowing users to enhance their experience across different devices and services. Whether you're a casual viewer, content creator, or business professional, connecting YouTube with other platforms can improve accessibility, engagement, and efficiency. In this section, we will explore the different ways YouTube can be integrated with various platforms, including social media, streaming devices, smart assistants, and productivity tools.

---

1. Connecting YouTube with Social Media Platforms

Social media plays a crucial role in content distribution, and integrating YouTube with popular platforms like Facebook, Instagram, Twitter (X), and LinkedIn can help users share videos more effectively.

1.1 Sharing YouTube Videos on Social Media

- Every YouTube video comes with a "Share" button below the video player. Clicking this button provides multiple sharing options, including direct links to Facebook, Twitter (X), WhatsApp, and more.
- Users can copy and paste the video link manually into social media posts to reach a wider audience.
- YouTube also allows embedding videos in blog posts, websites, or LinkedIn articles, making it easier for businesses and content creators to cross-promote content.

1.2 Linking YouTube to Facebook and Instagram

- While YouTube videos cannot be posted directly to Instagram, users can share links in their Instagram bio or stories using the "Swipe Up" feature (available for verified accounts or those with over 10,000 followers).
- On Facebook, YouTube videos can be posted as status updates, shared in groups, or included in advertisements for increased visibility.
- Facebook also offers an option to upload videos natively, but linking to YouTube is beneficial for driving traffic directly to a YouTube channel.

1.3 Sharing YouTube Videos on Twitter (X) and LinkedIn

- Twitter (X) allows users to share YouTube videos by pasting the link in a tweet, which automatically generates a clickable video preview.
- LinkedIn, which is popular among professionals and businesses, is an excellent platform for sharing educational or industry-specific YouTube content. Users can embed videos in posts, articles, and even LinkedIn Ads.

---

2. Using YouTube with Streaming and Smart TV Devices

Many people prefer watching YouTube on larger screens, and integrating YouTube with smart TVs, streaming devices, and gaming consoles makes it easy to enjoy videos from different sources.

2.1 Watching YouTube on Smart TVs

- YouTube is pre-installed on most smart TVs, allowing users to log into their accounts and access subscriptions, playlists, and recommendations.
- The YouTube mobile app offers a "Cast" feature that lets users send videos from their phones to smart TVs wirelessly.
- Voice-enabled remotes or virtual assistants like Google Assistant and Alexa can help control YouTube playback on smart TVs hands-free.

2.2 Streaming YouTube via Chromecast, Roku, and Fire Stick

- **Google Chromecast:** With a Chromecast device, users can stream YouTube videos from their phones, tablets, or computers directly to their TV screens. Simply tap the "Cast" icon on the YouTube app.
- **Roku and Amazon Fire Stick:** These streaming devices have dedicated YouTube apps that allow users to browse, search, and watch videos with a remote or voice commands.

2.3 Watching YouTube on Gaming Consoles

- YouTube is available on gaming consoles like PlayStation, Xbox, and Nintendo Switch. Players can watch gaming-related content, stream live events, or even broadcast their gameplay directly to YouTube using built-in streaming features.
- Linking a YouTube account to a gaming console ensures personalized recommendations and access to subscriptions.

---

3. Using YouTube with Smart Assistants and Home Devices

Voice-controlled assistants like Google Assistant, Amazon Alexa, and Apple Siri provide hands-free access to YouTube, making it easier to find and watch videos without manually searching.

3.1 Controlling YouTube with Google Assistant

- Google Assistant can be used to search for and play YouTube videos on smart devices by saying commands like:
    - "Hey Google, play cooking tutorials on YouTube."

  - "Hey Google, pause the video."
- Google Nest Hub and other smart displays allow users to watch YouTube videos while cooking, exercising, or working.

3.2 Watching YouTube with Amazon Alexa

- Although YouTube is not natively integrated with Amazon devices, users can access it via web browsers on Amazon Echo Show.
- Alexa commands can be used to open YouTube on Fire TV devices: "Alexa, open YouTube."

3.3 Using YouTube with Apple Siri and AirPlay

- Siri can help launch YouTube on Apple devices through voice commands.
- AirPlay allows iPhone or iPad users to stream YouTube videos wirelessly to Apple TV or compatible smart TVs.

---

4. Integrating YouTube with Productivity and Learning Platforms

YouTube is widely used in education and professional settings. It integrates with various platforms to enhance learning and productivity.

4.1 Using YouTube with Google Workspace (Docs, Slides, and Classroom)

- Google Docs and Slides allow users to embed YouTube videos for presentations and collaborative projects.
- **Google Classroom** enables teachers to assign YouTube videos as study materials, making remote learning more interactive.
- Google Meet and Zoom also support screen sharing for presenting YouTube videos in virtual meetings.

4.2 Embedding YouTube Videos in Websites and Blogs

- YouTube provides an **embed code** that allows users to insert videos directly into websites, making content more engaging.

- Blogs on WordPress, Medium, and other platforms support YouTube integration by simply pasting the video URL.

4.3 Using YouTube for Business and Marketing

- **YouTube Ads** can be integrated into Google Ads for targeted promotions.
- Businesses can link YouTube with e-commerce platforms like Shopify to showcase product videos.
- Email marketing tools like Mailchimp allow embedding YouTube videos in newsletters to increase engagement.

---

5. Automating YouTube with Third-Party Apps and Services

Automation tools can enhance YouTube's functionality by integrating it with various apps.

5.1 Connecting YouTube with IFTTT (If This Then That)

- IFTTT allows users to create automation rules such as:
    - Automatically sharing YouTube videos on Twitter when uploading a new video.
    - Saving liked YouTube videos to a spreadsheet for later viewing.

5.2 Using YouTube with Zapier for Business Automation

- Zapier helps automate workflows by linking YouTube with platforms like Slack, Trello, and CRM tools.
- Example: Posting a new YouTube video automatically on a company's Slack channel.

5.3 Integrating YouTube with Podcast and Streaming Platforms

- Some content creators convert YouTube videos into audio podcasts and distribute them on platforms like Spotify.
- YouTube can be connected with Twitch for cross-platform streaming.

Conclusion

Integrating YouTube with other platforms enhances its usability, whether for entertainment, business, education, or productivity. From sharing videos on social media to using YouTube with smart devices and automation tools, these integrations provide a seamless and efficient experience. By leveraging these features, users can maximize their YouTube interactions and make the most of this powerful video-sharing platform.

Conclusion

9.1 Final Thoughts and Summary

YouTube has become an essential part of our digital lives, offering a vast library of content that serves entertainment, education, and professional development purposes. Whether you are looking for music videos, how-to guides, movie trailers, or documentaries, YouTube provides an unparalleled platform where anyone can find something valuable.

This book has guided you through the process of using YouTube effectively, covering everything from navigating the platform to engaging with videos and creators. As we conclude, let's summarize the key takeaways and final thoughts on how to maximize your YouTube experience.

9.1.1 Recap of Key Learnings

Getting Started with YouTube

We began this book by exploring the basics of YouTube, including setting up your Google account, customizing your profile, and understanding the YouTube interface. Knowing how to navigate the Home tab, Subscriptions, and Library helps you find and organize content that suits your interests.

Discovering and Watching Videos

YouTube's search engine and recommendation system allow you to find new content effortlessly. By learning how to use filters, keywords, and browsing playlists, you can curate a watching experience that aligns with your preferences. Understanding video player controls, adjusting playback settings, and enabling captions can enhance your viewing experience.

Engaging with Videos and the Community

Interacting with videos through likes, comments, and sharing not only helps you express your opinions but also supports content creators. Subscribing to channels and enabling notifications ensures that you stay updated with new uploads from your favorite creators. Engaging in discussions and participating in live streams fosters a sense of community.

Managing Your YouTube Experience

We discussed various settings that help you personalize your YouTube experience. Features like Restricted Mode, autoplay management, and notification controls allow you to tailor the platform to your needs. If you have children using YouTube, enabling YouTube Kids or parental controls ensures a safer viewing environment.

Exploring Premium and Advanced Features

YouTube Premium provides an ad-free experience, background play, and offline video downloads. We also covered YouTube Music and YouTube TV, which extend the platform's capabilities beyond traditional video watching. Understanding these options allows you to make informed decisions about whether a premium subscription is right for you.

Tips for an Enhanced Viewing Experience

Learning about keyboard shortcuts, Picture-in-Picture mode, and playback speed customization can make watching videos more efficient. Reducing distractions by hiding comments, using focus mode extensions, and managing autoplay helps create a more enjoyable and immersive experience.

Using YouTube Across Different Devices

YouTube is available on a variety of devices, including smartphones, tablets, smart TVs, and gaming consoles. Learning how to sync your account across devices, use voice search, and cast videos to your TV provides greater flexibility in how you consume content.

9.1.2 Making the Most of Your YouTube Experience

Stay Updated with Platform Changes

YouTube is constantly evolving, introducing new features, layout changes, and updates to improve user experience. Staying informed about these updates helps you take advantage of the latest improvements. Following YouTube's official blog or subscribing to tech channels can keep you updated.

Explore Different Types of Content

While many people use YouTube primarily for entertainment, the platform also offers educational videos, TED Talks, coding tutorials, fitness guides, and much more. Expanding your content choices can turn YouTube into a powerful tool for personal growth and learning.

Be Mindful of Your Screen Time

With so much content available, it's easy to spend hours watching videos. While YouTube can be informative and entertaining, it's essential to maintain a healthy balance. Setting screen time limits and taking breaks can help you avoid overconsumption.

Support Your Favorite Creators

If you enjoy the content from certain YouTubers, consider supporting them by engaging with their videos, sharing their content, joining channel memberships, or contributing through Super Chats during live streams. Your support helps creators continue producing quality content.

Be an Informed and Responsible Viewer

Not all content on YouTube is accurate or reliable. Always verify the information you find, especially when watching news, tutorials, or health-related videos. Be cautious of misleading clickbait and misinformation. Using credible sources and checking multiple references can help you make informed decisions.

9.1.3 Final Words

YouTube is more than just a video-sharing platform—it is a community, a learning resource, and an entertainment hub. Whether you use YouTube for fun, education, or professional growth, understanding how to navigate and customize your experience ensures that you get the most out of the platform.

By following the guidance in this book, you now have the knowledge to explore YouTube confidently, interact with content in meaningful ways, and discover tools that enhance your viewing experience.

Thank you for reading **YouTube for Beginners: Navigate, Watch, and Enjoy**. We hope this guide has helped you become a more skilled and engaged YouTube user. Enjoy your journey through the vast world of YouTube!

9.2 Frequently Asked Questions (FAQs)

YouTube is a vast platform with countless features, and beginners often have many questions about how to use it effectively. This section covers some of the most frequently asked questions to help you navigate, watch, and enjoy YouTube with ease.

---

1. How do I create a YouTube account?

To create a YouTube account, follow these steps:

1. Go to YouTube.com.
2. Click on **Sign In** in the top right corner.
3. Select **Create Account** and choose **For myself** or **For business**.
4. Enter your name, email, and password, then click **Next**.
5. Follow the instructions to verify your email and set up your account.
6. Once verified, your YouTube account is ready to use!

If you already have a Google account, you can use it to sign in to YouTube without creating a new account.

---

2. Is YouTube free to use?

Yes, YouTube is free to use. You can watch videos, like, comment, and subscribe to channels without any cost. However, YouTube also offers a paid subscription service called **YouTube Premium**, which removes ads, allows offline downloads, and provides access to YouTube Music and YouTube Originals.

---

3. How can I watch videos without ads?

There are three ways to watch videos without ads:

1. **Subscribe to YouTube Premium** – This removes all ads from videos and gives additional features.
2. **Use an ad-blocker extension** – Some web browsers allow ad-blockers that can hide ads on YouTube. However, this is against YouTube's terms of service.
3. **Watch videos on YouTube Kids** – If you are looking for an ad-free experience for children, YouTube Kids has limited ads and a safer content selection.

---

4. How do I change the video quality?

To adjust the video quality, follow these steps:

1. Click on the **Settings (⚙□)** icon in the bottom right corner of the video player.
2. Select **Quality**.
3. Choose a resolution (e.g., 144p, 360p, 720p, 1080p, 4K).

Higher resolutions provide better quality but consume more internet data. If you are on a slow connection, select a lower resolution for smoother playback.

---

5. Can I watch YouTube videos offline?

Yes, but only in specific ways:

- **YouTube Premium users** can download videos to watch offline. Simply tap the **Download** button below the video.
- **YouTube Music Premium** allows downloading music videos for offline listening.
- Some regions allow free offline downloads via the YouTube app, but this feature is limited.

---

6. How do I subscribe to a YouTube channel?

Subscribing to a channel helps you stay updated with new content from your favorite creators. To subscribe:

1. Open a video from the channel you like.
2. Click the **Subscribe** button below the video.
3. (Optional) Click the **Bell icon (🔔)** to receive notifications when the channel uploads new videos.

---

7. How do I create and manage playlists?

Playlists help organize videos you want to watch later or group related content. To create a playlist:

1. Click on the **Save (📋)** button below a video.
2. Select **Create a new playlist**.
3. Name the playlist and choose a privacy setting (Public, Unlisted, or Private).
4. Click **Create**.

To manage a playlist:

- Go to the **Library** tab.
- Click on the playlist you created.
- Use the **Edit** button to add, remove, or rearrange videos.

---

8. Can I hide my YouTube watch history?

Yes, you can pause or delete your watch history:

1. Go to **YouTube History** (via the menu on the left).
2. Click **Manage all history**.
3. Choose **Pause watch history** or **Delete activity by date**.

Pausing watch history prevents YouTube from tracking the videos you watch, which can affect your recommendations.

9. How do I block unwanted videos or channels?

To block specific channels:

1. Go to the channel's page.
2. Click the **About** tab.
3. Click the **Flag (⚑)** icon and select **Block user**.

To block inappropriate content, enable **Restricted Mode** in the YouTube settings.

10. Why do some videos have age restrictions?

YouTube applies age restrictions to videos containing mature content, violence, or inappropriate language. You must be **signed in** and **18 years or older** to watch these videos. If you're unable to watch them, check if **Restricted Mode** is enabled on your account.

11. What happens if I report a video?

When you report a video:

1. YouTube's moderation team reviews it.
2. If it violates YouTube's **Community Guidelines**, it may be removed or age-restricted.
3. Reporting is **anonymous**, meaning the uploader will not know who reported their content.

12. How do I enable subtitles or captions?

To turn on captions while watching a video:

1. Click the **CC (Closed Captions)** button on the video player.

2. Choose the available language.
3. (Optional) Click the **Settings (⚙□)** icon > **Subtitles** > **Auto-translate** to select another language.

---

13. Can I watch YouTube on my TV?

Yes, you can watch YouTube on a **Smart TV**, **Chromecast**, **Apple TV**, or using an **HDMI cable** connected to your computer.

1. Open the YouTube app on your Smart TV.
2. Sign in or use the **Cast** button from your phone to connect.
3. Play a video, and it will stream on your TV.

---

14. How do I disable autoplay?

To disable autoplay:

1. Look for the **Autoplay toggle switch** (next to the video player).
2. Click to turn it **off** (gray).

Autoplay automatically plays the next video in the queue, which can be distracting if you want to watch only one video.

---

15. Can I control YouTube with voice commands?

Yes, if you use **Google Assistant** or a Smart TV, you can say:

- "Play the latest video from [channel name]."
- "Pause video."
- "Skip to the next video."

If you use YouTube on your phone, you can use **voice search** in the app.

16. How do I delete my YouTube account?

To delete your account permanently:

1. Go to **Google Account Settings**.
2. Click **Data & Privacy** > **Delete a service or account**.
3. Select **Delete your Google Account** (This will remove all Google services, including YouTube).

If you just want to **hide** your YouTube account, go to **YouTube Studio** > **Settings** > **Advanced Settings** and choose **Hide Channel**.

Final Thoughts

These frequently asked questions cover the most common beginner concerns on YouTube. As you continue using the platform, you'll discover even more features that can enhance your experience. Whether you're watching, creating, or exploring, YouTube has something for everyone!

If you have more questions, visit YouTube Help Center for official support.

Acknowledgments

First and foremost, I want to extend my heartfelt gratitude to you, the reader, for choosing *YouTube for Beginners: Navigate, Watch, and Enjoy.* Whether you're completely new to YouTube or just looking to refine your experience, I hope this book has provided you with valuable insights and practical tips to make your time on the platform more enjoyable and efficient.

In today's digital world, YouTube has become more than just a video-sharing site—it's a place for learning, entertainment, and connection. Your decision to invest time in understanding it better is truly commendable, and I'm honored to be a small part of your journey.

A special thank you to everyone who has supported this project—from friends and family who encouraged me, to the amazing online community that continuously shares knowledge and feedback. Without your inspiration and support, this book would not have been possible.

Finally, if you found this book helpful, I would truly appreciate it if you could share your thoughts by leaving a review. Your feedback not only helps me improve but also assists other readers in finding resources that may benefit them.

Thank you once again, and I wish you a fantastic YouTube experience!

Happy watching!

www.ingramcontent.com/pod-product-compliance
Lightning Source LLC
LaVergne TN
LVHW062302060326
832902LV00013B/2019
* 9 7 9 8 3 0 8 6 1 3 7 0 1 *